KUBRICK'S MEN

Kubrick's Men

Richard Rambuss

FORDHAM UNIVERSITY PRESS   NEW YORK   2021

Visit us online at www.fordhampress.com.

Library of Congress Control Number: 2020925119

Printed in the United States of America

23 22 21   5 4 3 2 1

First edition

Contents

KUBRICK'S MEN

Introduction

Kubrick and the Men's Film

Stanley Kubrick's body of work—from his early photography for *Look* maga-zine and short-form documentaries to his defining feature films—is preoccu-pied with men and the male condition. The persistent theme of that work, as I regard it here, is less violence or sex (as integral as those two subjects are to all the stories that Kubrick's movies tell and thus to any account of them) than it is the pressurized exertion of masculinity in unusual or extreme circum-stances, where it may be taxed or exaggerated to various effects, tragic and comic—or reconfigured, distorted, metamorphosed, and often undone. Pic-ture, then, as one iconic Kubrick image, the ass-backward rocket ride down to earth of Major "King" Kong at the apocalyptic end of *Dr. Strangelove Or: How I Learned to Stop Worrying and Love the Bomb*, his uniformed thighs clamped tight around the missile shaft: an emblem that is mega-phallic and suggestively sodomitical too (Figure 1): Strangelove for sure. And picture as another, no less iconic image the terrestrial return of astronaut Dave Bowman become the perhaps postgender Star Child at the likewise fateful end of *2001: A Space Odyssey*, where it is left ambiguous whether this further evolutionary iteration of man has come back to save or (like Major Kong) to destroy us. Or consider *A Clockwork Orange*'s devilishly charismatic Alex, psychologically rewired from a hypersexed, hyperviolent male juvenile delinquent to a mousy good boy without free will, before he's pleasingly turned back again into what he was. Or, to move from individuals to male groups, take the assorted Marine Corps recruits in *Full Metal Jacket* as they are all methodically broken down and re-fashioned into component parts of "Mother Green and her killing machine."

Kubrick's movies work out case study–like narratives—many of them clini-cal, even mechanistic in their feel, all of them highly aestheticized in their

Figure 1. Loving the bomb.

presentation—about masculinity with the screws put to it. "Torture the women" was Hitchcock's dictum on how to make a gripping movie. For Kubrick, the interest lay in men in extremis.

Kubrick's films have been branded masculinist, misogynist, and misanthropic. These are different sorts of charges, and I don't see them as necessarily coextensive. But they can all be made to stick here and there. My own inclination is to think of Kubrick as one of the great auteurs of the men's film— even though it has been said that there is really no such thing, that there is only cinema proper and the subsidiary form of the so-called woman's picture, which includes soap opera, the weepie, and melodrama.[1] Decades ago, feminist criticism set about expounding new ways of approaching (and appreciating) these genres directed toward a female audience and engrossed with, as Mary Ann Doane puts it, "problems defined as 'female.'"[2] One impulse animating this study of Kubrick is the concern that film criticism's treatment of problems regarded as "male" remains, ironically, less advanced conceptually and even descriptively by comparison: this notwithstanding, or perhaps because of, the sense that the default stance of cinema is male in subject matter and address. Let me be clear, however, that the notion of the men's film I mean to be honing here is not proffered as a dualistic counter to the women's film, but rather as something to be viewed alongside and even at times through it.[3] That is, *Kubrick's Men* has turned out to be very much a book about Kubrick and melodrama—one might even say, to get ahead of what is to come, Kubrick's male weepies. For few films of his, we shall see, go without male tears.

Kubrick's typically revisionary, often experimental way with genre is another of this book's principal concerns. And most of his filmmaking comes in the form of what may be thought of as male genres: the sports film (*Day of the Fight*); the heist film (*The Killing*); science fiction (*2001: A Space Odyssey*); the juvenile delinquent film (*A Clockwork Orange*, in which Alex addresses the audience directly as "my brothers"); horror (*The Shining*); and the war or military movie (*Fear and Desire, Paths of Glory, Dr. Strangelove, Full Metal Jacket*). Kubrick also mixes his male genres. *Killer's Kiss* is both a sports film about a boxer and a noir gangster movie. The Vietnam War movie *Full Metal Jacket* is also very much a male youth film. (The malleable recruits delivered to boot camp look to be little more than teenagers.) *A Clockwork Orange* is both Kubrick's first male youth film and a near-future science fiction successor/precursor to *2001*.

Consider too how Kubrick's two historical costume dramas—*Spartacus* and *Barry Lyndon*—are both titled for their male protagonists. Though one is about an ancient Roman populist hero and the other an eighteenth-century Irish gentleman-rogue on the make, both films scrutinize codes of manly conduct and play out various kinds of social, political, and sexual maneuverings among men (or among men and "boys"). Kubrick's sex comedy *Lolita* retains, of course, the female title character of the famous novel that it adapts for the screen. But both the book and the movie are about obsessional, illicit male desire. Indeed, Kubrick's *Lolita* frames the novel's perverse intergenerational love story more pronouncedly in terms of erotic rivalry—and with it of course a powerful doubling connection—between men, between Humbert Humbert and Claire Quilty, whose role as a star vehicle for Peter Sellers (more on Kubrick's actors in a moment) is much enhanced in the movie. Male desire and its discontents also churn in the undertow of the drifting plot of *Eyes Wide Shut*, Kubrick's final movie, which blends aspects of the male detective film and sex film.

The point of terming Kubrick's genres "male" isn't at all to stipulate their audiences or sphere of appeal. Nor, of course, is the men's film strictly the domain of male directors, as the career of Kathryn Bigelow compellingly illustrates.[4] My grouping of Kubrick's movies under the heading of men's pictures is to put forth a simpler claim about them. It is that his work amounts to a continuing reflection, through image and story, on maleness, not only in the present but also in history and the future. The stories that Kubrick's movies tell range from global nuclear politics to the unpredictable sexual dynamics of what appears to be a picture-perfect bourgeois marriage; from a day in the life of a New York City prizefighter preparing for a nighttime bout to the phases of human evolution. All of these stories center on men. Indeed, in a number of Kubrick's films—including several widely regarded as among his greatest: *Paths of Glory, Dr. Strangelove*, and *2001*—the world depicted is all but all male. Kubrick's movies are concerned with male sociality and asociality, especially apart from or notwithstanding the presence of women. They present male doubles, duos, pairs, rivals, and other forms of replication. They treat the romance of men and their machines, and men *as* machines. They elaborate intensely conflicted forms of male sexual desire. They spectacularize male violence and combat. They render male exertion and also exhaustion.[5] And they are also— though this dimension of Kubrick's work has thus far been less explored—very much about male manners, style, and taste.

I find that I keep returning in my work to Eve Kosofsky Sedgwick's observation that "some people are just plain more *gender-y* than others.'"[6] This book extends that notion to Kubrick's oeuvre: that it is especially "gender-y," and this in registers whose complexity and variability repay more sustained critical attention. Kubrick is a male director who made movies about men adapted from male-authored texts. This may sound like the makings of an ineluctably masculinist project. But what it means to be or to act or to feel like a man in Kubrick's movies is far too fractured, too dissonant, and ultimately too strange to be reduced to that.

There is another sense in which Kubrick is a men's picture filmmaker: a fairly obvious one, but worth pointing out here, I think, given that the title of this book is *Kubrick's Men*. It's that all the stars in Kubrick's movies are male stars. Kirk Douglas, Sterling Hayden, Laurence Olivier, Charles Laughton, Peter Ustinov, James Mason, Peter Sellers, George C. Scott, Ryan O'Neal, Jack Nicholson, Tom Cruise: that's the Kubrick firmament. There are no female stars in leading roles in any of Kubrick's films until the final one, *Eyes Wide Shut*, which costars Cruise's wife at the time, Nicole Kidman, and even then she hardly shares equal screen time with him. Otherwise, the parts for Kubrick's women are mostly roles for character actors the likes of Marie Windsor, Shelley Winters, and Shelley Duvall. They are all extraordinary in their way, and in the case of Winters scene-stealing, but the characters they play remain on the outside looking in on predominantly male narratives.

Although this study is not organized chronologically, the first chapter is devoted to Kubrick's earliest work. It opens with his photojournalism for *Look* magazine, where he landed a job right out of high school in 1945. At *Look*, Kubrick learned to tell stories through images. As a staff photographer— reportedly the youngest in the magazine's history—he had all kinds of assignments and took thousands of pictures, hundreds of which were published. I like to think that photographing male entertainers (Montgomery Clift, Leonard Bernstein, Frank Sinatra, Guy Lombardo, New Orleans Dixieland jazz musicians, etc.) and male athletes (especially boxers and wrestlers) were among Kubrick's fortes. Weegee (Arthur Fellig) and Diane Arbus are the names most likely to come up as reference points of comparison and inspiration for Kubrick, the young photographer. My consideration of his photography juxtapositionally brings in two later male portraitists, Robert Mapplethorpe and Bruce Weber (also, like Kubrick, a documentary filmmaker), as an angle onto other, less considered gendered aspects of Kubrick's early work.

This chapter next turns to the three surviving documentaries Kubrick made after he left *Look* in 1950 to devote himself to movies. They are quite different in their subject matter and genre: one is a sports short, another is a newsreel human interest story, and the third is a promotional film. I see these precociously stylish short-form film "exercises" as of a piece, however, for several reasons, especially because of their focus on male subjects. The most interesting of the lot is the first one, *Day of the Fight*, about a handsome Greenwich Village boxer named Walter Cartier. I surmise that for Kubrick a good deal of this subject's appeal—both visually and thematically—has to do with how Cartier comes with a twin brother, who (at least as Kubrick's documentary stages it) lives with him and manages his career in the ring. The Kubrick motif of the double or multiple takes root here, in the very first film that he made, and it gives this remarkable sports short an uncanny aura. Before he made a movie about Walter Cartier, Kubrick first shot him for a *Look* photo-essay titled "Prizefighter," which I also take up here at some length. Kubrick replicates images from both "Prizefighter" and *Day of the Fight* in *Killer's Kiss*, his second feature film, likewise about a New York City boxer. This chapter treats *Killer's Kiss* as an early illustration of the formal, thematic, and we might even say theoretical affiliations between Kubrick's three bodies of work: his photographs, his documentaries, and his feature films. The kinds of contact points found here also point to a notable aspect of Kubrick worth remarking from the outset: namely, the autoreferentiality of his art, which is markedly imitative of itself and quickly became its own main influence. That formal and thematic quality will make Kubrick's cinema very much a world unto itself.

Boxing is highly theatrical fighting—the ring, the audience, the Marquess of Queensberry rules—that is for real. It's the combat sport that comes closest in its aim, which is overcoming the opponent by way of injuring him, to war. And war is one of Kubrick's principal subjects. The war film is the most prevalent genre in his filmography, while battle scenes and military concerns also figure significantly in other kinds of Kubrick movies. Chapter 2 focuses on

Kubrick's first three war films: his little-seen debut feature, *Fear and Desire*; his World War I military melodrama, *Paths of Glory*, often heralded as one of the greatest antiwar films ever made; and *Dr. Strangelove*, his nightmare spoof about the war that ends all wars, along with everything else. I set up my treatment of Kubrick's war films with a glance at his unmade epic biopic about Napoleon, among the most storied of all military subjects. The chapter concludes with another Kubrick epic, *2001: A Space Odyssey*, contextualized here as a Cold War film. It locates mankind's disposition toward violence and war—by that time augmented with world-obliterating powers—in the process by which man became man.

Arousal is my way here into Kubrick's war films. Not just cinematic violence as itself a turn-on, though its stimulating properties are engaged as early on as *Fear and Desire* (reflected in the movie's libidinal title), and then given the most earth-shaking climax imaginable (or unimaginable) in *Dr. Strangelove*, which I see as a kind of terminal war film. (What do you do in that genre after this?) So there is the excitement of violence in Kubrick, of course. But I am also taken with how Kubrick's war films draw upon, how they activate *the stimulations of art*, including but not only their own filmmaking art. Here talk of weapons, troops, tactics, and casualties is juxtaposed with, and at times informed by, questions of beauty, style, and taste. All the show-and-tell of literature, architecture, furniture, and fine art that comes with the bravura combat sequences and rationalized military maneuverings is the stimulus for my attempt to work out aesthetical readings of Kubrick's war films. The point of such an approach is far from suggesting that his movies dignify, much less glorify, war. (Or art, for that matter, a point further considered in relation to *A Clockwork Orange* in Chapter 4.) But it does seem to me that none of Kubrick's war films really answer to any kind of antiwar war film imperative, if that's even what one here comes looking for.

Another way to say this is that in Kubrick politics tends to be subordinate to stylistics. For Kubrick's cinematic storybook about men in extremis also reads as an anthology of male types, roles, and gender styles, which are relentlessly counterposed in precarious, highly combustible relationship to each other. There may be no more consequential example in all of cinema of the clash of male types than *Dr. Strangelove*, where the film's over-the-top male satire also provides an alibi for what is concurrently a doting, technically detailed romance of men, machines, and the military.[7]

Chapters 3 and 4 on Kubrick and male sexuality take the matter of male difference in another direction. They offer the first detailed treatment of the homosexual content (mostly but not exclusively male) in Kubrick's work. Though he never made a gay-themed movie per se, hardly any Kubrick film goes untouched by something homosexual somewhere. Chapter 3 pursues that claim in *Lolita*, *The Killing*, and *Spartacus*, films that Kubrick put out while the Motion Picture Production Code was in effect. It banned, among so many things, any explicit acknowledgment of "sexual perversion," homosexuality naturally included. Chapter 4 turns to *Barry Lyndon*, *A Clockwork Orange*, and *Eyes Wide Shut*, three films that Kubrick made after the Production Code was replaced in 1968 by the Motion Picture Association of America film rating system. This chapter concludes with a short section on *The Shining*, from which the briefest of scenes provides, as I explain below, the inspiration for the line of inquiry followed here.

Chapters 3 and 4, paired, track where and how the homosexual shows up in a Kubrick film. We will find that homosexuality tends to be a marginal element, set at the sidelines of the movie's main story—though there, at the margins, the half-life accorded it can momentarily be quite spectacular. My term for this homosexual trace found throughout Kubrick's movies is *apparitional*, borrowed from an important book by Terry Castle on lesbianism and here given a local habitation (if not a name) in the two gay-acting ghosts ever so briefly glimpsed in *The Shining* once all hell has broken loose.[8] One might be tempted to say that homosexuality is the specter that haunts Kubrick's men's films—and, having said that, not only his various iterations of the men's film but just about all men's films. Yet with respect to Kubrick, I don't so much mean haunt in the sense of casting a shadow over, much less of looming fear or dread. Rather, I see the gay specter in Kubrick's movies more as a revenant, as something that keeps coming back—as recurring, though transient, visitations. (Perhaps this is why the prospect of a homosexual encounter comes up in both *Lolita* and *Eyes Wide Shut*, along with *The Shining*, in a hotel setting.) Sometimes the specter of homosexuality is *just there* in Kubrick. In other of his films, it emits some force, whether operative at the level of individual characters or (of more interest to me) narrative structure.

I originally conceived of this topic as material for a single chapter. The decision along the way instead to apportion Kubrick's treatment of male sexuality and homosexuality into two, historically organized chapters would, I presumed, set in sharper relief the differences between the Production Code–era films and those made when it was no longer in force. And some notable differences do in fact thus show up. But they are chiefly along the lines of the expected "progression" from insinuation in the earlier films (say, Crassus's encoded taste for "both snails *and* oysters" in *Spartacus*) to the various kinds of more explicit gay expression found in the later ones. The word "homosexual," for instance, is uttered for the first and, as it happens, only time in a Kubrick movie in *A Clockwork Orange*, which is also the first movie that Kubrick did after the Production Code's demise, part of that film's "showing off" its lack of restrictions. This X-rated art film is, as we shall further see, also flamboyantly decorated with spectral gay porn. But mostly the homosexual element appears rather the same across all these films: it is incidental to Kubrick's men's films, an accompanying feature, part of their (male) world-making. This, as I see it, is the paradox of homosexuality in Kubrick: same-sex interest and display are intriguing enough to these films always to make some kind of appearance, but not important enough to mean all that much of anything when they do. It may be just there, but it is there.

Another thing that the Kubrick films discussed in Chapters 3 and 4 have in common is that they are all adaptations from literary sources, novels in fact. The translation from page to screen is an issue of considerable interest in Kubrick, given that every one of his feature films, apart from the first two—*Fear and Desire* and *Killer's Kiss*, which he would subsequently all but disown—are adaptations. (Kubrick's literariness, no doubt, is part of my attraction, coming to these films by way of training in literary studies.) A remarkable feature of the movie adaptations pored over here is that the kind of minor, though fascinating, homoerotic and homosexual content referred to earlier has been *added* to them. That is, in most cases it isn't there in the source text—and what to make of that? These two central chapters twist their rereadings of an assortment of early to late Kubrick films around that added homosexual content, however peripheral, however superfluous. I suppose that what is on offer here could be described as a gay reading of male sexuality, and not just male homosexuality. The hope is that this aslant approach will provide some new perspectives regarding gender and sexuality in Kubrick's work, but also with them some different vantages onto narrative, style, and affect (which brings us back to Kubrick, the male melodramatist).

Kubrick's men are predominantly, but not exclusively, white. Male racial difference, noted throughout this study, comes more to the fore in the discussion of *Spartacus* in Chapter 3, in particular the character of the Ethiopian gladiator Draba, played by the towering former star athlete Woody Strode. And it comes again to the fore in the next chapter's consideration of *The Shining*, where Scatman Crothers's Dick Hallorann is a rival, second father to Danny through his and the boy's shared supernatural ability "to shine," to communicate telepathically. Kubrick studies (the work at hand included) has yet to deliver the extended study of race in Kubrick's movies that important topic warrants; but any account of Kubrick's men would be deficient without spotlighting Strode's Draba and Crothers's Hallorann. Their roles may be mostly shaped by the liberal trope of the "good man Black man." Indeed, *Spartacus* will hold up Draba (though in his death) as a new model for masculinity and the inspiration for the slave rebellion Spartacus himself (of course) will lead.[9] But the outsized impression made by Strode's and Crothers's performances exceeds their supporting roles as well as the stereotypes they seem meant to embody. (This is not unlike my argument about homosexuality's functioning here.)

Chapter 5 returns to Kubrick and the war film, a genre that he kept experimenting with throughout his career. One of the things the war or military movie is always about, on some level, is the relationship between men and their masculinity. War films put masculinity in question, throw it into crisis. What does it mean to act like a man, especially in extreme circumstances, war being the most extreme? This final chapter is given over to *Full Metal Jacket*, Kubrick's last war film, which I view as his most revisionary take on the genre and with it on gender. Earlier I proposed that Kubrick quickly became his own chief influence. This chapter also returns to the question of influence, now including *Full Metal Jacket*'s influence on works likewise concerned with the gendered dynamics of the military by other filmmakers and also writers.

Kubrick explained in a 1987 interview coincident with the release of *Full Metal Jacket* that he wanted "to explode the narrative structure of movies."[10] His bifurcated, two-act and pointedly "meta" Vietnam War movie does unusual things with structure, setting, and character. Instead of pursuing a main storyline (or a few interwoven narrative strands), *Full Metal Jacket* unfolds as a succession of nearly freestanding vignettes—a series of "dispatches" from the war (to invoke the acclaimed Vietnam War memoir of Michael Herr, a coauthor, with Kubrick and Gustav Hasford, of the screenplay). Similarly, this film, which Kubrick interestingly cast without a major star, has a fairly radical, one might say dissolved notion of what counts as a leading man in a military film, particularly—and this is germane to my consideration of *Full Metal Jacket*—a *Marine Corps film*. Also related to this, I think, is the way that *Full Metal Jacket* stands apart for its abnegation of the male melodrama that powers so many of Kubrick's films, as well as the war film genre more generally.

The aim Kubrick expressed of wanting violently to undo narrative structure can be extended to what happens in this film to our frameworks of gender. Whereas the plot and subplots of Kubrick's World War I movie *Paths of Glory* turn on the question of what is required of a man once he becomes a soldier, *Full Metal Jacket* starts off preoccupied with an antecedent question: How do you refunction the boy next door—just about any boy—into a hardhearted, semiautomatic killer, into a cog in "Mother Green and her killing machine," as this martial male family here refers to itself? On this account, the first third of Kubrick's Vietnam War film is spent on Parris Island at boot camp. There the Corps' micromanaged control technologies of discipline, drill, and regimentation are compellingly rendered—and also aestheticized—according to Kubrick's own masterful visual style. These transformative physical processes are matched with a methodical assault on the individual male self, and this most intensely so (at least in Kubrick's movie) around the especially vulnerable pressure points of gender and sexuality.

Hypermasculinity, including racialized hypermasculinity, would be one way to name the theoretical concern that animates this concluding chapter, with an understanding that here amplification turns strikingly transmutative, distortive. Nearly all of this book's overarching concerns—the all-male group or institution; male conflict and male-on-male violence; homoerotic/homophobic male homosociality; male sadomasochism; the male body in extremis; and especially male vulnerability—show up with a vengeance in Kubrick's late-'80s hyperviolent, hypersexualized Vietnam War film. Then factor in the highly ritualized, fetish-rich ethos of the Marine Corps: as represented here, its own totalizing male world. What does gender look like, how does it operate in this setting? Whatever it means to be or to act male here, it's not something, apparently, that the recruits naturally instantiate when they arrive at boot camp. "Sound off like you've got a pair," the film's Sergeant Hartman demands in his first scene with them in the barracks, insinuating that here they are taken, at best, as only notionally male.

Such mockery, along with the drill sergeant's interpellation of those in his charge as "ladies," "pussies," or "dick suckers," may strike veteran viewers of the military training movie as "merely" conventional. But the sexual effects mobilized in boot camp seem to me less assimilable to normative versions of maleness (however imagined) than is the case with the usual men-in-groups ritual fare of temporary, playfully derisory sexual reversal or inversion. Of course, the very conventionality of all this is itself of interpretive interest. To recognize that these are the commonplaces of male hazing, which is to say male fashioning, shouldn't entail that we then abstain from thinking about them as meaningful. *As conventions*, these terms and gestures may rather be seen as thick with significance.

Again, what does gender look like in such a setting? And what about sex and sexuality? Throughout this book I have tried to be sparing in my use of the word "queer," sometimes now a lazy shorthand in gender and sexuality studies.[11] Yet it is hard not to reach for that term when it comes to *Full Metal Jacket*. The question of sexuality in terms of this movie hardly answers to the models that bear on the readings of Kubrick's films offered in Chapters 3 and 4. Structurally speaking, male sexuality in *Full Metal Jacket* is not hetero or homo, and, while it melds aspects of both, bisexual doesn't really describe it either. The eroticism rhetorically activated around the film's marines, which plays no small part in making them marines, seems instead to point toward their own extreme alternative sexuality.

Ending *Kubrick's Men* with *Full Metal Jacket*, which isn't Kubrick's last film, only his last war film, may seem eccentric, perhaps even a touch perverse. So too (or maybe all the more) my giving this one film, not typically judged to be among the director's signal works, its own chapter. I do so chiefly because, as I have here begun to suggest, the articulations of masculinity in Kubrick's final war film seem to me both the most intense and estranging in his work. This privileging (if that's the word for it) of *Full Metal Jacket* may be indicative of the book as a whole, which proved to be idiosyncratic in several respects. Personal too. *Full Metal Jacket* is the first Kubrick film that I wrote about and taught. It is also the first Kubrick film that I saw in the theater upon its release. It seems fitting to return at the end of this reading of Kubrick's body of work to the place where this began for me.

Although this book considers all thirteen of Kubrick's feature films, plus his three documentaries, they are not accorded equal attention, and this for no one reason. As it happens, fewer pages are devoted here, for instance, to two of Kubrick's most widely discussed films, *2001: A Space Odyssey* and *The Shining*. And I found that I had as much or more to say about early Kubrick, lesser or even "bad" Kubrick (it's left to the reader to determine what film or films would go in that category), and also the Kubrick film often treated as not one (namely, *Spartacus*), as I do about what have come to be regarded as Kubrick's major works. In terms of generic classification, I wound up being especially drawn to his war films and his sex films, though of course those two groupings could be seen to embrace every film this director made.

I wouldn't say that this study of Kubrick quite qualifies as an expression of the "too-close viewership" named and dazzlingly exemplified in D. A. Miller's recent book *Secret Hitchcock*.[12] But my attention here, like Miller's, tends to fix on brief scenes, background matter, and minor details, including the occasional continuity error, along with allusions, puns, evocations, and other kinds of ghostly visual and textual traces. This is partly because my own tendency as a reader and viewer is to get caught up in the small—and, to use again a Kubrickian term, strange—particulars. It's also because I have found that such little things point to different interpretive paths into an already much written about filmmaker. As for the big picture, I recognize that I am hardly the only critic to remark the manifestly male orientation of Kubrick's work.[13] The same goes for its heightened aestheticism. In this book, I want to make even more of both matters, and at times to try to think about them in relation to each other.

1
Men's Pictures

I think he enjoys the male comradeship of making films. He's
surrounded by women at home and he likes to talk guns and sports.
—KEVYN MAJOR HOWARD ("RAFTERMAN" IN *FULL METAL JACKET*)

The first film that Stanley Kubrick made is a sports short. Titled *Day of the Fight*, this 1951 black-and-white documentary is about a man who, the film's narrator melodramatically declares, "literally has to fight for his very existence." He's a young, 5′10″ middleweight boxer (and Navy veteran) from Greenwich Village named Walter Cartier. Cartier is the first of Kubrick's men: the first of the male figures (some real, most fictional) in extreme, combative circumstances to whom Kubrick was drawn as a filmmaker and who predominate in his movies.

Day of the Fight was actually Kubrick's second camera study of Cartier. A few of years earlier, he shot a seven-page lifestyle spread on the photogenic boxer for the popular biweekly pictorial magazine *Look*, a rival to *Life*. Kubrick had landed a job as a photographer at *Look* fresh out of high school. (His poor grades, along with the influx of returning veterans availing themselves of the GI Bill, kept him from college.) There Kubrick honed his technique for storytelling by pictures, for stylizing narrative and feeling into serial images. "Prizefighter" was published in the January 18, 1949, issue. Like the documentary short film to which it led, Kubrick's *Look* photo-essay on Cartier takes us through the aspiring champion's morning to evening fight-day activities and then to the ring for his late-night bout.

Photography

Boxing is the most directly violent of athletic contests, the closest to a human blood sport. It's the sport least like a sport and the closest to combat. To injure, even incapacitate, is the aim. The chief target, Joyce Carol Oates points out in her entrancing book *On Boxing*, is the brain.[1] As in war, a "killer instinct"—the phrase originates in boxing—is prized. But the Sweet Science of Bruising can also be stylish, look sexy. Kubrick doesn't shy away from this contact sport's bared body, dark machismo glamor; his camera indulges in it. That Cartier is male-model handsome (if never quite a champ) doesn't hurt. Kubrick makes the most of those chiseled good looks in the story's lead picture, a three-quarter shot printed as nearly a full page (Figure 2). We come upon the fighter in the locker room. He is posed on a bench against the grid of a concrete brick wall, waiting for the summons to the ring: a portrait of brooding male anticipation. Kubrick's movies, starting with *Day of the Fight*, are full of images of men on the edge, waiting out some inexorable countdown. Cartier's manager, the legendary Bobby Gleason, is to the right of him in shirt and tie, making Cartier's semi-naked body seem more naked. Kubrick shoots the boxer's torso from below, monumentalizing the male form. An unseen overhead flood throws light across the expanse of Cartier's sculpted, hairless chest and shimmers on the black leather boxing gloves resting in his lower lap. The gloves touch, and the chiaroscuro effect there outlines, stigmata-like, a heart that is also a hole (Figure 3). As Roland Barthes would say, that detail—this photograph's *punctum*—is what pricks, what bruises. Kubrick's wistful boxer looks like a fighter and a lover.[2] Cartier's chiseled face is raised and slightly tilted left, as though, starlike, to find his light. Strong shadows set off his angular jaw and steep cheekbones. Dark planes render his heavy browed, deep-set eyes deeper—or masked, even made-up.

Kubrick's hard-contrast black-and-white photography has been compared to that of the noir New York photojournalist known as Weegee, who is an obvious influence on the young Kubrick. This particular photograph, though, makes me think ahead, impressionistically, to Robert Mapplethorpe and some of his statuesque male nudes and sexual exhibitionists. Again, it's that sensuous detail of the plush black-on-black of Cartier's crotch: black leather, black satin. This has the feel of what Freud terms a media fetish: that is, the fetishism of materials—leather, velvet, rubber, latex—of which Mapplethorpe was an artist-connoisseur. And it's not just that detail: everything about Kubrick's photograph—presented as photojournalism and yet as controlled in its own way as Mapplethorpe's studio portraiture—strikes me as dark and hintingly kinky. Both Kubrick's photo-essay and his documentary treat boxers as a breed apart

A grim resolve to win his fight grips young middleweight Walter Cartier as he waits with Manager Bobby Gleason the call to enter the ring.

Prizefighter

Walter Cartier is a young, strong middleweight struggling along in sport's toughest business

Photographed by STANLEY KUBRICK

THE prize ring is a cruel taskmaster. It demands harsh sacrifices. It brings rich material rewards to a few. But to the great majority, it offers only the bitterest future: Frustration. Disillusion. Exposure to bad surroundings. Physical beatings that frequently linger and sometimes kill.

A typical, struggling young fighter is 24-year-old Walter Cartier, middleweight from New York's Greenwich Village. He won 25 of his first 29 fights, then changed managers to make faster progress toward big purses. If they elude him another year, he plans to quit the ring and attend law school. It's a rare young fighter who sticks to such a wise decision.

(Continued on next page)

Figure 2. Prizefighter Walter Cartier's chiseled good looks.

Figure 3. Detail: the punctum.

among men, as somewhat fringe figures ("There are six thousand men like
these in America." "Why do they do it? . . . Where do they come from?" queries the film's narrator), even as their portfolio of images from Cartier's life
mixes in domestic interludes. The main event, however, is in the ring, which,
thrills another headline in "Prizefighter," is "filled with slashing blows of leather
on flesh." The picture-stories presented in *Look* were collaborative pieces. As
the photographer, Kubrick may or may not have had a hand in crafting that
stroke of pulpy prose. But the fascination of his early work with boxing and its
drama of punishment between the ropes is nonetheless of a piece with the various male sadomasochistic scenarios to come in his films.

     As for the fight scenes in "Prizefighter," they cut both ways. Cartier pre-
vails in one of the bouts pictured, but he loses the other on a TKO. Another
thing about Kubrick's fighters—not only his boxers, but also his soldiers, and
indeed just about all his men—is that their machismo, however ramped up,
is hardly indomitable. We see them take their beatings not just give them. In
a way that bears further comparison to Mapplethorpe, the more interesting
objectivity effects in Kubrick tend to accrue around his male figures and not
really so much the female ones, who, in any case, are almost always second-
ary, if present at all. That is in part because the kinds of narratives that Kubrick's films unspool—typically of clashes and journeys—are staked to a
vulnerable masculinity, to male identities that are treated as inherently pliant, physically no less than psychologically. This points to a general difference between Kubrick and Mapplethorpe as male portraitists. Whereas what
Richard Meyer refers to as the "stilling gaze" of Mapplethorpe's camera renders its male subjects and male scenes in the stasis of a "Perfect Moment,"

Kubrick's men tend toward a masculinity that is metamorphic, a masculinity that is pliable or in flux.[3]

Speaking of photographers known for their male portraiture, another, sunnier image in "Prizefighter" looks to me like something that Bruce Weber, working in one of his romantically retro modes, might have taken. The shot is of Cartier, again shirtless, though this time not in repose but rather with his corded muscles flexed in exertion on an afternoon outing to Staten Island with a girlfriend (Figure 4). "Rowing out to a friend's sailboat," blazons the caption, "emphasizes long, powerful muscles that give him punching power." Weber is known for his alfresco male youth physique photography, including his Abercrombie and Fitch "Bear Pond" fashion shoots of athletic boys cavorting in bucolic settings with big dogs and each other. Occasionally some girls are mixed in, but even then Weber's images feel homoerotic. Just so Kubrick's hunky picture of Cartier in the rowboat. Its caption doesn't remark the presence of the woman to whom he's turned his back—though not to gaze out at Kubrick's camera and thus also at the viewer, but rather to look down at his own powerful hands gripping the oars. Cartier's female companion (Dolores Germaine) is named in the caption for another, much larger photograph of the two on the same page, though it notes that the boxer "has no No. 1 girl friend." Cartier, again presented sculpturally in the foreground as a beautiful object to be admired, dominates this image too. His outsized recumbent head looks like a Brancusi "Sleeping Muse"—only a male one.

Two other, smaller photographs complete this single-page spread on the boxer at rest and at play. They are placed at the bottom, where they follow in a row after the rowboat photo. The friend's sailboat toward which Cartier is there pictured sculling comes back in the row's last photograph as a toy sailboat that he fixes at home for his "little nephew and leading rooter." This playful intergenerational male scene is staged in a way that quotes but reverses the brooding locker room picture of Cartier with his much older manager. This time the bare-chested figure on the left is the nephew, with Cartier now on right in the white shirt. The snapshot that comes between the two boat pictures singles out Cartier for once alone, while now casting him in the role of "rooter," as he cheers on the Boston Red Sox at a baseball game in Yankee Stadium. In Bruce Weber's "Bear Pond" idylls, the clean-cut male faces and toned bodies seem, in their invariable, fairly machinic perfection, interchangeable. Indeed, Weber likes using brothers, especially twins, as models. Kubrick too, we will see, is attracted to male doubles in their formal, objectifying capacity. For now, note that here it is the man/boy pictorial arrangements that serially repeat and the boy's toys that are interchanged.

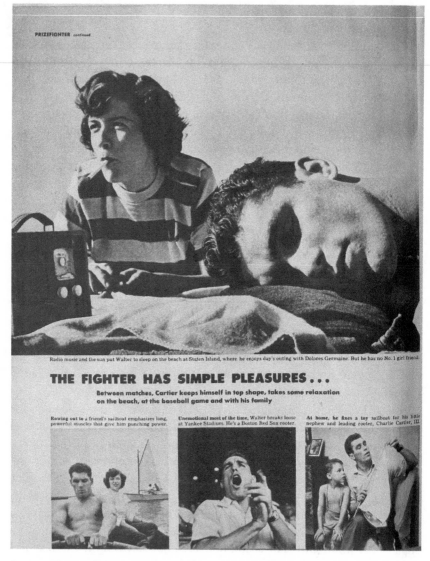

Figure 4. The prizefighter at play.

Admittedly it is whimsical, perhaps even perverse, to bring Mapplethorpe and Weber glancingly into a treatment of Kubrick's photography. I do so more as an opening gambit to reset the stage, to vary the frames of reference for thinking about male subjects and/as objects in Kubrick than to suggest direct lines of influence between artists. But it is notable that the homoerotic photographer Weber duplicates Kubrick in choosing an attractive, sensitive, young boxer as the subject for his own filmmaking debut: *Broken Noses*, a wistful, mostly black-and-white 1987 documentary about the coltish former Golden Gloves lightweight Andy Minsker. A still boyish coach and father figure, Minsker (shirtless through much of the film) runs a boxing club for ten- to sixteen-year-old boys (also often shirtless). Weber exchanges the boxing ring for the wrestling mat in his 2000 film *Chop Suey*, partly a coming-of-age story about a teenage wrestler and model named Peter Johnson, Weber's own muse at the time. Boxers and wrestlers, along with bodybuilders, were among the first male pinups.[4] Weber is mining that tradition here, as well as in his commercial work for Abercrombie and Fitch. These same masculine icons also crop up throughout Kubrick's *Look* work.

In between his two athlete homages, Weber made another highly stylized biographical documentary with a male subject: *Let's Get Lost* (1988), which is about the jazz trumpeter and singer Chet Baker, a dreamboat himself back in his youth. Kubrick's own enthusiasm for jazz—he played drums in a swing band in high school—led to assignments for *Look* like "Dixieland Jazz is 'Hot' Again." This June 6, 1950, entertainment piece has more of a sociocritical edge than is usually evident in Kubrick's work for the magazine. It intermixes images of Black musicians playing to well-dressed white audiences in New York nightclubs with scenes of those musicians back in their own homes in New Orleans. The juxtaposition suggests that the Dixielanders themselves weren't reaping much in the way of reward from the revival of their music. In one image from this shoot, Kubrick poses himself behind the drum kit—the white guy in a Black band—and looks right into the camera, with eyebrows arched (Figure 5). Kubrick also shot pictures for the magazine of jazz pianist and composer Erroll Garner, bandleaders Vaughn Monroe, and Guy Lombardo, and clarinetist Pee Wee Russell. Frank Sinatra and Leonard Bernstein were among his other subjects. And Kubrick got to photograph Montgomery Clift in his New York apartment for a story that ran in the July 19, 1949, issue of *Look* as "Glamour Boy in Baggy Pants." It is composed of nine pictures of the man whom the Barbizon Models of New York had just named America's Most Eligible Bachelor. In an interview many years later with Michel Ciment, Kubrick singled out this piece about the closeted actor as one of more interesting "personality stor[ies]" that he got to do at the magazine.[5]

Athletes, as I've been suggesting, appear to have been another Kubrick forte for *Look*. In addition to Walter Cartier, he photographed baseball stars Don Newcombe and Phil Rizzuto, along with decathlon champion Irving Mondschein, among others. Then there are his pictures of sports figures with a twist, such as the flamboyant professional wrestler Gorgeous George, dubbed "the Human Orchid" for his golden locks, fancy drag costumes, and practice of

Figure 5. Kubrick on the drums down in New Orleans. (Stanley
Kubrick, photographer, LOOK Magazine Photograph Collection,
Library of Congress, Prints & Photographs Division, LC-L9-50-
W99-C, no. 29. Used with permission of the Stanley Kubrick
Film Archives.)

perfuming the ring upon entering it. Or take Kubrick's 1947 piece "Baby Wears
Out 205 lb. Athlete." It playfully infantilizes a strapping ex-marine and Car-
leton College football player, Bob Beldon, as he tries to imitate and keep up
with an indefatigable toddler. This is just one of the many man-to-boy stories
in Kubrick, stories whose apotheosis will comes in 2001: A Space Odyssey, when
astronaut Dave Bowman returns home as the Star Child.

We see from Kubrick's marine jock and toddler photo-series that he had
a flair too for photographing children. Here the effect is comic. Kubrick's
unpublished "Tale of a Shoe-Shine Boy," also from 1947, is a Dickensian epic.
This is another one of Kubrick's day-in-the-life visual essays. Its subject is a
twelve-year-old from Brooklyn named Mickey—fetching enough to be a child
actor—who shines shoes to help support his nine younger siblings. Kubrick follows Mickey from the streets where he works to the tenement building roof-
top where he tends his homing pigeons. He also shows Mickey hitting both
his schoolbooks in the library and other boys in neighborhood boxing ring (Figure 6). In between his "Baby Wears Out Athlete" and "Shoe-Shine Boy" stories,
Kubrick landed the August 5, 1947, cover of Look with his shot of a little boy
gleefully dousing himself in the shower to cool off from the summer heat.
The following year Kubrick photographed five-year-old miracle boy Wally
Ward, who recovered from his infant paralysis to play with a football and spring
handstands.

Figure 6. Boy boxers. (Stanley Kubrick for Look magazine. Museum of the City of New York. Used with permission of Museum of the City of New York and Stanley Kubrick Film Archives.)

I am cherry-picking male images and storylines here, of course. In the five years that Kubrick worked at *Look*, he showed that he could frame an interesting, artful shot of nearly anything and anyone. He took thousands of pictures for the magazine, with more than nine hundred of them published in its pages.[6] Kubrick's assignments run the gamut from circus performers, including a tattooed man sporting enormous iron nipple rings, to showgirls and socialites; from rising star Doris Day to aspiring actress Betsy von Fürstenberg ("The Debutante Who Went to Work"); from the co-ed dating scene at the University of Michigan to nuclear scientists at Columbia; from "A Dog's Life in the Big City" to a baby boy's first look into the mirror.

Female nudity figures throughout Kubrick's movies.[7] There's a foretaste of that here in his *Look* photography: von Fürstenberg reading a script in her negligee; an undraped female sitter in front of an art class at Columbia; a man contemplating an enormous female nude hanging in a picture gallery; *New Yorker* sophisticate cartoonist Peter Arno in his studio with his own personal naked model, whom Kubrick shoots full-on from behind (Figure 7). The unexpected discovery is all the male bodies in states of undress in Kubrick's work. If "Art" serves as the cover for many of the naked female bodies in his photography, the alibi for nearly all of the beefcake here is sports.

Figure 7. *New Yorker* cartoonist Peter Arno with model. (Stanley Kubrick for Look magazine. Museum of the City of New York. Used with permission of Museum of the City of New York and Stanley Kubrick Film Archives.)

Figure 8. "Glamour Boy" Montgomery Clift.

Kubrick's *Look* work also presents more intimate male images, like snap-shots of the thirty-year-old, bare-chested Leonard Bernstein looking fit in his bathing trunks. Or Montgomery Clift sprawling on the bedroom floor in his boxer shorts, sucking on a bottle of wine (Figure 8). Another of Kubrick's bedroom pictures presents boxer Walter Cartier in nothing but his jockey shorts, yawningly just out of bed (Figure 9). His arms-akimbo pose echoes that of Arno's nude female model, connoting display, access. A second young man still lies there in Cartier's bed, wearing no more (perhaps less) than the boxer in his briefs. He too faces us, but his eyes are demurely closed. This private, behind-the-scenes "candid" is carefully composed: an erotic planar geometry of intersecting, if just now no longer touching, semi-naked athletic male forms. Thomas Waugh has searchingly analyzed the ways in which the male athletic photograph, ever since its late nineteenth-century emergence as a new genre, has "accommodated the homoerotic gaze."[8] Kubrick's own sports photography not only accommodates that gaze, it courts it.

Kubrick retraced the day-of-the-fight storyline of "Prizefighter" in a February14, 1950, photo-story for *Look* about the more famous middleweight Rocky Graziano subtitled "He's a Good Boy Now." Kubrick's camera follows a naked Graziano first into the ringside doctor's examination room and then the showers (Figure 10). *Look* didn't publish these locker room nudes of the one-time world champion, but it's something that Kubrick took them, just as he did of Walter Cartier. Kubrick's earlier photospread on Cartier reports that this fighter is headed to law school if he soon doesn't make it to the top in the ring. But when Cartier (who died in 1995) left the sport it was instead for act-ing, including a part in *Somebody Up There Likes Me*, Robert Wise's 1956

Figure 9. Boxer in briefs.

Oscar-winning drama about Graziano's hardscrabble life. Handsome Paul Newman plays Graziano.

Fight Films

Walter Cartier plays himself in Kubrick's debut film, *Day of the Fight*. Its title echoes a headline in "Prizefighter" that's also reused in the Rocky Graziano photo-story. The sixteen-minute documentary opened at the Paramount The-ater in New York on April 26, 1951—the bottom part of a double bill—and was widely distributed by RKO-Pathé for its *This Is America* series. Kubrick, then twenty-two, directed and shot the film himself, with the help of Alexander Singer, a high school friend, as the second cameraman. Gerald Fried, another acquaintance from Kubrick's schooldays, scored the film, providing a brass-heavy martial fanfare main theme, which later came to be called "March of the Gloved Gladiators."[9]

Richard Combs describes *Day of the Fight* as "Startlingly . . . not so much a rough draft as a perfect miniature of the feature films that were to follow."[10] Singer, who became a director himself, recounts how Kubrick "did that sports short as if he were doing *War and Peace*." "He was meticulous with everything, from scripting to editing. Stanley was a full-blown film-maker instantly."[11] Walter

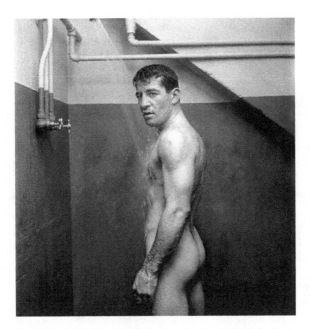

Figure 10. Rocky Graziano in the raw. (Stanley Kubrick for Look
magazine. Museum of the City of New York. Used with
permission of Museum of the City of New York and Stanley
Kubrick Film Archives.)

Cartier, not only the subject of *Day of the Fight* but also a technical consultant on
the film, makes a similar point in his own terms: "Stanley comes in prepared like
a fighter for a big fight, he knows exactly what he's doing, where he's going and
what he wants to accomplish. He knew the challenges and he overcame them."[12]
Michael Herr, a coauthor with Kubrick of the screenplay for *Full Metal Jacket*,
provides a variation on this theme in coming to the defense, many years after its
release, of Kubrick's other boxing movie, the not so well-regarded *Killer's Kiss*.
Herr reminds us that Kubrick made that early film "under severe time and money
limitations, which he addressed like a soldier." "And," emphasizes Herr, "not a
boy soldier either."[13] Such talk becomes a trope, a kind of Kubrick "thing"—a
male thing. We find versions of it in firsthand reminiscences of Kubrick's way on
the set, as well as in theoretical contemplations of his mode of auteurism. Kubrick, the director as a prizefighter. Or soldier. Or general. Then there's Kubrick
and his films as a brain (that's Deleuze)—or a computer. HAL, *c'est moi?*[14]

   The *Look* photo-essay "Prizefighter," the documentary *Day of the Fight*,
and the feature film *Killer's Kiss* make a mixed photography and film triptych
on boxing. In segueing from Kubrick's photographs to his films, I want to

dwell a while on *Day of the Fight* before turning to *Killer's Kiss*. I do so not
only because this now fairly obscure, short-form documentary made for such
an accomplished debut, a debut already compact with what will endure as
Kubrick's preoccupations, but also because (though this may be to say again
what I just said) the first film that Kubrick made is all about male display,
male contest, and male relations.

In turning his *Look* picture-essay on Cartier into his debut motion picture,
Kubrick repositions the boxer in an even more ritually intensive same-sex world.
A male voiceover narrator—a favored expository device of Kubrick's from the
beginning—takes us through it. Kubrick considered Montgomery Clift for the
part, but ultimately he decided on veteran CBS news reporter and later anchor Douglas Edwards. Cartier, Edwards has us know, shares his small Greenwich Village apartment with his aunt, but she is nowhere to be seen in the
film. Nor is the girlfriend who appears with him in two shots in the original
photo-piece. The narrator further informs us that Cartier's father is away and
that his mother died when he was a little boy. In the absence of these others,
the documentary narrows its focus to Cartier and his brother—his twin brother,
Vincent. Vincent is a lawyer in New Jersey and also Walter's manager. Singer,
who operated the second camera on the film, reminisces, "Walter Cartier was
good-looking and able. He surely looked good—and his brother, Vincent,
looked good—and the two of them together were really quite marvelous figures."[15] The nom de guerre under which Walter first fought was "Wally 'Twin'
Carter." Walter Cartier is the first of Kubrick's men; but he is also one in a
line of male duplicates—twins, doubles, doppelgängers—to be turned out in
Kubrick's movies. (Even HAL has a twin back on earth.)

The edgy hourly countdown to the late night bout begins at 6:00 a.m., with
Walter and Vincent waking up together in a double bed. "Walter is on the
right," the narrator must point out of the two "boys," as he calls them, who are
dead ringers for each other. (And it's twin brother Vincent in that bedroom
photograph in the *Look* magazine "Prizefighter" photo-essay.) We hear how
Walter and Vincent started exhibition boxing each other when they were just
little boys. Apparently inseparable, the twins continued to do so during the
war in the Navy, "where they were in the same outfit together." While the
voiceover relays this, the film supplies a neat visual pun. Out of bed and now
dressed, the brothers, still all but indistinguishable, are once again in the same
outfit. This time it's coat and tie (Figure 11). That's Walter now on the left,
"wearing the bowtie," the narrator indicates, as the boys sprint shoulder to
shoulder across a busy downtown street.

What am I insinuating? Simply that even as Kubrick's fight movie shapes up,
as others too have observed, as a formalist study of doubles—and this is Joyce

Figure 11. The Cartier twins, Walter and Vincent, in Greenwich Village.

Carol Oates's take *On Boxing* tout court[16]—it also comes to read as a kind of period portrait of a male "couple." The visual and thematic "homo"-ness of the encounter in the ring, including its homoeroticism, in this case bends back home as well. Kubrick's sports documentary is notable, we have already glimpsed, for the domestic vignettes that it stages. In addition to the uncanny image of the adult male twins side by side in a double bed in their pajamas, we watch Vincent serve Walter "a fighter's breakfast" in the apartment's cozy kitchen. This is where their aunt shows up in the corresponding picture in the "Prizefighter" photo-essay, but not here in the movie. "Now they live," pronounces the narrator, "as they used to years ago, the two boys—and Walter's dog." Fight day thus ironically occasions the irenic restoration of a fantasy of parentless fraternal exclusivity: brothers together, no others.

And dog makes three. The Cartier boys didn't have a pet; this was Kubrick's addition to the domestic storyline that he wanted to foster for them. Recall the decorative role that dogs play in Bruce Weber's work, which culminates in the 2004 documentary *A Letter to True* about his own beloved pack of handsome golden retrievers. Dogs are what Weber's sportive boys have—that and each other, if not girls. A later scene in the film of the Cartiers killing time alone at home before the fight shows Walter cuddling his spaniel, while Vincent, puffing on his pipe, approvingly looks on. Just as the twins double one another, Vincent plays a second, doubly gendered double role—a brother who is both mother and father—in this day-of-the-fight male household.

While Walter's pet plaything kisses his face and he affectionately blows in the dog's ears, we hear how tonight he will "go to work [in the ring] with these same kind, playful hands." Fast forward to Walter in the locker room just before the fight:

> Walter isn't concerned with the hands of the clock now, just his own hands. As he gets ready to walk out there in the arena, in front of the people, Walter is slowly becoming another man. . . . The hard movements of his arms and fists are different from what they were an hour ago. They belong to a new person. They're part of the Arena Man: the fighting machine that the crowd outside has paid to see in fifteen minutes.

The mind/body processes of becoming machinic are another abiding interest of Kubrick's work, stretching from this sports short through all his war films. Walter Cartier wielded a knockout punch both in his right hand and his left hand, twin engines of unconsciousness. The boxing claim to fame of this "fighting machine" was knocking out an opponent in the first round in less than one minute with one punch.

There is another personal dimension to this boxer—and something else the brothers share—that the film is interested in. The soulful middleweight Walter and his twin are both devout. A holy picture and crucifix hang above their bed. Later in the film, just before he is called from the dressing room to the ring, Walter gives Vincent the saint's medal that he wears around his neck for safekeeping. And the scene on the street where the two boys are all but identically dressed up has them on their way, not from any of the Greenwich Village bars seen in a row in the background, but rather to church. There they kneel alone and side-by-side (again looking so good together) at the altar rail. "It's important for Walter to receive Holy Communion," intones the narrator ominously, "in case something should go wrong tonight." A low, tilt angle shot of a Pietà—Jesus, his loincloth comparable to what little a boxer wears, laid out stone cold dead over Mary's lap—feels foreboding.

After receiving the host from a priest and breakfast from his brother in paired, consecutive scenes of feeding—soul, then body—Walter undergoes another kind of day-of-the-fight rite: the mandatory prefight weigh-in and physical by a doctor. This scene, also pictured in both of Kubrick's boxing photo-stories for Look, returns us to the question of bodily display. As I remarked earlier, there may be more female than male flesh on view in Kubrick's movies, especially when it comes to nudity in an explicitly sexual context. But there is another kind of male exhibitionism that recurs in his art, both the photography and the films. These are scenes of looking at the male body as it is put on display for examination and handling, whether in athletic, military, or medical contexts: scenes imbued with their own, principally disciplinary, erotics. The most revealing comes in *A Clockwork Orange* when Alex is being processed for incarceration. "Get undressed . . . and bend over," he is ordered by the Chief Guard, in a scene that Kubrick's film adds to Anthony Burgess's novel. Consider too in this context the scene in *Full Metal Jacket* where facing rows of marine recruits stand at attention on their footlockers in their white boxers and T-shirts. Their drill inspector moves slowly down the line to inspect the recruits' outstretched hands, nails, and feet. In *Spartacus*, it's teeth: "As the teeth go, so go the bones." Thus declares the slave trader Batiatus as he peers into the mouth of a brawny slave he considers purchasing for his gladiator school. Then he learns that Spartacus has used his teeth to hamstring a slave guard. "How marvelous!" he says, and buys him on the spot. *Spartacus* is another one of Kubrick's fight films; it features both the ring and the battlefield. During one of its own "boot camp" scenes, different colored paints are swiped across Spartacus's bared body to target the most vulnerable areas. "You get an instant kill," says the trainer, "on the red"—the gladiator's version of the boxer's knockout punch, which also on occasion proved fatal. "For the blue you get a cripple." For the yellow "the slow kill."

In *Day of the Fight*, the combatant's body is not scored with paint but rather slicked with Vaseline. Vincent rubs Walter's bare chest and face with it before Walter is called from the dressing room to the ring. That Vaseline is part of the boxer's kit—along with his robe, satin trunks, gloves, tape, and icepack— carefully laid out on the bed back in the apartment and filmed by Kubrick in a slow, hovering pan. (A large jar of Vaseline also appears on the dresser of the boxer protagonist of *Killer's Kiss*.) The fetishistic shot of the boxer's things in *Day of the Fight* dissolves into a close-up of him regarding his face, artifact-like, in a mirror (Figure 12). This scene may be the strangest in Kubrick's altogether strange take on the sports short. With Walter—now both viewer and thing viewed—we watch the man in the mirror go from coiffing his hair (so as to look his best for a fight?) to curiously tracing his finger across the lines of his eyebrows and then pressing it into the spongy tip of his nose, a nose that looks to have been broken before. Recall that Bruce Weber's own boxing documentary movie debut is titled *Broken Noses*, signaling that form of facial disfigurement—sexy, it might be thought, in its way—as this sport's calling card. "Before the fight, there is always that last look in the mirror," muses the narrator of *Day of the Fight*, "time to wonder what it will reflect tomorrow." In Cartier's self-objectifying lingering farewell look we again see double—double in more ways than one. The boxer who once fought as "Twin Carter" now re-doubles himself, all alone. Forms of replication multiply: two who are as one

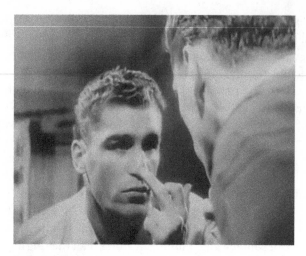

Figure 12. The boxer's magic mirror.

and one who here appears as two. We also see at once in Cartier's reflection both what is and what may be, as he plies his own waxwork countenance with a hand that has the power to alter another's. And therein is another double image, one of male vulnerability (not to say vanity) coupled with awesome brute force.[17]

The mirror scene of *Day of the Fight* mirrors an even queerer looking double image from the "Prizefighter" photo-essay, which depicts the two twins face-to-face in profile, as Vincent again makes up Walter's visage with that Vaseline (Figure 13). If the film's mirror scene has a surreal, dreamlike aura, this one looks like an ecstasy. Literally so. The two boys, one another's best, appear to be transported together outside themselves—and everything, as intimated by the lack of any background in the photo. The caption reads, "His expression reveals depths of fondness he has for his brother." Whose "his" is this? Vincent's? Walter's? Who can say? On this account there is no need to tell them apart. For just before he enters the ring we are told how "every blow that Walter takes" is "going to land on Vince too." "But," the narrator deadpans, "they don't talk about that."

These mirror scenes involving the Cartier boys also double back to another of Kubrick's *Look* pieces: a photo-essay I mentioned earlier on a baby's first encounter with a mirror, published in the May 13, 1947, issue. The opening picture in this six-shot narrative sequence shows a tentatively smiling baby boy in his short pants waving or reaching out to what looks to him like a new playmate, one who replies in kind (Figure 14). Kubrick sets the angle of the shot so that we can't see the front baby's left arm: a perspective that creates the impression of two separate figures.[18] Behind this baby boy lies a hairbrush: an

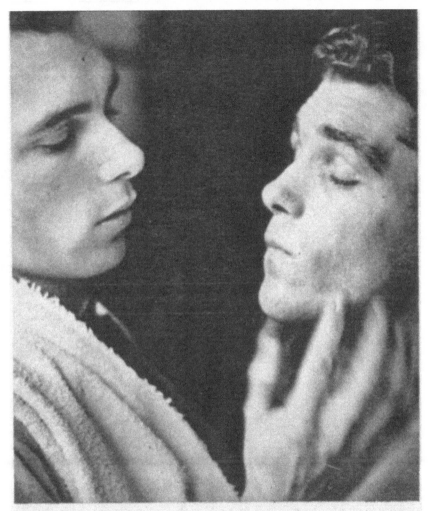

Vincent rubs Vaseline on Walter. His expression reveals depth of fondness he has for his brother.

Figure 13. Fraternal ecstasy.

intriguing single prop I take as a pointer to the all the scenes of male grooming forthcoming in Kubrick's movies and not only *Day of the Fight*. In the third picture, the baby seems to offer his fellow that brush, only to see himself copied again. In the final picture, the child has turned away from the mirror, his mouth open in a wail of bewilderment or frustration. The evocatively pop-psych caption reads: "It's beyond me, and I want no more of it. Mom—get me out of

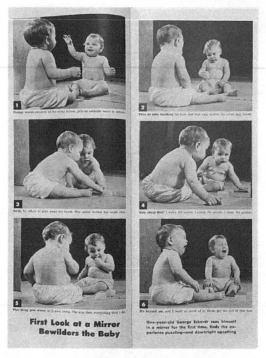

Figure 14. Seeing double: A boy's first look in the mirror.

this fast."[19] The bare, artificial setting, the supersized mirror, and all the black box–like negative space that it creates suggest the controlled environment of an experiment—a not altogether benign one. It will be my argument here that Kubrick's films never stop experimenting with their men and boys, with forms of masculinity and male identities.

To return to *Day of the Fight*, Walter Cartier, once in the ring at last, is matched with another "boy" (as the narrator calls him too): Bobby James, who is Black. The pair of welterweights makes for a different kind of play on sameness and difference. Compare again the fight film *Spartacus*, which will pit Kirk Douglas in the ring against the awesome Woody Strode, former college athlete and then professional wrestler. (The flamboyant Gorgeous George, another Kubrick subject for *Look* magazine, was a frequent opponent of Strode's on the professional wrestling circuit.) *Day of the Fight* devotes two kinetically photographed and edited minutes of screen time to the fight itself, shot live by Kubrick operating a handheld Eyemo camera (which he thrust through the ropes right into the ring) and Singer using a camera on a tripod. Cartier wins with a knockout in the second round. A day's work, reports the narrator, and there the film ends.

"Matched pairs of men will get up on a canvas-covered platform and commit legal assault and lawful battery," the film's narrator had heralded in his script's most lyrical flight, "hammering each other unconscious with upholstered fists." But Kubrick's sports short, as we have seen, has two stories to relay at once. "One man . . . skillfully, violently overcom[ing] another": "this is for the fan, short for 'fanatic,'" we are informed in the opening segment of the film. That first, four-and-a-half-minute-long, tabloidlike introduction speeds us through the mechanics and also the annals of the sport, culminating in a shot of a boxing record book that fills the screen. A close-up of a hand belonging to Nat Fleischer, publisher of *The Ring* magazine and boxing historian, flips through the pages until we come upon the name and picture of Kubrick's own "Prizefighter," Walter Cartier. "What would *his* story be like?" asks the narrator, as the film cuts to a fight poster adorned with Cartier's face attached to a lamppost. The film's remaining twelve minutes are devoted to him. And it is around Cartier, plus his twin, that this other story unfolds: an inside story paired here with the public spectacle of the fight—a story about structures of bonding and male intimacy, of male doubling, but also coupling. A (brotherly) love story, if you will, to go with the nighttime call to battle.

Four years after he made *Day of the Fight*, Kubrick returned to the ring for his second feature film, *Killer's Kiss* (1955): an atmospheric sports/crime pulp piece about another white, twenty-something boxer, soon to become a has-been, named Davey Gordon (Jamie Smith). This time there is no authoritative male voiceover to call him "boy," the way that the narrator of *Day of the Fight* refers to Walter Cartier. But the puerile "y" tacked onto Davey's name does the trick. The faltering welterweight is left to tell his troubled tale in a flashback that begins with the day of the fight—which itself begins with images that flash back all the way to Kubrick's debut sports short. The first is a close-up of a poster with a photograph of Davey on it advertising his bout that night, just like the fight-night poster that presents Walter Cartier to us in the earlier film. The next shot, however, shows another of these posters in a puddle of rain, where this boxer's image is forebodingly trampled underfoot. The second flashback to *Day of the Fight* occurs when we come upon Davey alone in his forlorn studio apartment, looking in a mirror. There, like Cartier, Davey tentatively pokes and pulls at his face as though it were made of putty, speculating about what it will look like after that night's fight. "As hard a puncher as they come," reports a TV sportscaster of this boxer; "but he's been plagued by a weak chin"—"a glass chin," it will later be recast.

Kubrick, who showed a flair for repetition from the beginning and quickly became his own chief influence, not only cites himself in this recycled mirror scene, but also adds to his repertoire of uncanny subjective shots. For here the

Figure 15. Davey, boxer with a "glass chin."

boxer's magic mirror is pasted with photographs. They picture his uncle and
aunt (Davey appears to be an orphan: an intensification of Cartier's circumstances, with his absent father and deceased mother), along with the family
ranch in Washington State, from which he presumably came and to which he
intends to return at the film's end. What a curious image, when you think about
it, this mirror adorned with snapshots, with freeze-frame mementos from another time. It layers and suspends there in a single look the present, past, and
possible futures (one of which would be a return to the past, to the family home
of sorts out west). At a further remove, we might also reflect upon the pictorial-
ized looking glass as an early auteurist signature: another marker that for this
director everything here looks back to the photograph—to how these fight films
originate in the 1949 "Prizefighter" *Look* photospread Kubrick did on Cartier
(and then did over again on the even more successful prizefighter Rocky Graziano). Both Cartier and Davey first appear in their movies in the form of
photographs, in images of images. This is true for Cartier twice over. Recall
that we first see his picture in a close-up of a boxing record book, followed by
that shot of his fight night poster.

There are photographs planted all over *Killer's Kiss*. Reflective surfaces, too.
Later, when Davey heads downstairs, we see him doubled in a gleaming row of
metal mailboxes. But before that, in the scene that we were just considering,
Davey goes from considering himself in his dresser mirror, to getting a glass
of water from the sink over which hangs a second mirror, to then looking
through the looking glass of a fish bowl. The reverse-angle close-up is Kubrick's
witty literal take on a "fisheye" lens (Figure 15). Bill Krohn sees this "deforming"

Figure 16. Dave, metamorphic astronaut.

image as making Davey look like "a battered pugilist"—even before the fight that night, which, no surprise, he loses.[20] I see that here as well, along with a sense of both loneliness (Cartier has a twin brother and a dog; Davey's only companions are a couple of goldfish) and confinement. But there is also something else to see reflected in this watery mirror image of the boxer with the glass chin. It's a metamorphic image of dissolving and with it the possibility of *becoming*—one that is weirdly proleptic of the blank, expectant face of another Dave, astronaut Dave Bowman of *2001*, in his amphibious-looking spacesuit and on the brink of his deep space transformation (Figure 16). Dave will metamorphose into the Star Child. But what of this earlier Davey? What may become of him, of this about-to-be-battered boxer, with the pliable putty face? "It's crazy how you can get yourself in a mess sometimes," he begins his story—the same old story (but then again perhaps not).

Killer's Kiss has a weak script. The acting is stilted. And the post-dubbed dialogue stutters in and out of sync with the image. But then there is, as we've been considering, Kubrick's photography. The film's feature length allows him to show off his own handheld camerawork, this time in two extended one-on-one fight scenes. The first takes place in the ring, where Davey is soundly beaten. As in *Day of the Fight*, Kubrick sticks his own hand through the ropes, rendering an array of shaky-cam close-ups that make us feel as though we are right there too. The rest of the world falls away. There are no establishing shots of the crowd in the stands here because there actually isn't one. (Kubrick couldn't afford the extras.) Martin Scorsese draws upon this visceral, right-there-in-the-ring-with-him effect, adding sprays of blood to the flying sweat, in his own tour-de-force boxing movie *Raging Bull* (1980), about Jake LaMotta, the one-time world middleweight champion. LaMotta and Kubrick's *Look* photographic subjects Walter Cartier and Rocky Graziano were all friends and occasional sparring partners.

Kubrick's cinema verité boxing footage is virtuosic and cinematically influential, and not only on Scorsese. This is something that commentators on *Killer's Kiss* routinely remark, even those who have nothing else good to say about this bare-bones budget early feature. What also needs to be said is that Kubrick's cinematic visualization of the fight is not only impressive but arousing too. It's hard to imagine a more erotic shot selection from inside the ropes. Before the bell, Kubrick's camera peers through the seated Davey's legs all the way across the canvas to his opponent, Kid Rodriguez, in the far corner. This unusual crotch-shot point of view is also directly copped from *Day of the Fight*. In the extreme low angle frame that Davey's bristly calves afford, we watch Kid Rodriguez's trainer push in the boxer's mouthpiece and then snatch away his stool. Rodriguez's imposing form pops up in deep focus from between the still seated Davey's splayed legs. The bell sounds, and the two dance around and court each other. Here it is "the two game boys" (as the TV commentator dubs them) matched in the ring, not the boys in the sheets and in the streets as in *Day of the Fight*, who double each other. Davey and his opponent come together hard in another striking shot that lops them off at their necks and knees, while centering on their bare, sweaty torsos in a tight male embrace, groin to groin. When they untangle their bodies from each other, Kid Rodriguez puts Davey down for the first of two eight counts. Another powerful blow hurtles Davey backward into the ropes, which is to say ass-forward into the frame and smack into our faces. "Go on home, Gordon; "You're a bum," someone in the crowd calls out. "You're all through!"

"Surely boxing derives much of its appeal," Oates insists, "from [its] mimicry of a species of erotic love in which one man overcomes the other in an exhibition of superior strength and will."[21] Kubrick might not have put it quite like that himself. But his *Killer's Kiss* proffers the encounter in the ring between the dominating young Kid Rodriguez and the overmastered veteran Davey as pornography for the morose crime boss Vincent Rapallo—note the reuse here of Walter Cartier's twin brother's name—and his moll Gloria Price. The Jamaican-born, mixed-race actor Frank Silvera, the only real professional in the cast, plays Vinnie in darkening makeup. Irene Kane, who had done some modeling for *Vogue*, is the bottle-blond Gloria.[22] Along with the washed-up prizefighter Davey, they constitute the dismal masochistic erotic triangle of a movie to which Kubrick, when he rewrote Howard Sackler's first-draft screenplay, gave the working title *The Nymph and the Maniac*.[23]

Gloria, who lives in a one-room apartment directly across the way from Davey's, works as a "hostess" at Pleasure Land, the taxi-dance hall that Vinnie runs in Times Square. The sole windows in Gloria and Davey's matching apartments face one another, affording their inhabitants nowhere else to look. Early on in the film we see that they are the unknowing (or perhaps not so unknowing) objects of each other's rear-window voyeurism. In Hitchcock's movie *Rear Window*, which came out the year before *Killer's Kiss*, the photographer Jeffries (James Stewart) doesn't become aroused by his glamorous girlfriend Lisa (Grace Kelly)—so notes Laura Mulvey in her influential schematization of the cinematic gaze—until she leaves his apartment and crosses over to the other side of the courtyard: that is, into the field of vision for his scopophilia.[24] Kubrick reworks this arrangement by placing Gloria (his poor man's Grace Kelley), over there on the other side from the beginning. Kubrick further plays with the erotic gaze, routinely indicated, following Mulvey, as male, by having the woman steal the first long, lingering look, one that also takes in the boxer's backside. Gloria becomes the object of his gaze that night, after he returns home from the fight. We see Davey sitting alone in the dark and shirtless once again, staring at Gloria, who has taken off her blouse.

Still later that night, Gloria's scream summons Davey from his place to hers to save her from the rapacious Rapallo's unwelcome advances. The next morning she recounts her life story: a sorry family drama steeped in Freudianisms (incestuous desire, sibling rivalry, and the like). Kubrick sets Gloria's voiceover to a bizarre solo ballet interlude on an empty stage by his then wife Ruth Sobotka, a Viennese-born dancer, painter, actor, and set designer, who moved through the New York avant-garde art scene. She figures Gloria's ballerina older sister, Iris: the image, we hear, of their mother and their daddy's favorite. We also now learn that Gloria, like Davey, is now an orphan. Parallel edits earlier in the film of them readying themselves for work—the boxer and the low-rent dancer are both professional entertainers, the kind who offer up their bodies for others' pleasure—have already established them as another of the film's multiple sets of doubles. These paired scenes culminate in Gloria and Davey arriving downstairs, with their coats and bags (hers a purse, his a duffle), at precisely the same moment. They silently exit the courtyard to the street walking side-by-side in a way that harks back to the Cartier twins. Even as they go their separate ways, the parallelism continues. Davey waits in the locker room and has his hands taped up by his trainer. Then his manager (in another replay of *Day of the Fight*) glazes Davey's face and bare chest with Vaseline before giving him a prefight rubdown. I find these silent, dutiful scenes of handling and preparing the fighter's body among the most intensely intimate male images in all of

Kubrick. In between those male ministrations, the film cuts to Gloria alone in the dressing room at Pleasure Land. She is also shown undressed, getting ready in front of another mirror for her own night's work. A close-up of the dresser strewn with her makeup, tweezers, brush, and high-heel shoes recalls that fetishistic slow pan across the boxer's kit laid out on the bed in *Day of the Fight*.

Once Gloria is out on the floor, Vinnie roughly cuts in on a soldier with whom she has been dancing to steal her away to his office so that they can watch Davey's bout on TV. At the end of the film, Davey and Vinnie will, in another of Kubrick's race-inflected duels, face off. That fight Davey manages to win. But here the film intercuts the beating that Davey takes in the ring with shots of Vinnie and Gloria in an outward-facing embrace, their eyes locked, not on each other but instead on the boxers. Socially censured in many quarters and on occasion even outlawed, boxing has never altogether shed its underworld association with organized crime and vice trades such as gambling.[25] This sport's allure for Vinnie is another aspect of his sordidness. But the film shows Gloria no less transfixed than he is by what she spies on his television, with its small, round, peephole-like screen. The killer's kiss in the ring—the smack that lays out Davey for the count—leads to Vinnie's lip lock with Gloria ("Her soft mouth was the road to sin-smeared violence," cries the movie poster), and then the screen fades to black.

Looking back on *Killer's Kiss* in an interview many years later, Kubrick lamented the "slight zombielike quality" of the acting.[26] The awkwardly post-synched dialogue mentioned earlier may be blamed in part for that effect. But the robotic performances feel right for a movie whose climax is staged in a Garment District mannequin factory and warehouse. It is there, in the second fight scene of *Killer's Kiss*, that Davey and Vinnie battle to the death over its femme fatale, this pearl of great price. Kubrick abandons the gritty realism of the film's first fight scene for a warped expressionism evocative of Orson Welles's *The Lady from Shanghai* (1947), though he replaces the multiplying mirrored forms of that movie's famous funhouse sequence with heaps of plastic molded ones. This principle of reduplication, first iterated with the shots of Davey doubled in not one but two mirrors at home, has been building on itself throughout the film. Take the kitschy drawing of the two guffawing clowns hanging in Vinnie's office, in which Vinny sees himself mirrored as the object of derision and so he flings his glass at it. Or the two drunken, madcap Shriners who steal Davey's scarf, causing him to give chase and thus saving him from Vinnie's two henchmen, who then mistakenly target and kill Davey's manager Albert instead. The hoods corner the doomed man in a dead-end alley, next to a huge "Notice" that declares "No Toilet." (Not a good sign in a Kubrick movie.) This compulsion on the part of the film to make everything double is now, in its climax in the mannequin factory, hyperbolized in a stockpile of nude human figurines and unattached body parts: heads, hands, legs, trunks, set out in orderly rows or amassed in overflowing piles. Its humanoid mise-en-scène is prefigured earlier in the film by a wonderfully strange Times Square storefront montage that includes a mechanical Santa Claus sticking out his tongue to lick the candy apples that he holds, one in each hand, and a wind-up plastic naked baby paddling around in a bowl: artificial persons in a surreal city.

"I gotta get out of here," Vinnie murmurs to himself, once he takes stock of where he is. But Davey, whom we watched manipulate his own features as though they were putty—Davey, the boxer with the glass chin—turns out to be made of stronger stuff. He fits in better than Vinnie does among these abstract, pseudo-bodies. Davey first crouches for cover, lining up himself in a row of male heads all facing the same way. And then he defends himself against the ax-wielding Vinnie by prosthetically arming himself with whatever plastic dummy body part he can lay his hands on. (A *Clockwork Orange* pornographically tropes on this, first in the female-form fiberglass furniture of the Korova Milk Bar, and then Alex's murder of the Cat Lady with a giant sculptured cock and ass.) Eventually Davey takes up a spearlike hooked window pole. He stabs Vinnie to death with it, gladiator-like, as the film shock-cuts to a shattered mannequin face. Catherine Malabou, working at a conjunction of philosophy and neuroscience, credits humans with brains that are plastic.[27] Kubrick renders synthetic men in glass and plaster-molded parts.

And it is a world of plastic people who pose as the impassive audience for this final struggle between men, an audience that went missing from Davey's first fight back in the boxing ring. Not even Gloria is there to see it. After Davey's botched attempt to rescue her in the scene before, she remains tied up in Vinnie's nearby hideaway. (The film has prefigured this too, in the form of a doll tied up to the bedpost back in Gloria's studio apartment.) Some of the mannequins are male; others are ungendered. Most of them, however, are female. Indeed, there are more female forms here than anywhere else in Kubrick, until we arrive at the orgy scene in *Eyes Wide Shut*. These mannequins are the only spectators for Davey and Vinnie's mortal faceoff, and they are a mute, unimpressed crowd. Some dummy eyes seem trained on the combatants, others not. But as things, none of them sees anything. Their presence as blank witnesses undermines the performance of masculinity for anything at all—literally any "thing."[28]

This stunning scene makes for a queer penultima to what may look like the most conventional Hollywood ending in Kubrick. *Killer's Kiss* concludes with Davey waiting for Gloria at the old Penn Station, where they are to catch a train that will carry them far away to a new life together at his uncle and aunt's horse ranch in Washington. The film has thus returned to where its story began (this time-loop trick will be repeated in Kubrick's *Lolita*), which is with this very scene of Davey nervously pacing at the train station, two small pieces of luggage at his feet. As he waits, he tells his tale in a flashback that (to repeat myself) flashes us all the way back to Kubrick's first boxing film. In its seedy noir romance replay of *Day of the Fight*, *Killer's Kiss* recasts the self-sufficient, idyllic male "couple" of that sports short into an agonistic heterosexual love triangle and increases the number of character parts in the revamped ring-side drama. One example: the prefight ritual of oiling the boxer's body is performed in *Killer's Kiss* not by his twin but by his manager Albert—though, as we saw, he himself is tragically taken for the boxer by Vinnie's thugs, who murder him instead. Another is that it's Gloria who, after Davey has chased Vinnie away from her apartment, makes breakfast for him—just as the other Vincent, Vincent Cartier, does for Walter in *Day of the Fight*. This redistribution of roles is necessary for *Killer's Kiss* to enact its boxer meets, saves, and wins girl plot, however ham-fisted it is.

But what in the end does this boxer have to show for himself in the exchange of the fraternal devotion of a male double for a woman? Well, Gloria does not leave Davey alone at the station. She at last arrives and dashes across the platform into his embrace. They kiss. Yet the train to Seattle has already left, while Gloria, unlike Davey, has shown up empty handed. And to invoke *Rear Window* once more—specifically, the verified "feminine intuition" of Grace Kelly's Lisa—what woman would really be intending to go off anywhere with no bag, "without packing make-up, clothes, and jewelry"?

A parting shot: Irene Kane, the actress who plays the slightly tomboyish Gloria Price in *Killer's Kiss*, remembers Kubrick as (Hitchcock-like) "all for sex and sadism." She also recalls how Kubrick talked her into the role—her first in a movie—by saying that he "loved my voice," "a little-boy voice," as it was described.[29]

Documentary

In between the boxing movies, Kubrick made his first war film, *Fear and Desire*. It was also his first feature film. But before he took that step, Kubrick did two other documentaries: *Flying Padre* (1951) and *The Seafarers* (1953). Like his sports short about prizefighter Walter Cartier, *Flying Padre* is a male human-interest story. So in its own way is *The Seafarers*.

Day of the Fight cost Kubrick $3,900 to make, and he sold it to RKO-Pathé for $4,000. But the studio also gave Kubrick his next film project and a $1,500 budget to do it. *Flying Padre* presents Father Fred Stadtmueller, a Catholic priest who makes his pastoral visits to his far-flung flock, spread out over four thousand square miles in New Mexico, via his own single-engine airplane. Though he later developed a fear of flying and refused to travel by plane, Kubrick himself held a pilot's license when he did this nine-minute movie, which he wanted to call *Sky Pilot*, a pun on a slang term for a priest. *Flying Padre* employs the same "day-in-the-life" narrative framework as *Day of the Fight*, though here it's two days. Another carryover from Kubrick's first documentary to his second is a concern with religious rites and objects. He films Fr. Stadtmueller in full priestly regalia, conducting "solemn services" for a deceased ranch hand. His fancy cope and pomped biretta flamboyantly stand out within the desert cowboy mise-en-scène of the humble mission church and dusty gravesite. Stadtmueller then wings his way back to his home parish church in time to lead evening devotions. There, now dressed in his chasuble, we watch him in a peculiarly extended sequence brandish the monstrance right and left and back again for his mostly Hispanos congregants to venerate.

Day of the Fight humanizes Walter Cartier, a "fighting machine" in the ring, by giving him a dog at home. In *Killer's Kiss*, Davey has pet goldfish. The padre raises canaries as his hobby. But we are made to understand that he, too, is a man's man. The narrator, Bob Hite, informs us that Stadtmueller is a "good shot" and that he likes to hunt, as well as to work on his Piper Cub, which he has named the *Spirit of St. Joseph* after Jesus's earthly father. *Flying Padre* is more conventional than the arty *Day of the Fight*, with all that film's noir shadows, extreme angles, and double images. But its exciting final shot—a long, fast backward track of Stadtmueller posing proudly beside his aircraft—stands out as a harbinger of the man-and-machine images for which Kubrick will be known.

It would be interesting to know whether Kubrick got the assignment for *The Seafarers*, a promo film about the men who crew American ships, because of his way with male subjects in his first two shorts. In any case, this industrial documentary for the Seafarers International Union has its place, however minor, among Kubrick's men's films. Not only is the film's subject—this "brotherhood of the sea," with its quasi-military hierarchy and traditions—male, but so too is its specified audience of new or prospective union members. This half-hour-long color film (Kubrick's first) is as much a recruitment tool for the union as it is a depiction of the seafaring life, or "calling" as the movie has it. "I see guys doing other things together," says one fellow, rendering in simple words the film's stylish visual solicitation, and "I want to be part of it."

Nearly all of the film is shot on shore, and mostly at a union hall: one of many such places, declares the film's narrator, CBS news reporter Don Hollenbeck, "built by seafarers to meet the needs and suit the tastes of seafarers." (The matter of male taste will come back in the next chapter on Kubrick's war films.) The movie takes the viewer on a tour of places in and near the union headquarters, starting with the hiring hall, where seafarers put in for berths on ships that take them around the world. It next looks in on the union offices, where Kubrick juxtaposes the narrator's assurance that all "the machines and the files and the figures are there to serve the seafarers and not the other way around" against a striking constructivist montage of those many machines automatically whirring away. We also visit the cafeteria, barbershop, bar, the "Sea Chest" clothing store, various game rooms, a library, even a small art gallery. There the camera finds two nudie drawings that, along with a topless pin-up calendar in the barbershop shown full screen—"a pleasant sight after any voyage," the narrator chimes in here—give this inhouse documentary a slight stag flavor now and again.

Whatever the port, these union halls serve as a "second home" for seafarers, "where no man off the ship is stranger to the rest." (More brotherly love.) As such, that port-of-call second home makes for another of the all-male settings— the armed forces, athletics, prisons, spaceships—where so many of the stories that Kubrick's movies tell are placed or pass through. Here his gliding camera movements about the invitingly homosocial spaces of *The Seafarers* are punctuated by some striking working-class male portraiture of seafarers in suits and others in short sleeves that show off sailors' tattoos.

We see from the photographs, documentaries, and features touched upon in this chapter that Kubrick's art from early on was deeply absorbed with men and with forms of masculinity: this in ways, as we will further see, more various and complex than has been reckoned in Kubrick criticism.

2

War Films

Napoleon, Fear and Desire, Paths of Glory, Dr. Strangelove,
2001: A Space Odyssey

There is more to say about war than it is just bad.

— STANLEY KUBRICK

Stanley Kubrick is one of the great genreists because his way with a genre is
so idiosyncratic, one might even say strange. No genre occupied him more
extensively than the war film. Four of the thirteen features he directed are war
movies, the most for him in any genre. *Fear and Desire*, Kubrick's 1953 feature
debut (which he directed, shot, and edited), is a war film: an arty, abstract allegory that the director himself would come to disavow as too pretentious.
Four years later, Kubrick made another war film, *Paths of Glory*, a World War I
male melodrama. This was the twenty-eight-year-old director's breakout. (The
aborted *Aryan Papers*, an adaption of Louis Begley's semiautobiographical
novel *Wartime Lies*, published in 1991, would have been his World War II and
Holocaust film.) In 1964, Kubrick released his third war movie, *Dr. Strangelove Or: How I Learned to Stop Worrying and Love the Bomb*, a nuclear war
nightmare comedy. Kubrick returned to the war film for the last time with
1987's *Full Metal Jacket*, his most revisionary take on the military genre.

War, weapons, and tactics play an important part in other kinds of Kubrick
movies too. An uneasy Cold War détente provides the backdrop of his futurist
epic, *2001: A Space Odyssey*. Martial training and the battlefield also figure
prominently in *Spartacus*, Kubrick's historical saga about an ancient armed
slave revolt that shook Rome and required the full force of its mighty army to
suppress. Kubrick would turn his back on this film too, over which he didn't
have total control. But its two training sequences, first in Batiatus's "School
for Gladiators" and then in Spartacus's rebel army camp, served as a dress

rehearsal for passages from the Parris Island part of *Full Metal Jacket*. Kubrick's other historical drama, *Barry Lyndon*, is partially set during the Seven Years' War. The film features two extraordinary battle scenes and is bookended by duels. ("War," theorized Clausewitz, "is nothing but a duel on a larger scale."[1]) Speaking of military matters, it may be worth noting here that it is a handsome naval officer for whom Alice considers leaving her husband in *Eyes Wide Shut*, Kubrick's last film.

Maximal Kubrick

Kubrick's most ambitious unrealized film project—a colossal biographical movie about Napoleon Bonaparte, for which he wrote a treatment in 1968 and a screenplay in 1969—also has a military subject, indeed among the most storied of all. Whether by happenstance or design, the date of Kubrick's screenplay for his "Napoleon" coincided with the bicentennial of Napoleon's birth: a banner year for a figure whom Kubrick (as he jotted down in one of his countless project development notes to himself) regarded as "the most interesting historical subject that there has ever been."[2] In an interview from this time with Joseph Gelmis, he boasts of having tried to see every film ever made about Napoleon (none were to his liking) as well as having consulted hundreds of books on him.[3] Kubrick himself eventually amassed one of the largest private archives of Napoleon material, comprising five hundred books and some eighteen thousand period illustrations, including portraits and maps, but also pictures of hats (of course) and hairstyles, weapons and medals, furniture and tableware.[4] Kubrick's Napoleon collection would continue to grow even as his hopes of making his own "Napoleon" languished.

"I've ransacked all these books," the imperious director tells Gelmis, "for research material and broken it down into categories on everything from his food tastes to the weather on the day of a specific battle, and cross-indexed all the data in a comprehensive research file."[5] For his own on-call consultant on the film, Kubrick contracted the services of Oxford University historian Felix Markham, a leading Napoleon specialist. He also purchased the rights to Markham's biography of Napoleon. Kubrick, moreover, employed Markham's graduate students as foot soldiers for tracking down and recording on chronologically cross-referenced, color-coded file cards the whereabouts and actions of more or less everyone connected to Napoleon. "Between 1967 and 1969," Eva-Maria Magel ascertains, "Kubrick thus acquired just about all the available knowledge" on his subject.[6]

In the same interview with Gelmis, Kubrick comments on how Napoleon's life "has been described as an epic poem of action."[7] Elsewhere Kubrick makes it sound more like an opera: "It has everything a good story should have. A towering hero. Powerful enemies. Armed combat. A tragic love story. Loyal and treacherous friends. And plenty of bravery, cruelty, and sex."[8] As for Napoleon's sex life, Kubrick terms it "worthy of Arthur Schnitzler," the Viennese author whose 1926 novella *Traumnovelle* decades later became the basis for *Eyes Wide Shut*, Kubrick's sex film.[9] His Swinging Sixties "Napoleon" may have turned out to be even more explicit. A stage direction in the script labels a full-frontal nude sex scene between Josephine and Captain Hippolyte Charles, whom she takes as a lover while her husband is away in Italy, "Maximum erotica."[10] The scene is set in her boudoir on the Rue Chantereine in Paris, where previously she had similarly received Napoleon on the eve of their marriage. "The candlelit, oval bedroom," Kubrick's script details, "is completely encircled with floor-to-ceiling mirrored panels, which multiply the erotic images of Napoleon and Josephine, making love."[11] Imagine Audrey Hepburn *in flagrante delicto*, from all angles and sides, here coupled with the groovy David Hemmings, fresh from Michelangelo Antonioni's *Blow-Up* (1966) and Roger Vadim's *Barbarella* (1968). Or instead Hepburn with Ian Holm, or (weirder) Jack Nicholson. They were among those whom Kubrick, at one time or another, considered for the leading roles, though Hepburn herself politely begged off. Kubrick also had his eye on Jean-Paul Belmondo and Charlotte Rampling for supporting parts. Earlier in the script, while Josephine is still Napoleon's mistress, Kubrick has the pair watch a live sex act involving three copulating couples put on for them in the music room of Paul Barras. "Napoleon, still the provincial," the script indicates, "can scarcely believe his eyes."[12]

As for the film's battle scenes, they too were to be nothing short of maximal. In another of his handwritten notes to himself about the film, Kubrick tallied that "Napoleon fought more battles than Caesar, Alex and Hannibal combined."[13] He thus envisaged an array of meticulously reconstructed clashes involving as many as ten thousand cavalry and forty thousand infantry. A stage direction for a scene of the Grande Armée on the march calls for "Maximum numbers."[14] Both in view of its gigantism and its attention to minutiae ("Yes, I'd like a lot of details," Kubrick admits to Markham—*quelle surprise*—in one of their tape-recorded dialogues[15]) this historical epic, had it ever been realized, would have dwarfed even *2001*, Kubrick's Homeric space epic. Or at least Kubrick himself wanted it to. In an eleven-point memo that he typed up for potential investors in 1971, he declares as item 3: "It's impossible to tell you what I'm going to do except to say that I expect to make the best movie ever made."[16]

No less remarkable than the sheer scale of the proffered "best movie ever made"—this unmade/unmakeable film of films—is Kubrick's manifest pleasure in hypothetically working out its staggering logistics, especially with regard to the battle scenes. Where do you get fifty thousand male extras? (Inquiries were made into renting the Romanian and Yugoslav armies.) How do you then transport all these bodies to a shoot? (An armada of a thousand trucks, each carrying forty to fifty men, would be needed. Or better, find a battle site "contiguous to a . . . barracks area where the troops we'd use are already bivouacked.")[17] How do you costume them? (Kubrick found a New York company that could cheaply mass-produce fire-resistant paper uniforms that would still look good in the long distance shots.) He also calculated the need for 200,000 gallons of Technicolor blood.[18] The film's running time? "At least 199:40 minutes."[19]

This director's fascination with numbers, systems, and strategies—all evident on an epic scale in his designs for his "Napoleon"—has been remarked before. Kubrick's commitment to painstaking accuracy is likewise well known. But there is also an aesthetics in play here to which I would venture everything else is subordinate, especially with regard to the battle scenes. "From a purely schematic point of view, Napoleonic battles are so beautiful, like vast lethal ballets," Kubrick explains to Gelmis, "that it's worth making every effort to explain the configuration of forces to the audience."[20] On that account, he was willing to let naturalism fall by the wayside at times and resort to artificial devices such as animated maps in order to render the "flows" of Napoleon's most complex, most "choreographic" battles. "I think it's extremely important to communicate the essence of these battles to the viewer," Kubrick further expounds,

> because they all have an aesthetic brilliance that doesn't require a
> military mind to appreciate. There's an aesthetic involved; it's almost
> like a great piece of music, or the purity of a mathematical formula.
> It's this quality I want to bring across, as well as the sordid reality of
> battle. You know, there's a weird disparity between the sheer visual and
> organizational beauty of the historical battles sufficiently far in the
> past, and their human consequences.

Kubrick, the director-general, then waxes hawkish: "It's rather like watching two golden eagles soaring through the sky from a distance; they may be tearing a dove to pieces, but if you are far enough away the scene is still beautiful."[21]

This opus on Napoleon, for Kubrick the greatest of all military figures, remained perforce notional. I have lingered over it here, at the beginning of this chapter on the well-trod subject of his war films, because his conception of it brings to the fore another set of terms for thinking about them, in addition to each film's historical particularity and relevance.[22] "The scene is still beautiful," Kubrick muses over the complex patterns, the figures in the carpet, of his Napoleonic battlefields that were to be dyed incarnadine with those hundreds of thousands of gallons of Technicolor blood. As with boxing, the subject of Kubrick's very first (combat) film, *Day of the Fight*, it's the style that arouses. This is the premise for my aesthetical reading of Kubrick's first three war films—*Fear and Desire*, *Paths of Glory*, and *Dr. Strangelove*—a rereading that is as much concerned with style, culture, taste, and stimulation as it is with military tactics and outcomes. How are these aesthetic concerns raised, and what do they mean, in the male domain of the military, where, in Kubrick's work, we encounter a variety of warring masculinities? All this is related to another overarching question of this chapter: a question about war films, specifically Kubrick's (oxymoronic) "antiwar" war films. Let me be clear from the outset that this approach is not meant to imply that Kubrick's movies glamorize war, or any kind of masculine battlefield heroism—which, let it also be noted, is, like patriotism, here in short supply. But I would say that Kubrick was all but incapable, formally speaking, of making what could simply be called an antiwar film.

Generic War

Fear and Desire, Kubrick's little seen first feature, is a generic war film, so generic as to be abstract. It presents a discordant quartet of soldiers from an unidentified army in an unnamed country during an unspecified war. "Its structure: allegorical. Its conception: poetic," explains Kubrick in a 1952 letter to independent and foreign film distributor Joseph Burstyn. "A drama," Kubrick continues, "of 'man' lost in a hostile world deprived of material and spiritual foundations seeking his way to an understanding of himself, and of life around him."[23] In contrast not only to his obsessively historical "Napoleon" project, but also to all Kubrick's other war movies, this first one is posited outside history—or so we are told in the free-form poem, intoned by a male voiceover (David Allen), that opens the film:

> There is a war in this forest.
> Not a war that has been fought, or one that will be,
> But any war.
> And the enemies who struggle here do not exist
> Unless we call them into being.
> This forest, then,
> And all that happens now

Is outside history.
Only the unchanging shapes of fear and doubt and death
Are from our world.
These soldiers that you see keep our language and our time,
But have no other country but the mind.

There is a literary term for this kind of war story—*psychomachia*—that comes from a medieval allegory about the spiritual battle for the soul. *Fear and Desire* secularizes and updates that internal combat in terms of a then fashionable existentialism. This is to say that Kubrick's 1953 film, made near the end of the Korean War and amidst the Cold War, is both "outside history" and very much inside it, inside what the narrator invokes as "our time," "our world." The movie makes that point visually in its use of a mélange of military uniforms, gear, and insignia gathered from different twentieth-century wars, including World War II. Thus, as Geoffrey Cocks notes, one of the soldiers wears an American leather bomber jacket and an Air Force cap, but with a Nazi-esque emblem on it.[24] The film's evocation of place is likewise juxtapositional. Aspects of its forest setting—the palm trees and ferns—evoke the tropics. The film's prelude insists that these soldiers have no country but the mind, but the maps in enemy outpost show Europe and Africa.

These soldiers are not only dislocated in time and place, they also find themselves stranded behind enemy lines after their plane goes down. They devise a plan to make a raft to carry them downriver to rejoin their own side. As they set to work, shirts are doffed (Figure 17). (If you have eyes for it, there is no shortage of bare-chested men in Kubrick.) "All we need is Huckleberry Finn," quips Private Fletcher (Steve Coit), in his stage southern drawl. The film's script by budding poet-playwright Howard Sackler, Kubrick's friend from their high school days, seizes every opportunity to emit literariness. Sackler, as I noted earlier, also wrote the first draft of the screenplay for *Killer's Kiss*. These two movies—Kubrick's first features—are the only ones he made from original screenplays. (His "Napoleon" would have been the third.) All the films that come after are adaptations of literary works.

The forest through which these soldiers trudge in Kubrick's head-trip war movie is meant to be an externalization of their own battle-addled psyches. These expressionist woodlands are all mist and fog, deep shadows, and slants of light. A cacophony of more voiceovers makes us privy to each soldier's thoughts. Like the fantastical island setting of Shakespeare's *The Tempest*—the film's principle literary intertext—this forest is "full of noises."[25] But here, instead of the kind of "sounds and sweet airs, that give delight and hurt not" to which Caliban is attuned on his native island, we are bombarded with the

Figure 17. Soldiers out of their shirts.

anxious inner murmurings of these four lost soldiers: "Are they watching me?"
"Don't die here." "Nobody's safe!" "We're all gonna hang from the trees tonight."
Later Sergeant Mac (Frank Silvera, in his first of two roles for Kubrick) taunts
the skittish boy soldier Sidney (a New Yorker, by his accent) about the unseen
enemy lurking in the forest: "What's the matter, sweetums? I heard that they're
cannibals." Then, chucking the youth's chin and feeling up his skinny body,
the sergeant adds: "Even if we get caught, *you're* pretty safe." The pretense of
this peril suggests another association with *The Tempest* by way of Montaigne's
early modern anthropological essay "Of Cannibals," a stinging critique of
European savagery.[26] Shakespeare draws upon it for his play, which features
an island native, Caliban, whose name is an acronym of "cannibal," a term that
was then also related to "Carib."

Shakespeare's island play, like Kubrick and Sackler's forest film, seems to
be located in two places at once—the Mediterranean and the Caribbean—
while staking itself on a tenuous border between "primitive" and "civilized,"
concepts Montaigne's essay satirically interrogates. *Fear and Desire* has in mind
to work that conceptual territory too, beginning with the scene (speaking of
eating) when the men happen upon a cabin where two enemy soldiers sit at a
meal. They viciously stab them to death and then wolf down the leftovers.
When a third enemy soldier shows up with firewood (this is one of Caliban's
tasks in *The Tempest*), he is killed too. "Cold stew on a blazing island. We've
just made a perfect definition of war, Mac," Corby says, waxing philosophical
while he eats: "Of course. A blazing island with a tempest of gunfire around
it that fans the blaze." The lieutenant is the first of Kubrick's fighter-philosophers;

the Jungian Private Joker of *Full Metal Jacket* will be the last.[27] "No man is an island?" Corby further reflects. "Perhaps that was true a long time ago, before the ice age. The glaciers have melted away, and now we're all islands—parts of a world made of islands only." (So much, then, for John Donne.) Corby offers this antisocial vision of contemporary life while contemplating the three corpses scattered on the cabin floor. Repeated shots render them in parts: a formalized zigzag geometry of wrenched uniformed legs; a close-up of a clawlike open hand, oozing stew; and shadowed faces fixed in dead stares, juxtaposed with round crocks of gruel. It's horrific—and highly aestheticized. Kubrick's rapid montage editing here showily evokes Eisenstein, as does the device of having the soldiers thrust their trench knives directly at the camera, which is to say right at us.

The twenty-five-year-old cineaste who sought to see everything that came to New York had yet to contrive a style of his own. Here he's channeling Soviet cinema, as he does in *The Seafarers*, the documentary he made around the same time to help fund this, his first feature film. When the soldiers the next day happen upon some women wading waist-deep in a light-stippled stream, it's Kubrick doing Kurosawa, whose own forest fable, *Rashomon* (1950), had recently won the Golden Lion at Venice and a special Oscar from Hollywood. The soldiers capture one of the women when she spies them hiding in the underbrush. They gag her and bind her to a tree using their belts. Mac suspects that she had been foraging for fish and strawberries to take to the enemy general. "I'll pluck thee berries; / I'll fish for thee," Caliban offers to Trinculo and Stephano in *The Tempest* (2.2.157–158). "Thou . . . wouldst give me / Water with berries in't," Caliban remembers to Prospero (1.2.334–335).

The "native" girl of *Fear and Desire*, its beautiful she-Caliban—the film's racy promo poster dubs her "a strange half-animal girl"—is played by Virginia Leith, a fashion model in her acting debut. Leith, the minor starlet-to-be, is the first of Kubrick's women. "The Girl," as she is simply identified in the credits, is also the first incarnation of that sole female figure in a world of military men: a scenario that repeats as theme and variation in all of Kubrick's war movies. "She's quite nice, don't you think so, boys?" Corby drools over their mute captive. (The film gives "The Girl" but one word of dialogue: "Boat?" she bleats uncomprehendingly.) "Even though we're lost in the woods, let's try to remain civilized," Mac says sarcastically, repeating what Corby had said to him earlier, when he brought up cannibals. "No one's going to punish her. I simply want to tie her up," Corby replies, now sounding kinky. Fearing that she would discover them to the enemy, they leave Sidney to guard her at gunpoint despite signs he is already becoming unhinged. While Corby, with his philosophical bent, anticipates *Full Metal Jacket*'s Private Joker, Private Sidney foreshadows

that movie's deranged Private Pyle. "If we're not back by night, just get in touch
with her old man about a wedding," Mac again teases Sidney; "maybe you can
settle down in a tree house and raise some monkeys." Go primitive, that is;
turn "half-animal," like the native girl with whom he has been left. "The
wolves," pants the movie poster, "are breathless about Virginia Leith."

With its "strange," exciting "half-animal girl," Kubrick's high-concept allegorical war film shows a streak of sexploitation, typical of a time when, in
Naremore's words, "art cinema rubbed shoulders with a softly pornographic
sensationalism."[28] The title *Fear and Desire* advertises the film's "adult" nature. Its working title had been *The Shape of Fear*, and before that the Camu-
sian *The Trap*. Now called *Fear and Desire*, it was released in New York City
as the top part of a libidinous Joseph Burstyn double bill with a foreign film,
The Male Brute: "a story of Sin, Sex and Passion!" Kubrick's first feature earned
a "B" rating—"objectionable in part"—from the Legion of Decency because
of the bondage and how the soldier grows aroused by his female captive. This
scene was also apparently quite a turn-on for Mark Van Doren, who was then
writing film criticism for the *Nation* and whose world literature class Kubrick
had audited at Columbia just a few years before. "The incident of the girl
bound to a tree," the professor gushes in a puff piece for the fledgling new
director, "will make history once it is seen; it is beautiful, terrifying and weird;
nothing like it has ever been done in a film before, and it alone guarantees
that the future of Stanley Kubrick is worth watching for those who want to
discover high talent at the moment it appears."[29]

Shakespeare's *The Tempest* shows up most explicitly in *Fear and Desire*'s perverse sex scene. The twenty-year-old, baby-faced Paul Mazursky—also here in
his first acting role in a movie—plays Sidney, the soldier about to lose it who's
left alone with "the Girl." Far better known for his work later behind the camera, Mazursky made his own contemporized film adaptation of *The Tempest*
in 1982. He dates his long "obsession" with the play to *Fear and Desire* and the
twisted Shakespeare monologue that his character Sidney delivers in this
scene.[30] "Look, I'll make you laugh," he says to his captive audience of one.
As if spirit-possessed by Shakespeare's magic-infused romance, the lunatic soldier mangles some lines of Ariel's about shipwreck, spliced together with off-
kilter references to the war scene in which he finds himself. "I'm the general,"
Sidney jests. "Orderly! More fat fish that the girl caught for me." "Listen to
me," he continues. "I'm lost, lost on this terrible island." "Do you want to hear
more?" Sidney asks his prisoner. "Alright. Then the spirit in the magician's
power goes back to the island and tells Miranda that her father's dead. The
spirit sings how he's dead at the bottom of the ocean. His bones are coral. His
eyes are pearls. And *Miranda*—her father's dead. Dead!" "Can't you understand

anything? Dead . . . Dead! Dead!" he squeals, pantomiming with his hands around his own neck.

"Now do you understand?" asks Sidney. Though he has removed her gag, "The Girl" remains mum, unresponsive throughout to the soldier's manic one-man Shakespeare performance. Apparently she is unlearned in the language of Shakespeare, perhaps even altogether "unlettered," as Montaigne's "Of Cannibals" has it of the New World inhabitants. Sidney brings her water in his cupped hands, which, animal-like, she laps up and then licks his hand enticingly. "Now you like me, don't cha?" He kisses her and then frees her from the tree. Those who know their Shakespeare may here be thinking of how the magician Prospero releases Ariel from the pine where the witch Sycorax had imprisoned him. But whereas Prospero wants another slave, Sidney's intentions are sexual. But that also evokes something of *The Tempest*, which has its own rape pretext in Caliban's desire to "violate" Miranda and "people" "This isle with Calibans" (1.2.347–351). Recall how his fellows tease Sidney about raising monkeys with the "half-animal" native girl.

When she tries to run away—"You're going to tell the general!" Sidney screams—he shoots her in the back and kills her. "Where's the girl?" Mac wants to know when he returns. "What have you done?" In response, Sidney continues dissociatively to spout forth a hodgepodge of figures from Shakespeare's play. "It wasn't my fault. The magician did it! Honest. Prospero, the magician. First, we're a bird. And then we're an island. Before I was a general. And now I'm a fish." "What have we here? a man or a fish?" Trinculo wonders of Caliban, at their first encounter (2.2.24). "Hoorah for the magicians!" Sidney howls hysterically. Then he darts into the forest.

We do not see Sidney again until the film's dreamlike final scene. He reappears then, floating down the river on the raft with the mortally wounded Mac: a cinematic evocation of Géricault's homoerotic (and cannibalistic) painting, *The Raft of Medusa* (Figure 18). The film ends with Sidney on all fours, brute-like as predicted, though ultimately paired not with "The Girl" but with the older soldier, the one who had called him sweetheart. Sidney is crooning to the moon Ariel's dirge from *The Tempest*: "Full fathom five thy father lies;/ . . . /Sea nymphs hourly ring his knell:/Ding-dong" (1.2.397, 403–404). Kubrick's film's ending is in Shakespeare's play's pre-beginning: Prospero and Miranda in a frail bark, exiled from Milan and put out to sea. But the film recasts *The Tempest*'s father and daughter scene as all male—a dying gruff lieutenant and a mad boy soldier—even as Shakespeare here gets the last word in Kubrick's first film.

Before that, while Sidney is guarding the captive girl, the other three soldiers hatch an impromptu plot to kill the enemy general and then make their escape to their own side of the battle lines. For Mac, whose idea it is, this act

Figure 18. "Full fathom five."

has less to do with any specific military objective than with his own desire for existential validation. "Here I am. I'm 34 years old. I've never done anything important," he explains, talking aloud to himself. "When this is over," he rambles on, "I'll fix radios and washing machines. And they'll say, 'Good boy, Mac.' That's all." But now, a general has been "dangled in front of me, like magic." Killing the general—that one extraordinary act—would, Mac feels, give some meaning to their meaningless lives.

At nightfall, Mac floats by the enemy outpost on the raft, yelling "Come on out of your cage, you half-witted cannibals." While he draws away the sentries, Corby and Fletcher stalk the general, who has stayed behind at headquarters, drinking with his captain and uttering lugubrious lines like "Waiting to kill. . . . Waiting to die." Fletcher, firing through a window, wounds the general and kills the captain. That the general whimpers his surrender before Corby finishes him off at close range troubles the scene, revalencing that act with a moral uncertainty that prefigures the "mercy killing" of the female Vietnamese sniper at the end of *Full Metal Jacket*. The general's head hits the floor with a sickeningly amplified thud, and we see—if we hadn't seen it already—Corby's own countenance in that of the man he has just killed. The same goes for Fletcher and the enemy captain, each the other's shadow self.

I am less sure than are other commentators, however, that Corby and Fletcher share in that recognition.[31] Corby's reaction shot to what he has done seems more blank than comprehending, and Fletcher isn't even afforded one. Whatever this fable-like film's moral—"We are our own enemy," "We're all linked," "War is futile"—the soldiers themselves are denied any kind of epiphany, which will turn out to be typical of Kubrick's war films.

Fear and Desire amounts to a negativist take on male doubling, also the principal visual theme of Kubrick's very first film, *Day of the Fight*: his uncanny sports short about a handsome Greenwich Village prizefighter, Walter Cartier, who—and I think that this is what most drew Kubrick to Cartier as a subject—has a twin brother Vincent. In moving from that short-form documentary to the feature format of *Fear and Desire*, Kubrick, we find, doubles his male doubles. He also imparts to their twinship a heavy sense of "the duality of man"—"man" very much meaning men here, as it just about always does in Kubrick. That premise is another pointer from this, his first war film, to *Full Metal Jacket*, his last. There, Private Joker, adorned with a peace button on his uniform and the motto "Born to kill" scrawled on his helmet, tries to educate a dim colonel about "the duality of man. The Jungian thing, sir!" *Fear and Desire* materializes its own lesson about the duality of men by casting Kenneth Harp and Steve Coit, who play Corby and Fletcher, in twinned, abstract roles as self and other, protagonist and antagonist, killer and killed, while offering Mac and Sidney as another kind of male pair or couple.

The contrivance of casting the same actor in multiple roles derives from the stage, including countless performances of Shakespeare. Kubrick redeploys this device in other movies, and never to greater effect than with Peter Sellers, the most protean of Kubrick's men. Sellers first appears in *Lolita* as playwright Clare Quilty, Humbert Humbert's archnemesis and man of many guises. Sellers reappears in Kubrick's next film, *Dr. Strangelove*, now in three completely different roles as a British RAF exchange officer, the US president, and the former or not so former Nazi title character. There they make for a perfectly exaggerated ensemble of wildly contrasting male styles, (which, to show my hand, I find more compelling than the "Jungian thing").

Kubrick is said to have wept during a preview of *Fear and Desire* when the audience laughed at parts of the film.[32] Even though we can now see *Fear and Desire* as, in part, an arty study for the war films to come, especially *Full Metal Jacket*, Kubrick himself turned on his own feature-film debut, dismissing his experimental brush with Shakespeare as "little more than a thirty-five-millimeter version of what a class of film students would do in sixteen millimeter." This is essentially what he said too about his follow-up feature, *Killers Kiss*—that it was just a student film.[33]

Stories are told that Kubrick bought up all the prints of *Fear and Desire* he could find and even oversaw the negative's destruction. One print, however, safely found its way into the motion picture collection at the George Eastman Museum in Rochester, New York, where I first saw the film. Another is preserved in the Library of Congress, which in 2012 had it restored and remastered for release on DVD, making it now widely available. Kubrick certainly was aggressive in trying to prevent new screenings of his first feature while he was alive. When *Fear and Desire* showed up on the bill as part of a 1994 program called "The Young Stanley Kubrick" at the Film Forum in New York, the director refused comment to the press. But he issued a statement through his longtime studio Warner Brothers repudiating the movie as "a bumbling, amateur film exercise, written by a failed poet, crewed by a few friends" and "a completely inept oddity, boring and pretentious."[34]

Fear and Desire's interpolation of material from *The Tempest* contributes, no doubt, to that sense of pretentiousness. Though the play is weirdly integrated here and there into the film—which does not really qualify as a Shakespeare adaptation or even a spinoff—the play hardly seems essential to it. Here the Shakespeare looks like literary window dressing. But, then, what's wrong with that? We might find the film's citations of *The Tempest* interesting precisely as a form of decoration. Shakespeare will next appear in Kubrick as an actual piece of decoration, as a venerable white marble bust atop a classical column: this in the opening scene of *Lolita*, which is set in Quilty's trashed mansion and also littered with references to Kubrick's own work. We can take that 1962 film as marking how literary decoration in Kubrick's first film had developed into the practice of literary adaptation in his later ones. But all that said about the "merely" decorative Shakespeare, I also wonder whether on another level—let's posit the film's own unconsciousness—that *Fear and Desire* hasn't also deeply absorbed something from Shakespeare's late play in terms of an abiding undercurrent of dislocation, paranoia, sorrow, and loss. In any case, the mannered artfulness that the young Kubrick recoils from here is never dispelled from his work. Rather, it is reformatted in his subsequent films, including his war films, as a marked concern with fine art, architecture, décor, and taste—male taste.

What Becomes a Man: Decoration and Decorum

The other part of a director's job is to exercise taste. (Stanley Kubrick)

Kubrick's next war film, the much-lauded *Paths of Glory* (1957), exchanges the allegory of *Fear and Desire*, with its Renaissance literary trappings, for martial melodrama. The film's title comes from a line—"The paths of glory lead but to the grave"—in another, though later, well-known work of English literature: Thomas Gray's 1751 "Elegy Written in a Country Churchyard." Gray is one of two eighteenth-century authors to figure proverbially in *Paths of Glory*. (Samuel Johnson, we'll see, is the other.) The eighteenth century—both the so-called Age of Enlightenment and a time when theories of taste began to proliferate and the philosophical discipline of aesthetics received its name—would from this film forward have a hold on Kubrick's imagination. The fullest realization of Kubrick's concern with the period, given that his "Napoleon" never left the drawing board, is *Barry Lyndon*, a 1975 film version of William Makepeace Thackeray's nineteenth-century picaresque novel about eighteenth-century European society. Kubrick turns Thackeray's book into a gorgeous succession of motion picture paintings—cinematic Gainsboroughs, Hogarths, Reynolds, and Zoffanys—rendered "in period": that is, without the use of electric light, this by means, paradoxically, of the latest super-fast camera lens technology courtesy of NASA. I broach *Barry Lyndon* here, and in this way, to suggest something of the once and future quality of Kubrick's eighteenth-centuryism. The director's juxtapositional historical sensibilities spectacularly come into view in another way near the end of *2001: A Space Odyssey*. After astronaut Dave Bowman has passed through the psychedelic "Stargate," he finds himself in a bedroom plus bathroom suite (also an observation cage) that counterposes an ultramodern fluorescent white light grid floor with neoclassical art and Louis XVI–style furnishings. This scene, which morphs into nothing less than the next evolution of man, illustrates that Kubrick's absorption with the eighteenth century is not strictly bound to the period itself, that its ethos and aesthetics suffuse other of his historical and even futuristic works. *Paths of Glory* provides the first example of this: a military narrative about ritualized and rigidly hierarchical male relations set in World War I that Kubrick furnishes with an eighteenth-century décor and eighteenth-century literary allusions.

The film is an adaptation by Kubrick, Calder Willingham, and Jim Thompson of the 1935 novel of the same title by Humphrey Cobb, himself an army veteran of World War I. Kubrick came across *Paths of Glory* when he was a teenager. "It was," he recollects, "one of the few books I'd read for pleasure in high school."[35] Cobb's novel, based on a true story, reads as sheer polemic, stridently antiwar and antimilitary.[36] Kubrick's film, however, is not strictly so, by which I mean that it also treats, through the form of a war story, other of his fascinations with male culture. But in the first of his many encounters with censorship, it was Kubrick's movie, not Cobb's polemical book, that was long banned both in France, where the story is set, and also on US military bases in Europe.[37]

Near the end of the film, in a scene not in the novel, a couple of highly decorated French generals—Mireau (George Macready) and Broulard (Adolphe Menjou)—sit at breakfast in an opulent drawing room in the palatial eighteenth-century chateau that Mireau has taken over as his field headquarters. While they eat, they converse about proper manly comportment in the face of death, but not in this case death in combat. There are numerous such deaths in the film's one stunning battlefield scene, which lasts just three minutes. The generals instead reflect upon the court-martial execution that we have just witnessed with them in the previous scene: a highly ceremonial performance of extreme military discipline staged in the chateau's own manicured parterre gardens. Its mazy footpaths are a verdant obverse of the funk hole, zigzag system of trenches that is ironically just a few miles removed from the deluxe domain of the generals. Both settings, even more ironically, turn out to be killing fields for French soldiers. Here, back in the chateau, croissant in hand, Mireau coos with pleasure to Broulard that this terrible "scene," as he terms it, had "a kind of splendor, don't you think?" "I've never seen an affair of this sort handled any better," concurs Broulard. Kubrick's generals come across like two *grand-guignol* theater queens enjoying a post-performance meal at their gentlemen's club.

Mireau and Broulard's breakfast is interrupted by the blustery arrival of another French officer, Colonel Dax. In contrast to the suavity of the generals, Kirk Douglas—the biggest star with whom Kubrick had yet worked—plays Dax aflame with righteous male indignation. (It's tempting to give Dax/Douglas his own, albeit perhaps more benevolent, place in the roll call of Kubrick's male hysterics: a line that stretches from Private Sidney in *Fear and Desire* to Jack Torrance in *The Shining*, with HAL from 2001 in that company too.) "Colonel Dax, your men die very well," Mireau greets him provocatively, referring to the morning's ritual executions. Over Dax's heated protests, three of his men were made group scapegoats for a failed assault on an impregnable, heavily armed German outpost known as the Ant Hill. (In Cobb's novel it's called, more grotesquely, "the Pimple.") Mireau had ordered the attack at Broulard's urging. "Paul, if there's one man in this army who can do this for me, it's you," Broulard sweet-talks him, man-to-man, during his visit to the chateau in the film's second scene. Mireau at first brushes aside any thought of taking the Ant Hill as utterly infeasible, given the debilitated, battle-weary state of "my men," who, he paternalistically declares, "come first of all, George." But that sentiment quickly falls by the wayside when Broulard temptingly dangles a promotion before him, and the scene ends with Mireau repeating: "We might just do it. . . . We might just do it."

The film then dramatically shifts from General Mireau's rococo drawing room in the chateau to Colonel Dax's Spartan bunker in the trenches. There this scene of military seduction is replayed with a difference. "You are the man to take the Ant Hill," Mireau tries to entice Dax, just as his superior Broulard had enticed him. And just like Mireau Dax at first balks: "You know the condition of my men," he protests. But then Dax, again like Mireau, eventually warms to the idea, though he is motivated not by the prospect of a promotion but rather by the threat of a furlough, of being separated from the troops. "You can't take me away from my men. You can't do that to me," Dax protests, and thus the scene ends with him likewise repeating: "We'll take the Ant Hill. . . . We'll take the Ant Hill." Internecine conflict is a hallmark of Kubrick's military movies, and Mireau and Dax, however, quickly turn into enemies who wear the same uniform. "I'll break you . . . I'll ruin you, and it will be just what you deserve!" Mireau, his voice rising, melodramatically vows during a later encounter between the two men on the chateau's grand marble staircase—but not before this unsparing story first sets them up, in certain respects, as two of a kind.[38]

As for the notional "real" enemy—the Germans—they never actually appear in the film. Their numbers are represented only by the tremendous firepower that they unleash during the next day's ill-conceived French offensive. The galvanized Dax can lead his troops only a few yards across a cinematically expressionist no man's land before the few survivors fall back in disarray. Whole other companies are unable to leave the trenches under the German bombardment and the piling up of bodies all around them. Even so, the generals fault Dax's troops, though not Dax himself, for the mission's embarrassing failure. "If those little sweethearts won't face German bullets, they'll face French ones!" Mireau thunders. "Little sweethearts" is the screenplay's revision of "bastards," as Cobb's novel has it (136): a detail that's in line with the film's structuring concern with acting male, to which we will return. Mireau thus comes up with a plan to execute a representative number of soldiers for group cowardice and mutiny. This, Broulard agrees, will be "a perfect tonic for the entire division." First a hundred soldiers are proposed, then a dozen. When Dax offers himself up as an expiatory sacrifice of one for the many, Broulard quickly brushes him aside: "Come, come, Dax. I think you're overwrought. This is not a question of officers." (It is commonplace, indeed irresistible, to read the kind of war story *Paths of Glory* unfolds as also one of class warfare. More later on this too.) The generals' administrative arithmetic finally fixes on a token three: one man to stand for each company.

Paths of Glory is well supplied with the kind of mathematical thinking— an interest in persons or bodies as numbers and percentages, a concern with calculations, measurements, statistics, and odds—that will become a leitmotif of Kubrick's military films.[39] This one begins (as will *Dr. Strangelove*, his next war film), with another male voiceover. It tersely relays the only history lesson that Kubrick's World War I movie will provide: "By 1916, after two grisly years of trench warfare, the lines had changed very little." "Successful attacks were measured," the voiceover portentously continues, setting the stage for all the computations to come, "in hundreds of yards, and paid for by lives in the hundreds of thousands." Later, Mireau abstractly works his way to envisioning how Dax's already severely depleted troops can still manage to take the Ant Hill—itself named in the film as a figure of sheer numerosity—not in terms of tactics, but simply by crunching the numbers: "Five percent killed by our own barrage," he estimates to Dax. "Ten percent more in getting through no man's land, and twenty percent more in getting to the wire. That leaves sixty-five percent, with the worst part of the job over." "Let's say," Mireau goes on, "another twenty-five percent in actually taking the Ant Hill—and we're still left with a force more than adequate to hold it." Alexander Walker aptly describes the general's calculations as "almost a pilot study for *Dr. Strangelove's* nuclear overkill."[40] That's right; but the numerical conceptualization of war in both films, especially their concern with statistical persons, should also be seen as an escalation of the interest displayed in Kubrick's work from the beginning in human multiples: in twins and doubles (*Day of the Fight, Fear and Desire*) and other forms of somatic replication and destruction (the mannequin factory fight scene at the end of *Killer's Kiss*).

On his way to Dax's bunker, Mireau makes a show of visiting with the men in the trenches. He pauses to greet a few of them one by one, but all according to the same script: "Hello there, soldier. Ready to kill more Germans?" And then, curiously, as the next item on his soldierly checklist, "Are you married?" (Not all of them are.) The general's "personable" interaction with the soldiers has the effect of momentarily individuating them, but only as replaceable component parts in a French killing machine ever primed for killing. This lethal man/machine figuration is further technologized in *Full Metal Jacket*, Kubrick's Vietnam War film about "Mother Green and her killing machine," where it is also queerer. (No one here is married save to his phallicized/feminized weapon.) When alone with Dax in Dax's private bunker, Mireau pragmatically reconceptualizes the troops in his command not as killers but as fodder for the enemy's own killing machine: "They'll absorb bullets and shrapnel," he explains, "and by doing so make it possible for others to get through." The soldierly body is so readily refashioned—from hard, metallic to receptive, spongy. Again, *Full Metal Jacket* will hyperbolize this paradox of the hard/soft, invulnerable/vulnerable male warrior body to its breaking point.

Paul Fussell's indispensable *The Great War and Modern Memory*, a literary-historical study of World War I, makes irony the conflict's master experiential trope.[41] *Paths of Glory*—in this case, both the novel and the film—is shot through, as I have been suggesting, with a similar ironic sensibility. It's never more jarring than during this walk of Mireau's through the trenches when his lackey Major Saint-Auban (Richard Anderson) flatters the general about how "these tours of yours have an incalculable effect upon the morale of these men," men whose deaths he so methodically calculates and later even orders himself.

Mireau's calculations are, no doubt, meant to come off as appalling. Not that the director-cum-general Kubrick was a stranger to thinking of soldiers as numbers and bodies as objects. Despite the apparent havoc of the actual war-zone in *Paths of Glory* and the raw, documentary-like feel of the footage (with Kubrick himself wielding a handheld camera, its zoom lens trained on Douglas), he wanted the film's no man's land to have a certain kind of "look," a fairly precise *concordia discors*. "For this sequence," Kubrick explains to Walker, "we had six cameras, one behind the other on a long dolly track which ran parallel to the attack. The battlefield was divided into five 'dying zones' and each extra was given a number from one to five and told to 'die' in that zone, if possible near an explosion."[42] Here his extras were, ironically, six hundred German police officers in French army uniforms. Kubrick employed a similar "decorative" numerical scheme on an epic scale in *Spartacus*. One can only imagine the aesthetic arithmetics he would have worked out for his Napoleonic battlefields—a martial Kubrickian mathematical sublime—had he been able to make that supra-epical, ultimate experience film.

Some have speculated that Kubrick was attracted to boxing (which he voyeuristically made the subject of his first film) and chess (which he starting playing at the age of twelve, a year before his father gave him his first camera as a birthday present) because these contests are, in ways, like war. But perhaps Kubrick was drawn to war as a subject because he saw war as being like boxing and chess: highly stylized and abstractly tactical. Chessboards, large and small, figurative and literal, are placed all over his movies. Kubrick sets the court-martial scene in *Paths of Glory* in a grand hall in the chateau with a black-and-white checkered marble floor that makes the three soldiers on trial look like pawns on a giant chessboard. The Ant Hill figuratively looms over the game board–like proceedings in the form of a giant wall-size painting of a mound rising out of a landscape. In the film, though not the novel, Colonel Dax just happens also to be "the foremost criminal lawyer in all France," and he takes it upon himself to represent the defendants. But his best lawyerly maneuvers are for naught. All three soldiers are summarily convicted of cowardice for refusing to advance, even though two of them had indeed left the trenches, while the other, with a nasty head wound to prove it, had been knocked unconscious when another soldier's body was blown backward upon him.

Early the next morning the three prisoners are ceremoniously conducted from their makeshift cell in the estate's animal stalls. That one of them is now unconscious and needs to be conveyed to his execution on a medical stretcher makes this scene more ritually macabre. These dead men walking (or being carried) pass through the assembled ranks of their own regiment. The silent spectators have amassed on both sides of the estate's broad avenue in orderly row upon row. The visual field here, as in much of Kubrick's film, is rigorously geometric and the action within it highly choreographed. The chateau lines the top of the shot, its imposing stone façade a massy horizontal bar that extends beyond the frame in either direction. The camera follows the grim procession relentlessly downward toward the tall vertical spikes of the three evenly spaced stakes to which the condemned men will be tied. Behind each stake is a square neatly constructed of sandbags to absorb the spray of bullets. To the side, three rectangular coffins await. Once the men are secured to the stakes, three details comprising two rows of four riflemen each—those in front kneeling, those behind standing—line up facing them. In what will become a recurring signature effect, Kubrick places a photographer in the scene to shoot pictures. "When the killing happens," observes Naremore, the film "gives the audience nowhere to look except at the executed men."[43] But would one look away even if he could from such a precise, aesthetic composition, masterfully taken in the long shots for which Kubrick would come to be known? Then to the generals' breakfast, with which I began, as the film cuts directly from the clap of the rifles and the soldiers' slumping bodies to Mireau and Broulard's elegantly laid table, with its clinking silver and china. "The men died wonderfully," Mireau exalts. "There's always that chance," he muses, "that one of them will do something that will leave everyone with a bad taste. This time you couldn't ask for better."

The question of taste keeps coming up in Kubrick's movies, going all the way back to *The Seafarers*, which showcases the union hall "built by seafarers to . . . suit the tastes of seafarers." Mireau's table talk also anticipates the gustatory turn of the mini disquisition on male sexual tastes offered by Crassus (another general) to his "body servant" Antoninus in a similarly palatial setting in Kubrick's next film, *Spartacus*, a scene that we will save as fare for the next chapter. But Mireau's concern with tastefulness also harks back to the beginning of *Paths of Glory* when Broulard pays that fateful call on him at the chateau and prevails upon Mireau to assay the Ant Hill. This scene, which follows on the heels of the opening voiceover tally of the grim cost of real estate along the Western Front, begins, astonishingly, with chitchat about connoisseurship.

BROULARD: Well, this is splendid! Superb!
MIREAU: I've tried to create a pleasant place in which to work.
BROULARD: Well, you've succeeded marvelously. I wish I had your taste
   in carpets. And pictures.
MIREAU: You're much too kind, George. Much too kind.

What military brass talk like this? None do—or rather they only do in Ku-brick. The entire scene is another invention of the screenplay. "I really haven't done very much," Mireau, flattered, goes on. "The place is much the same as when I moved in." Mireau does seem, however, to be doing some redecorat-ing. In the background of a later scene, we catch three of his men hauling an-other of the chateau's huge landscapes from room to room. Only after such "cultured" talk, do the generals turn to military matters and the prospect of Mireau's own decoration with another star, should the Ant Hill be taken. Dur-ing this tense encounter—part verbal duel, part dance—Mireau and Broulard have two turns, arm in arm, about the grandiose salon and a prominently fea-tured tufted round sofa (Figure 19). The camera gracefully waltzes with them in a pair of fluid long dolly shots: an homage, Kubrick declared on set, to Max Ophüls, who had died that day. The generals' pas de deux is a prelude to the fancy dress ball Broulard callously puts on in the chateau's ballroom the night before the court-martial executions. That brief scene, incidentally, is the only one in the film, apart from the final one, which isn't all male.

In her essay "Décor as Theme," Vivian Sobchack calls attention to the abun-dance of art in the mise-en-scène of Kubrick's A Clockwork Orange. The film, she points out, is full of paintings and statuary not present in Anthony Burgess's "less-decorated" novel, which provides "relatively little description of places and objects."[44] Sobchack might as well also be describing the earlier Kubrick film Paths of Glory, which is given a similar decorative makeover in the translation from page to screen. In the film, the bulk of this war story's action takes place in the chateau—with its salons, ballroom, library, and stone staircases, every space grandly ornamented with art and architectural detail—or on its park-size land-scaped grounds.[45] And it is here, at the chateau, that Kubrick begins the film. In the novel, by contrast, there's no mention of the chateau until midway through the story. That's when it occurs to General Assolant (as the Mireau character is there named) that the chateau "happened to possess the best parade ground in that part of the country" and would thus make for an ideal natural theater in which to stage the court-martial executions (137–138). As for the chateau itself, Cobb's novel allots less than two pages of description to it, most of which con-cerns how "since it had been built in the late eighteenth century, [it had] seen its share of war and of warriors" (203). Napoleon, it is noted, spent two nights there,

Figure 19. Waltzing generals.

"and it was in honour of this that its name had become Château de l'Aigle." No mention of this is made in the film. But during the last scene at the chateau Dax leans up against a desk upon which stands a china figurine of Napoleon, the Emperor-General himself. Like the citations of Shakespeare in *Fear and Desire*, it's another piece of the film's male décor.

War films put masculinity in question, in crisis. What does it mean to act like a man in extreme circumstances, war being the most extreme? "What kind of a man do you think I am?" a lieutenant in *Paths of Glory* defensively retorts to a corporal. "Pull yourself together. Act like a man," the same corporal is later exhorted as he faces a firing squad of his fellow soldiers. By decentering actual combat from its storyline, Kubrick's film dislocates its treatment of masculinity from any kind of military "humanism" that hallows such battlefield virtues as male comradeship—a powerful commonplace of Great War literature and film—to say nothing of heroism, chivalry, and patriotism. *Paths of Glory* instead accentuates military culture's taste for the trappings of hierarchy and ritual. What becomes a man appears here to be principally a function of various ordering protocols.[46] Apart from one notable exception, we never see the essentially all male cast of the film except in the uniforms—and, in the case of

the officers, the decorative medals—that sartorially sort them according to
rank. Always in uniform, Kubrick's soldiers are also ever marching in formation, standing at attention, saluting, or waiting upon their superiors, even if
they are but once shown engaging the enemy in combat.

A *digression:* Dax, the film's star, is of course that one exception. In his
first scene he appears stripped to the waist, bathing himself in his
bunker: a fairly strapping harbinger of Kirk Douglas's next starring role
in a Kubrick-helmed film as the renegade warrior Spartacus, where
he will wear even less. Perhaps because that male body on display in
Paths of Glory is a movie star body, perhaps because its display here is
gratuitous, this particular slice of beefcake has garnered some notice
in Kubrick criticism. Krohn mentions it in passing as "a sop to Douglas's female fans," while Walker, who views Dax as "a man among his
fellow men," seizes this occasion to remark admiringly the actor's
"strong bone structure and physique."[47] Naremore notes that the scene
has no equivalent in the novel. He attributes Dax's shirtlessness to
Douglas's star image and its "unwritten rule that virtually every one of
his pictures after his breakthrough role in *Champion* had to contain a
scene in which he takes off his shirt."[48] But the male exhibitionism in
this case is not only a predicate of Kirk Douglas; it is also, as we have
seen, a feature of Kubrick's work, especially the early Kubrick. *Day of
the Fight, Fear and Desire, Killer's Kiss, Spartacus,* and *Lolita*: every
one of these films features its leading man without his shirt. Sterling
Hayden, the physically imposing star of Kubrick's noir heist movie *The
Killing*, keeps his shirt on, but two of his accomplices doff theirs: Mike,
a middle-aged regular Joe played by Joe Sawyer and, more spectacularly,
the gargantuan wrestler Maurice played by he-man Kola Kwariani. And
why should we think that all this male bodily display of various sorts is
there just for what female fans Kubrick's sports, military, and crime
dramas might attract? Women don't make up the only audience that
locates visual pleasure or interest in the sight of men out of their
clothes. This streak of male exhibitionism continues beyond *Paths of
Glory* and *Spartacus* into *2001: A Space Odyssey*. Kubrick's astronaut
movie shows off the former UCLA quarterback turned actor Gary
Lockwood as Frank Poole, shirtless in his white short shorts, matching
white tube socks, and orange goggles rolling over on a purple vinyl
tanning bed [Figure 20]. Barry Keith Grant finds Kubrick's astronauts
robotic, this image "sexless."[49] Looking back on it now, I'd say instead
that it seems more like a groovy '60s turn-on.

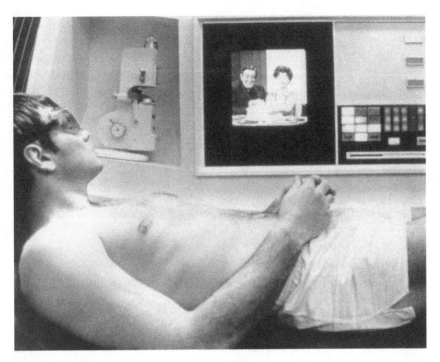

Figure 20. Hot jock astronaut.

Military life is nothing if not regulated and ritualized. What's striking about *Paths of Glory* are all the affronts, major and minor, to protocol and male decorum patterned into its narrative. These military men repeatedly forget, slight, even flout the formalities that are supposed to govern their interactions with each other. Mireau becomes so taken with the prospect of winning the Ant Hill as his own path of glory that he helps himself to a glass of cognac, before he recovers his manners in mid-gesture and offers that first pour to Broulard, his guest but also the higher-ranking officer. ("Not before dinner," Broulard, superiorly, declines.) A similar lapse of manners plays out in the reverse direction hierarchically when Corporal Paris (Ralph Meeker) grumbles that if Lieutenant Roget (Wayne Morris) is going out on a nighttime reconnaissance mission drunk, the least he could do is share the bottle with Paris and the other corporal ordered to accompany him.[50] Then there is Dax's declaration that, in defending his men against Mireau's charges, he is "not going to mince words and stand on ceremony." Mireau indignantly threatens Dax with arrest for insubordination, until Mireau is himself put in his place by Broulard. Or take the prisoners' snub of their chef-prepared ritual final meal of duck that is presented with a flourish to them on a silver tray, courtesy of the general. (They suspect the food to be drugged.) Later one of them punches Father Du Pres (Emile Meyer), who is sent to hear their last confessions. The most significant breach of protocol occurs during the court-martial: a trial so pro forma that the colonel-judge dispenses with formalities like reading aloud the indictment against the soldiers.

These incidents return us to the matter of class, a predominant theme in the film as well as in the novel that it adapts. But in Kubrick's movie (if not so much in Cobb's book) class struggle is crosshatched by another form of social struggle—a gendered struggle between men, between warring masculinities. This is personified in the contrast, soon outright conflict, between Dax and his bravura virility and the urbane, mannered Mireau and Broulard, with their chateau talk of taste and well-executed "scenes." Those two would not be out of place as cultured villains in a Hitchcock movie.[51] In an essay on war films and military masculinities, Yvonne Tasker writes astutely about "different and distinct ways of 'being a man,'" of "diverse male identities."[52] In Paths of Glory, it feels more like diverse male stylistics. Here the clash between these gender styles is further overcoded by the way that Douglas plays his true-grit French colonel as "American," while Macready and Menjou (both themselves Americans) put on "foreign" airs for their roles, their crisp line readings a pronounced contrast to Douglas's gruff murmurs and growling.

And yet the divide between these gender styles—or at least between Dax's and Mireau's instantiation of them—may not be as polarized as it seems from their antagonism to each other. There are no paintings or carpets in Dax's bunker, but one small decorative touch calls attention to itself in this setting: a painted porcelain bowl—"a memento," Thomas Allen Nelson sees it, "from the chateau."[53] The shirtless Dax—another decorative feature—bends over it to wash himself in a scene I digressively referred to earlier (Figure 21). Images of men washing and grooming themselves are another staple of Kubrick's movies. Kubrick's men tend to be fastidious about such matters. (When Jack stops shaving in The Shining we know that everything is really about to fall apart.)

"Well, quite a neat little spot you have here," Mireau commends Dax's quarters when he visits, recycling a diminutive version of the compliment that Mireau himself received from Broulard in the scene before this one in the chateau. Nor does Mireau, who has a reputation for being "a fighting general," appear altogether out of place on the frontlines. "If a man's a ninny, let him put on a dress and hide underneath the bed," he pronounces to Dax. "But if he wants to be a soldier," Mireau continues, "then he's got to fight. And he can't do that unless he's where the fighting is." In this respect, Mireau stands

Figure 21. Male grooming.

apart from Broulard, whom the film only shows in or around the chateau. The curved scar that adorns Mireau's face also marks him as no stranger to combat. (Macready's scar was real, the result of a car accident. Kubrick had it accentuated to make his character look more sinister.) What Mireau is a stranger to—ironically, given his air of cultural refinement—is literature. Or at least he has never heard of Samuel Johnson, whose famous adage that patriotism is the last refuge of a scoundrel Dax cites in this scene, deflating the general's grand talk of France.

Broulard certainly thinks that Dax is cut from the same cloth as Mireau— and for Mireau. "Don't deny it, Paul. You've been hiding this man, keeping him for your own," he teasingly chides Mireau, upon first meeting Dax. Later, Broulard approvingly, albeit incorrectly, assumes that Dax is angling for Mireau's position when he informs him that Mireau had ordered artillery fire on his own troops during the Ant Hill offensive to drive them out of the trenches. Broulard thus concludes the generals' elegant postmortem breakfast by nonchalantly (which is to say theatrically) indicating that he has come to learn of Mireau's order and that a public inquiry must now follow. With that, as Mireau grasps immediately, will surely come the end of his military career. From here on, the brakes are off. The movie becomes an all-out melodrama. Throwing down his napkin, the disgraced Mireau denounces Dax, his subordinate, as treacherously disloyal. But his furious final words are reserved for Broulard, his superior: "I have only one last thing to say to you, George: the man you stabbed in the back is a soldier." Of all the volatile emotions sparked

over the course of this scene—shock, indignation, hatred, Broulard's condescending pity—the most charged may be wounded male pride. It registers here
in the form, ironically, of downward class movement, as Mireau exits proudly
recasting himself as a (mere) soldier, and more of a man as such.

Dax is also provoked to insist upon his own, no less touchy male honor immediately thereafter, when Broulard does indeed offer him Mireau's command in a deep focus shot richly layered with the salon's fine art and furnishings.
"Come, come, Colonel Dax," Broulard cajoles him. "You've been after the
job from the start. We all know that, my boy." Dax rejects the older, more
powerful man's proposal, seizing on that last word: "I may be many things,"
he spits out, "but I'm not your *boy*." When Broulard naturally disavows any
familial meaning, Dax hysterically repeats himself, his voice rising: "I'm not
your boy in any sense." Men are frequently designated boys in Kubrick's movies, and this in many senses. "Boy" is Crassus's term—Spartacus's preferred
term too—for Antoninus, the young man on whom the epicurean Roman
general has designs in the next Kirk Douglas/Kubrick collaboration. Kubrick
took over *Spartacus* when Anthony Mann, the film's first director, was fired
two and a half weeks into the production for, among other things, his criticism of Douglas's overacting. In his autobiography *The Ragman's Son*, Douglas describes the on-set scene in which he presented Kubrick as the film's new
director.

> Monday morning, the principals, in costume, were sitting in the balcony
> of the gladiator arena. Rumors were flying. I took Stanley into the middle
> of the arena. 'This is your new director.' They looked down on this
> thirty-year-old youth, thought it was a joke. Then the consternation—
> I had worked with Stanley, they hadn't. That made him 'my boy.'"

"They didn't know," writes Douglas, rescripting a line written for him as Dax,
"that Stanley is nobody's boy."[54]

Dax declares that he is not Broulard's boy *in any sense*. Is it grasping at straws
to reach for a (disavowed) sexual implication here in *Paths of Glory*'s climactic scene? Not if we take our cue from the scene's table-turning end. "Sir, would
you like me to suggest what you can do with that promotion?" Dax shoots back
to the general—this before he calls out Broulard as a "degenerate, sadistic old
man." It's hard not to surmise that the colonel (nobody's boy) has something
buggery-like in mind.[55]

Paths of Glory is routinely hailed as one of the greatest antiwar movies ever
made. But Kubrick's film seems too little interested either in the particular war
in which it is set or in war generally to be political in that way. The movie's
vantage onto the subject of war rather derives from its rendering of relations

WAR FILMS   69

among men in extreme circumstances, ordered and disordered by ritual and a lockstep male social hierarchy. *Paths of Glory* is institutional melodrama. The all-male society of the military, with its various gender styles, is a hothouse for exaggerated emotion and clashing male temperaments; for plots and subplots of ambition, rivalry, and treachery; for flaunting and flouting male taste and manners. Call it Kubrick's *The Men*—and I don't mean this evocation of George Cukor's 1939 film *The Women* the least bit derisively.[56] Kubrick's movie is catty from the beginning—"If I had the choice between mice and Mausers, I think I'd take the mice every time," Dax quips to Mireau—and then becomes backstabbing and crude in the end.

And even then Kubrick's military movie has one more melodramatic turn to take in its final scene. The mute native "Girl" from *Fear and Desire* comes back here as a captive German woman, played by Susanne Christian, née Christiane Harlan—a year later Kubrick's wife. She is hauled out on stage in front of a punchy crowd of Dax's men who have gathered in a tavern after the morning's court-martial executions. With tears running down her cheeks, the frightened woman begins to sing, her murmur at first barely audible above the catcalls. But her song—"*Der treue Husar*," "The Faithful Hussar," a German folk ballad about love, death, and fidelity during war—subdues them. The men don't know the words, but they hum along its plaintive melody and are themselves reduced to tears. This cabaret makes for the most nakedly sentimental scene in Kubrick. It turns *Paths of Glory* into a tearjerker, a male weepie. Dax has been watching it all, voyeur-like, from the street outside through the shutters on a window. He is informed of orders to move the troops back to the Front immediately. For all his manly force, Dax was unable to take the Ant Hill as well as unsuccessful in court. But his finest moment, such as it is, has been saved for now. "Well, give the men a few minutes more, sergeant," Colonel Dax says solemnly and then walks away as the film ends.

At the beginning of his 1987 *Rolling Stone* interview with Kubrick upon the release of *Full Metal Jacket*, Tim Cahill relays to the director how this final scene of *Paths of Glory* brought tears to his eyes on four separate viewings.[57]

The Essence of Men, or Loving the Bomb

> God willing, we will prevail, in peace and freedom from fear, and
> in true health, through the purity and essence of our natural fluids.
> (General Jack D. Ripper)

Recall that a preview audience laughed during parts of *Fear and Desire*, Kubrick's first war film, and that made the director himself cry. *Paths of Glory*,

Kubrick's next war film, incorporates male tears into its melodramatic story-line as well as occasions them. Kubrick's third war film, *Dr. Strangelove* (1964), continues to experiment affectively with the genre. This "nightmare comedy"—Kubrick's name for it—of thermonuclear apocalypse now sets out to make the audience laugh when we all should be crying, screaming.[58] And, in its perfectly insane way, *Dr. Strangelove* winds up being, scene upon scene, one of the most masterfully sustained satiric comedies ever made. Though it is altogether different tonally from Kubrick's previous war films, Kubrick's nuclear arms movie reiterates many of the same obsessions. Weapons, tactics, command, numbers, projected casualties: these military concerns are so exponentiated here that there is no way further, terrestrially speaking, to play them out. Even the film's thirteen-word, two-part title—among the longest in the annals of film—is a form of overstatement. To begin, then, with the obvious: *Dr. Strangelove Or: How I Learned to Stop Worrying and Love the Bomb* is a terminal war film. Kubrick's doomsday movie is at once the ecstatic summation and the utter undoing of this genre that so occupied its director. And the same could be said for *Dr. Strangelove*'s manic treatment of gender.

Gentlemen, sometimes a cigar is just a cigar (Figure 22). It is doubtful that Freud ever actually said that. Certainly no such delimiting literalist herme-neutic obtains in the hyper-sexualized, hyper-virilized male world of *Dr. Strangelove*. Cigars, cigarettes, sticks of chewing gum, microphones, pencils, planes, guns, bombs: there is hardly a phallic symbol, large or small, that this parodic paean to arms and men does not reach for. Even before the opening credits roll, Kubrick points a giant metal penis right in our face (Figure 23). It takes a second to figure out that this thing is the airplane-refueling boom of a Boeing KC-135 Stratotanker. Enthralled, we voyeuristically watch the boom's midair insertion into the sleek silver body of a B-52 bomber, while the dreamy strains of an orchestral version of "Try a Little Tenderness" rise and fall on the soundtrack. The two aircraft, with their massive phallic fuselages, stay mated until the credits end. This awesome aerial feat of male/male machinic copu-lation is extraneous to the film's narrative. It is pure techno-sexual phallic spec-tacle. But this prefatory image sets the stage for our story's "wargasmic" conclusion, precipitated by Major "King" Kong's ass-backward rocket ride to earth, the shaft of the H-bomb, with the cruisy pickup line "HI THERE!" painted on it, protruding from his crotch.[59] What is strange (or not) about love in *Dr. Strangelove* is how a nuclear strike makes for the ultimate hard-on and the definitive "fuck you."

The atom bombs that the United States dropped on Japan at the end of World War II were given male code names: "Little Boy" and "Fat Man." Ku-brick's movie seizes on this kind of jocular puerility and shamelessly runs with

Figure 22. The proverbial cigar.

Figure 23. The ultimate hard-on.

it as though there were no tomorrow, what with its General "Buck" Turgidson (George C. Scott), Group Captain Lionel Mandrake (Peter Sellers), General Jack D. Ripper (Sterling Hayden), President Merkin Muffley (Sellers again), General Faceman (Gordon Tanner), and Colonel "Bat" Guano (Keenan Wynn)—"If that really is your name" questions Mandrake—along with Major T. J. "King" Kong (Slim Pickens), and Dr. Strangelove himself (Sellers yet again). This film, which is followed in sequence by 2001: A Space Odyssey and A Clockwork Orange, marks Kubrick's career-propelling move in the direction of science fiction and futurism—or rather, as it turns out here, "no futurism." But there are retrospective dimensions to the movie as well. The way, for instance, that Dr. Strangelove gives its dramatis personae sexually emblematic names—including a Soviet ambassador called Alexi de Sadesky (Peter Bull)—that seem to come from an especially debauched form of eighteenth-century comedy or vaudeville opera, with a Jack D. Ripper in place of a Mack the Knife and without, of course, the ladies. Or perhaps a martially set Swiftian lampoon. As for that eighteenth-century satirist, "Laputa," the name of Major Kong's bomber's primary target in Russia, an ICBM complex, is lifted from Gulliver's Travels, Swift's proto-science fiction fable, where it names a flying island. The term itself—la puta—means "whore" in Spanish. The movie's approach to its characters (or caricatures), along with its reuse of the conceit of casting the same actor in multiple contrasting roles, also harks back to Kubrick's own debut feature and first war film, Fear and Desire. That movie was a cinematic psychomachia about the existential battle for the soul of four different takes on Everyman. Dr. Strangelove satirically worries the fate of all mankind and the entire planet.

In Dr. Strangelove, Kubrick made a film that is at once fantastic and fact-based, highly stylized and technologically realistic. This was the fullest materialization thus far of his soon to be legendary perfectionism and attention to detail. It was said that on set Kubrick "scarcely let as much as a trouser pleat go unsupervised."[60] (So much attention to every male detail!) More significantly, the film's recreation of the interior of the bomber was such a close replica of an actual B-52, the design of which was then still classified, that it triggered an FBI investigation. But there had been no leak. Production designer (and World War II veteran RAF pilot) Ken Adam gleaned from technical flight magazines what he needed to construct his own model. Adam was also responsible for the heavily shadowed, expressionist War Room. Monumental landscapes decorate the chateau where the French generals machinate in Paths of Glory. Here, in place of all those oil paintings, are towering electronic military maps of the world. The cavernous War Room, with its "Big Board" (as Turgidson reverentially refers to it), is chiefly the film's invention. Adam's convincing set fooled Ronald Reagan, however. It is reported that right after he took office in 1981 Reagan asked to be shown the real War Room. The Hollywood movie actor become militarist American president was disappointed to learn that no such place existed. "You must be joking," Adam scoffed when told of this.[61]

In contrast to Kubrick's allegorical *Fear and Desire*, a war film that posits itself "outside history" and world politics, *Dr. Strangelove* addresses two questions—What is the risk, the likelihood of nuclear war? Is such a war winnable?—that were extensively analyzed and hotly debated in the 1960s by politicians and defense establishment intellectuals. As he later did when he set out to make a film on Napoleon, the autodidact Kubrick put together for himself an extensive personal research library of books about nuclear war, weapons, and strategy. He also started subscribing to military magazines. Chief then among treatments of the subject was the systems theorist and founding futurist Herman Kahn's *On Thermonuclear War*, an Atomic Age successor to Carl von Clausewitz's nineteenth-century classic *On War*. Published by Princeton University Press in 1960, Kahn's nearly seven-hundred-page tome became a minor bestseller and was pored over on both sides of the Iron Curtain. Kubrick took so many lines and ideas directly from Kahn's book—most crucially, the hypothetical "Doomsday Machine"—that Kahn, after a special advance screening, asked him: "Doesn't that entitle me to a royalty?" Kubrick, Kahn reports, pretended at first not to hear him. Then, when asked again, the director snapped: "It doesn't work that way."[62]

Can one side prevail in a large-scale nuclear war? Kahn's *On Thermonuclear War*—which the *New Statesman* called "pornography for officers"—lays out the case that such a war is indeed winnable in terms of (as one of Kahn's notorious tables blandly enumerates it) "Tragic But Distinguishable Postwar States," involving a range of deaths from two million to 160 million.[63] George C. Scott's General Turgidson makes that case too in the film, and in just such terms, even the though the film itself ultimately shows otherwise. The general, his arm propped on a black binder labeled *World Targets in Megadeaths*—more porn for warriors and war hawks—urges "catching [the Russians] with their pants down" with an all-out preemptive strike. (As this story gets underway, Turgidson himself is found offscreen in the bathroom, presumably with his own pants down.) Doing so, he maintains, would eradicate 90 percent of the Soviet Union's missiles before the Russians could retaliate and thus keep the number of American casualties within an "acceptable" range: "No more than 10–20 million killed. Tops. Depending on the breaks." "You're talking about mass murder, General," President Muffley retorts, "not war." "I'm not saying," Turgidson concedes, "we wouldn't get our hair mussed."

Another digression. Kubrick's hair-raising nightmare comedy has a thing about hair. "Is it that bad?" Colonel Mandrake questions General Ripper, who has just ordered him to issue "Wing Attack Plan R": a nuclear airstrike against Russian military targets. "It looks pretty hairy," Ripper replies. Two scenes later, we find Turgidson (who will argue against issuing a recall of that order) in his Pentagon private quarters in his Bermuda shorts and with his leisure shirt unbuttoned to the waist, his hairy chest and potbelly on display. Later, in the War Room and exasperated by the way that President Merkin Muffley dons a hair shirt in his dealings with the Russians ("I'm very sorry. . . . I am as sorry as you are, Dmitri! Don't say that you're more sorry than I am, because I'm capable of being just as sorry as you are"), Turgidson is shown nervously running his hands through his flattop crew cut. Peter Sellers plays Merkin Muffley in a prosthetic skullcap that renders him bald, but the character's name means a pubic hairpiece, a wig for the muff. Mandrake's distinctive physical feature is his bushy British moustache. And then there's Strangelove's wavy white shock of hair, as kinky as his irrepressible black-leather-gloved hand.

Just before the film ends, Strangelove has the top politicos and military leaders assembled in the War Room fantasizing about a new, select survivalist underground society to be seeded in the deepest American mineshafts, with a 10:1 female to male ratio. The female of the "species" would be handpicked, Strangelove further specifies, for "their sexual characteristics, which will have to be of a highly stimulating nature" and the males for their ability to "breed prodigiously." "Wouldn't that necessitate the abandonment," Turgidson excitedly grasps, "of the so-called monogamous relationship—I mean, as far as men were concerned?" But despite Strangelove's arousing calculations, what we actually get in the film is what we always get in Kubrick's war movies: one woman in a world of men. Here the leggy Tracy Reed (stepdaughter of the director Carol Reed) plays her. She first shows up in the form of a nudie centerfold that Major Kong indifferently considers before dropping off to sleep in the cockpit of the B-52 he pilots. (Porn isn't just a recurring element in Kubrick's movies, it's part of their culture.) A copy of the magazine *Foreign Affairs* is strategically draped across her upturned behind as she's posed on a white bearskin rug, a Venus on fur. For the purposes of the film, this prop centerfold was inserted within the pages of the actual June 1962 issue of *Playboy*, whose cover announces "A Toast to Bikinis" inside. And when "Miss Foreign Affairs" comes to life in a later scene as Turgidson's secretary and mistress, Miss Scott, she is in a mod two-piece, catching some rays (ominously, it turns out) under a sun lamp. These bikini dreams in the film amount to a mordant pun on the Bikini Atoll, the site of numerous American nuclear tests in the 1940s and '50s. *The Leper Colony*, Kong's B-52 bomber, has been decorated by its crew with pinups of mushroom clouds that would make toast of anything. Those photographs portend the spectacular montage of atomic ejaculations skyward—no *petites morts*, these—that will end the film and with it the world, as Strangelove's wet dream of a subterranean new phallocratic master civilization goes up in flames. The World War II hit "We'll Meet Again," sung by Vera Lynn, known as "the Forces' Sweetheart," provides the deadly ironic soundtrack: "Don't know where, don't know when, / But I know we'll meet again, some sunny day."

The extensive *Stanley Kubrick* traveling show I saw in 2012 at the Los Angeles County Museum of Art—the first retrospective of Kubrick's artistic career from photography to filmmaking in an art museum setting—included a March 20, 1964, academic fan letter from a Cornell University art history professor, LeGrace G. Benson, which Kubrick had saved in a scrapbook. Benson compliments Kubrick on what he discerns as the Pop Art (then a fledgling movement) sensibilities of *Dr. Strangelove*, along with how the film appears to be "structured formally as a kind of duplication of sexual intercourse." This form, opines the art historian, "is entirely appropriate to the [film's] iconological content." The show also included Kubrick's reply of April 6, 1964. "Seriously, you are the first one," the director writes, obviously pleased, "who seems to have noticed the sexual framework from intromission to the last splash." Benson may possibly have been the first to observe the film's coital superstructure, but he certainly wasn't the last. Just about every commentator on *Dr. Strangelove* comes to the conclusion not just that militarism and war can be arty, stylish, even sexy, but that here *war is sex*. And, not to put too fine a point on it (though this one tends to go unremarked), such sex as there is here is principally between men, or machines, or men and machines.

Another way to put this is that for all that it smacks of male potency and phallic display, *Dr. Strangelove* is strangely about sexual deferral and denial—when it comes to men with women. In this respect, it falls in line with Kubrick's other war films. Midway through *Fear and Desire*, a soldier grows aroused by the female captive he has been left to guard; when she tries to run away, he kills her. The threat of sexual assault also hangs in the air during the tavern scene in *Paths of Glory*, when the captured German woman is first hauled out on stage to sing for the hooting and whistling French soldiers. But it quickly evaporates, as we saw, into a wellspring of male tears all around as the film comes to its overwhelmingly mournful conclusion. In *Dr. Strangelove*, General Buck Turgidson leaves Miss Scott alone in bed, prematurely smoking the cigarette that is supposed to be had after sex. "You just start your countdown, and old Bucky'll be back here," he promises when he leaves her to join the other brass gathering in the War Room, "before you can say 'Blast off!'" Miss Scott has more lines than the all-but-silent native "Girl" in *Fear and Desire* and the unnamed petrified chanteuse in *Paths of Glory*, who quietly sings not speaks. Miss Scott even gets to interrupt "Bucky" with an illicit phone call to the War Room. ("I told you never to call me here," he grumbles into the receiver; "My president needs me. . . . Of course it isn't only physical.") But the kind of blastoff that this bombshell is left waiting for with her man remains forever on hold.

As for heterosexual denial, however, nothing can top General Ripper, played (in his second role for Kubrick) by the statuesque Sterling Hayden, who had once been dubbed by Paramount "The Most Beautiful Man in the Movies" and "The Beautiful Blond Viking God." "Women, uh, women sense my power, and they seek the life essence," Ripper murmurs to Mandrake, whom he holds captive in his stylish midcentury-modern, bachelor pad–like barracks office, which includes a full bar. (Compare how in Kubrick's *Lolita* Charlotte tries to entice Humbert to take the room for rent in her house by pronouncing this "semi-studio affair" as "very male.") Ripper continues: "I do not avoid women, Mandrake," who is named after a plant mythically thought to be an aphrodisiac. "No," Mandrake, the scene's straight man, replies uncertainly. "But," says Ripper stutteringly, "I, I do deny them my essence."

While it keeps women at a distance, Kubrick's film is bent on finding weird ways to couple the men. When President Muffley gets Premier Kissov on the hotline (a replay of Turgidson's War Room phone call from the antsy Miss Scott), the two world leaders come off like an old married couple having another of their spats. Then Turgidson and de Sadesky are caught in a dancelike scuffle that leads to the Russian ambassador falling backward onto the lap of the American general, who wraps his arms tightly around the other man's ample waist. They maintain this preposterous position while the president ridiculously scolds them for their lack of decorum: "Gentlemen, you can't fight in here. This is the War Room!"

The scene anticipates an extended encounter between Ripper and Mandrake on the leather sofa in Ripper's well-appointed office, with the lights turned low. The general, chomping on another gigantic, iconic cigar, drapes his arm around Mandrake's uniformed shoulder and places his other hand on Mandrake's knee, while Mandrake nervously fiddles with a stick of gum still in its foil. Like the condom in the flight survival kit for the crew of *The Leper Colony*, it is never unwrapped (Figure 24). Ripper then proceeds to unfold further his personal theories about essences and fluids—male essences and fluids. "Mandrake, do you realize that 70% of *you* is water?" "You and I," he goes on,

Figure 24. A man-to-man on "our precious bodily fluids."

"need fresh, pure water to replenish our precious bodily fluids." "Are you beginning to understand?" Ripper asks Mandrake, who, to humor him, will
later "out" himself as "a water man." So too, of course, is Ripper, who professes
to drink only distilled water or rain water—that, and pure grain alcohol. (It's
the milk of human kindness that's in short supply in this fluid-obsessed film.)
When their man-to-man is interrupted by a burst of gunfire that leaves Mandrake face down, butt up on the couch, Ripper pulls a machinegun and ammo
belt out of a bag of golf clubs. "Come here and feed me this belt, *boy*," orders
Ripper, employing a designation that carries a sexual charge, we have noted,
in other Kubrick films around this time. "Now feed me," demands Ripper,
"Feed me!" "I haven't had much experience with those sorts of machines,"
Mandrake demurs, but he gets down on the floor with Ripper and does it.

   Whether themselves homosexual or not, the hypermasculine, misogynist
General Jack D. Ripper and the slightly sissified, unavailing President Merkin
Muffley embody the era's stereotypical polarities of gay male gender expression.[64]
It is easy to see *Dr. Strangelove* as satirizing, even pathologizing both styles. But
the film also wickedly lampoons the homophobic Cold War ideology that
associated political subversion with sexual perversion. After the bodily fluids–
obsessed Ripper shoots himself in his bathroom (where else?) and just as
Mandrake is figuring out the recall code for the attack, Colonel "Bat" Guano

bursts into the general's locked office. Mandrake's foreignness—his affected English male manners and RAF uniform—reads as queer to the American: "What kind of suit do you call that, fellah?" he demands. Earlier in the film, Turgidson denounces Premier Kissov as "a degenerate, atheist commie." Here Guano suspects Mandrake of being "some kind of deviated *pre-vert*," who is "organizing some kind of mutiny of *pre-verts*." Mandrake's British reserve will finally give way in a threat that returns us to the matter of male attire, but also to the site of Ripper's suicide: "You'll be lucky," he warns Guano, whose name means shit, "if you end up wearing the uniform of a bloody toilet attendant." Also on display in the LACMA *Stanley Kubrick* show was a page from one of Kubrick's notebooks containing his jottings about possible titles for the film, "Dr. Strangelove's Secret Uses of Uranus" among them.

Even as the batshit American colonel relents and permits Mandrake to enter the base's closet-like phone booth in order to dial in the recall code—P-O-E for "Peace on Earth"/"Purity of Essence"—Guano warns back: "If you try any *pre-versions* in there, I'll blow your head off." ("Peace on Earth" is taken from George's novel. The acronymic play on it—"Purity of Essence"—is the film's psychotic invention.) The major is made to pay a slapstick price for his sexual paranoia as the scene's climax. When Guano unloads his gun into a Coke machine to get Mandrake the little bit of change that he still needs to place his urgent phone call to save the world, the beverage dispenser discharges not only a stream of coins, but its fluid contents as well—smack into Guano's mustached face (Figure 25). This image is the displaced stand-in for the deferred "money shot" during the office scene between Ripper and Mandrake, with all its unresolved male sexual tension.

We have observed how invocations of taste bookend *Paths of Glory*, Kubrick's World War I melodrama. The film opens with one French general complimenting another on his taste in carpets and pictures. And near the film's end, the same two generals express their pleasure that the execution of the court-martialed soldiers didn't leave a "bad taste" for those who watched. Taste also weirdly emerges as a concern in *Dr. Strangelove*, Kubrick's biopolitical nuclear war black comedy. General Ripper becomes unhinged at the thought of "a foreign substance [being] introduced into our precious bodily fluids without the knowledge of the individual." (No doubt, then, that "Miss Foreign Affairs" would not be this fellow's cup of tea.) What is maddeningly insidious to Ripper about the communist fluoridation plot is that this dangerously enervating contaminant doesn't leave a bad taste. Tasteless, fluoride can secretly be added to anything: not just water, he hysterically relays to Mandrake, but "salt, flour, fruit juices, soup, sugar, milk, ice cream . . . *children's ice cream!*"[65]

Figure 25. The money shot.

Tasteless—dangerous too—is also what some critics said at the time about Kubrick making a laugh fest out of the Cold War and its attendant threat of thermonuclear annihilation. Bosley Crowther begins his *New York Times* review by declaring *Dr. Strangelove* to be "beyond question the most shattering sick joke I've ever come across," adding in another piece for the *Times* that he finds the film "a bit too contemptuous of our defense establishment for my comfort and taste."[66] That kind of personal response becomes political in Chalmers M. Roberts's *Washington Post* article on *Dr. Strangelove*, in which Roberts opines, "No Communist could dream of a more effective anti-American film to spread abroad than this one."[67] Nora Sayre, another *New York Times* film reviewer, reports that she too came away from *Dr. Strangelove* feeling that Kubrick had "defied the traditions of taste and subverted our institutions." But to her that was good thing.[68]

Dr. Strangelove's plot derives from the novel *Red Alert*, a solemn 1958 Cold War thriller by Peter Bryan George about a fictional American general who goes rogue and orders an unprovoked nuclear attack against the Soviet Union. George, like the film's set designer Ken Adam, was a World War II RAF veteran. That may partly explain why he published this technically detailed cautionary tale about the failure to understand the dangers of a nuclear war under a pseudonym, Peter Bryant. Kubrick explains in an interview that when he started working on a screen adaptation of George's novel he had every intention of making a serious film. But then he came to the realization that a story about nuclear war, in which two opposing superpowers have it in their means to wipe out not only each other but possibly all life on the planet, couldn't be treated along the lines of a conventional war drama. That sense pushed his conception of the film further and further in the direction of the absurd. Kubrick says that he kept telling himself, "I can't do this. People will laugh."[69] But he brought on board the dark, edgy satirist Terry Southern to help him and George revamp George's white-knuckle suspense drama into a satiric black comedy. George's original characters were all renamed and turned into a variety of male caricatures. General Quinten from *Red Alert* became General Jack D. Ripper; Major Clint Brown became Major "King" Kong; General Steele became General "Buck" Turgidson; and so on. A brand new titular character for the movie, Dr. Strangelove, was also concocted. Most importantly, their screenplay stunningly took away the novel's hopeful ending, in which the world barely manages to survive intact and the nuclear superpowers, Russia and the United States, learn from this brush with doom a great lesson. Not so in the film.

Kubrick's movie had competition. Sidney Lumet was at work on a rival nuclear war film, *Fail Safe*, which would also be released in 1964, though not until after *Dr. Strangelove* had its run. *Fail Safe* garnered favorable reviews. But it disappointed at the box office, whereas *Dr. Strangelove* was a hit. Lumet's movie closely followed its source: the novel of the same title by Eugene Burdick and Harvey Wheeler. George, the author of *Red Alert*, felt that the plot of Burdick and Wheeler's book was so similar to his that he sued them for plagiarism. They settled out of court.

Lumet's *Fail Safe* is deadly serious, a straightforward suspense thriller. Kubrick's Last Night Revel, his this is how it all ends epiphany, is hardly that. But while *Dr. Strangelove* represents a return to experimentation with the genre that Kubrick undertook in his first war film, the heavily allegorical *Fear and Desire*, the film does not altogether abjure the kind of melodrama that animates *Paths of Glory* either. (That abnegation will come in *Full Metal Jacket*.) Earlier in this chapter I proffered *Paths of Glory* as a male, military counterpart to George Cukor's women's film *The Women*, in which, famously, no male character appears on screen, not even in the background. But Kubrick's third war film is a far more delirious male ensemble piece, its manic mood powered by all those contrasting, often conflicting ways of being a man, each radiating its own considerable tragicomic force. Here we find variations of hypermasculinity (Ripper, Turgidson, Kong) and variations of—what to call it? what's the obverse of hypermasculinity?—hypomasculinity or amasculinity

(Muffley, Mandrake)? And what to do on this account with the heterosexually lecherous but physically mangled Strangelove himself? What kind of alternative masculinity does he present? Here are varieties of varieties of acting like a man, the contested meaning of which is a principal concern of all war movies, not just Kubrick's. That several of these diverse, indeed divergent male styles are rendered, in Peter Sellers's three-point star turn, by the same actor heightens the sense here that masculinity is quite the performance. Sellers was originally slated to play the part of Major Kong too, but he begged off complaining that he couldn't get the accent just right. As good as the metamorphic Peter Sellers is here, a daffy, way over-the-top George C. Scott and a deadly, deadpan Sterling Hayden nearly steal the show in this movie that features more male star power than Kubrick had ever worked with before or after.

Somewhere in between all the extremes in the world of men of *Dr. Strangelove* are the soldiers manning the locked-down Burpelson Air Force Base, whom General Ripper sentimentally refers to as "my boys," "my children"—this before he kills himself after they "let down" their dad by surrendering to the Army troops sent to wrest control of the base from him. The firefight between these two branches of the American military—shot, documentary-style, by Kubrick himself again with a handheld camera—provides this film's internecine conflict, a hallmark, I noted earlier, of his war movies. And then there are all those unindividuated government suits and military brass arranged around the War Room's own "Round Table." Most of these Cold War knights in khaki or wool simply sit there in place in silence, smoking, while they keep watch on what turns out to be the world's final night. *Planet Earth, mon amour.* These silent witnesses make for what I find to be one of the film's most indelible images: those plumes of smoke from their cigarettes and cigars, trailing upward and vanishing into the darkness beyond the ring of light suspended overhead. Peter Baxter takes these men as indicative of the film's "obsessive," "frantic" "serial multiplication of male figures," which he reads as symptomatic of castration anxiety.[70] It is hard to argue with that, when we have General Ripper worrying about the expenditure of male essence. But I am also inclined to see Kubrick's fascination with male multiples and male seriality in more formalist, less heavily psychologized terms as an abiding aesthetic impulse. This is something that can be tracked all the way back to Kubrick's first film, *Day of the Fight*, starring those good-looking Cartier twins.

Dr. Strangelove works a mildly sociopolitical variation on the theme of male sameness and difference in the third of the film's three enclosed spaces: the B-52 bomber. Its crew wears identical flight suits and crash helmets that outfit them all as versions of each other. They predict the duplicated, difficult to distinguish astronauts, Frank and Dave, of 2001. But this band of brothers also seems to have been assembled, like *Fear and Desire*'s quartet of "Everymen," as a male cross-section of American society, including the Texan pilot, Major Kong, the Jewish lieutenant and navigator B. Goldberg (Paul Tamarin), and the Black lieutenant and bombardier Lothar Zogg (James Earl Jones, in his movie debut.)[71]

As with *Paths of Glory*, this male melodrama's setting is institutional not domestic. But here the stakes are no longer chiefly personal or even national. They are mega-global, apocalyptic. And things could not turn out worse. Crowther ends his review with the end of the film—and the world: "The ultimate touch of ghoulish humor is when we see the bomb actually going off, dropped on some point in Russia, and a jazzy sound track comes in with a cheerful melodic rendition of 'We'll Meet Again Some Sunny Day.' Somehow, to me, it isn't funny. It is malefic and sick."[72] Nor was Pauline Kael, never keen on Kubrick, amused. "*Dr. Strangelove,*" she observes in *The New Yorker*, "ridiculed *everything* and *everybody* it showed."[73]

This may be the only thing Kael would ever really get right about Kubrick. And perhaps this is the only way that Kubrick could make a real antiwar war movie: that is, by making an anti-everything (apart from his own perfect art) war movie. Certainly *Dr. Strangelove* shows Kubrick at his most misanthropic, his most contemptuous of men.

Homo Bellicus

War is over . . . if you want it. (John Lennon)

What comes next, if you're Kubrick, after *Dr. Strangelove*? What do you do after you have made, in your third take on the genre, the terminal war film, the film whose ending is the end of everything? As it happened, what Kubrick did following his doomsday satire was to begin all over again on the subject of men, this time at the very beginning—at "The Dawn of Man," as the first segment of his next film, *2001: A Space Odyssey* (1968), is titled. Imagistically relaying the passage of man from the prehuman to the human to the posthuman (and perhaps also the postgender), Kubrick's evolutionary epic still stands as the most ambitious movie with regard to its scope in the history of cinema all told. In the context of Kubrick's war films, specifically the one that he subtitles *How I Learned to Stop Worrying and Love the Bomb*, *2001* can be taken not only as a kind of replay with an alternative ending of that prior dead-ending film, but also as a *longue, longue durée* ontological reflection on our bellicose, war-oriented species. *2001* unfolds as a meditative picture book on how man

got himself to this point where a nuclear Armageddon seemed not just imaginable but imminent, and how he might further evolve to transcend that threat.
Kubrick, that is, had by no means gotten his worries about "the Bomb" out of
his system as a filmmaker with *Dr. Strangelove*. Like the devastating tragicom-
edy that precedes it by four years, Kubrick's epochal *2001* is very much a period film for the nuclear age.

Interviews Kubrick gave in connection with *2001* indicate that the threat of
nuclear conflict continued to weigh heavily on him during this film's making
and its release. The superpowers had taken some steps toward deescalating hos-
tilities in the years since *Dr. Strangelove* came out—including a 1967 UN
"Outer Space Treaty" that banned the placement of weapons of mass destruction in space—though this apparently gave Kubrick cold comfort. "If anything,"
he told Eric Nordern in a long, wide-ranging interview for *Playboy* in 1968,

> the overconfident Soviet—American *détente increases* the threat of
> accidental war through carelessness; this has always been the greatest
> menace and the one most difficult to cope with. The danger that
> nuclear weapons may be used—perhaps by a secondary power—is as
> great if not greater than it has ever been, and it is really quite amazing
> that the world has been able to adjust to it psychologically with so little
> apparent dislocation.

"It's improbable," Kubrick further worries, "but not impossible that we could
someday have a psychopathic president . . . who . . . starts a war."[74]

Set at the beginning of the new millennium, *2001* registers early on both
the further progress of the United States and the Soviet Union toward détente
and the persistence of their conflict by means of a brief encounter in passing
between Dr. Heywood Floyd (William Sylvester) and a group of Russian scientists aboard International Space Station 5. They exchange polite small talk
until the one male Russian scientist in the group, played by Leonard Rossiter,
brings up the subject of Clavius, the American lunar settlement to which Floyd
is en route. When Floyd refuses to address "the extremely odd things" the Russians have been hearing about goings-on at the base, including a (planted)
story about an epidemic, the formal pleasantries give way to a suggestion of
treaty violations and veiled threats of retaliation. The American-Soviet conflict may be subdued here in comparison with *Dr. Strangelove*, but it still hangs
ominously in the air. Indeed, that confrontation has been elevated from earth
and sky to outer space, even as it has migrated out from politicos and military
brass to scientists and colonists.

This politically telling scene may be most remembered, however, for its décor. The film stages the friendly, turned frosty exchange between Dr. Floyd

and his suspicious Russian counterparts in a lobby outside an orbital Hilton Hotel, its curving white floor eye-poppingly appointed with Olivier Mourgue's henceforth iconic cherry red Djinn chairs. (What a way for Kubrick to make a visual statement in his first feature film in color!) This low-slung, one-piece upholstered seating—something between an upright chair and an abbreviated, gestural chaise lounge—super-stylishly underscores the contortedness of this emblematic edgy Super Powers mini-faceoff that settles nothing. The highly expressive use of décor harks back to *Paths of Glory* and with *2001* now becomes characteristic of the Kubrick mise-en-scène. As does art, here in the form of the mysterious alien monolith, which appears throughout the film and looks like a piece of minimalist sculpture. Black, black paint mixed with pencil graphite gave this rectangular slab, made of fine-sanded wood, its mesmerizing dark metallic glint. The alien ultramachine of *2001* seems at once out of this world and of a piece with the hand-painted standing slats of wood that Anne Truitt had been making, or John McCracken's plank sculptures.

In this film's version of the twenty-first century, Americans and Russians will have come to share, if uneasily, some stylish celestial accommodations. But this high-design outer space way station is not the only thing that has been launched into the heavens by the turn of that century. There are also those sleek, ray gun–like orbiting nuclear weapons, placed up there, not just by Russia and America, but other countries too. Indeed, a satellite nuclear platform is the first thing the film shows us when, near the end of "The Dawn of Man" segment, it spectacularly cuts across millions of years in one breathtaking edit, advancing the story of man from hominid to human. While this epic film's subtitle alludes to Homer, Kubrick is here also cinematically translating Virgil, lifting both arms and men to the firmament. More than that, in this origin myth it is arms that make the man. It all begins when the pensive prehuman called Moon-Watcher (Daniel Richter), jumpstarted by some force emanating from that sculptural monolith, takes up an animal bone as the first tool, which is here to say weapon. Soon the enlightened ape-man and his clan are killing animals to eat and then, before you know it, orgiastically clubbing to death the weaponless chief of a rival clan to take over a contested waterhole: history's first homicide. Or as Kuberski pointedly puts it, "Moon-watcher has invented war"—and with it planted the seeds of civilization as we know it.[75] This Ur-warrior triumphantly hurls that bone heavenward. This primitive first tool/weapon, through the magic of what may be the most famous jump cut in cinema, becomes as it falls back downward an elongated, bone-white nuclear weapon spacecraft: the apotheosis of the human war machine.[76]

In Arthur C. Clarke's novelization of *2001* (published after the release of the movie), the first order of business for astronaut Dave Bowman (played in

the film by the blandly handsome, baby-blue-eyed Keir Dullea) when he returns to Earth as the Star Child is to detonate those orbiting nuclear weapons,
"a slumbering cargo of death"—this, because "he preferred a cleaner sky."[77]
"History as men knew it," the novel further informs us, "would be drawing to
a close." But what that means—has this Star Child, now "master of the world,"
come back to save mankind from itself, or to wipe it out for a new start?—is
left unresolved. All that is said, as the novel's final line, is that "he would think
of something." The ending of Kubrick's movie is even more enigmatic. When
the embryonic Star Child approaches the Earth in his planet-sized, sky blue
amniotic sphere, all he—though it's impossible to tell in the movie that he is
still a he—does is slowly turn his supersized head to stare out at us. And that's it.

"Kubrick was drawn to science fiction," Grant posits, "for the same reasons
he was attracted by the war film": technology, violence, and masculinity.[78] 2001
works its own way with the one woman in a world of men trope deployed in
Kubrick's other war films. Though there are far more parts for women in this
film than any of his previous works, those parts are all minor. Three of the
four Russian scientists who briefly detain Dr. Floyd on his way through that
stylish International Space Station are women: a small, forward-thinking, perhaps even slightly feminist touch. We will also see two American female scientists in attendance at the moon base briefing to which Floyd is heading,
though these are not speaking roles. Apart from televisual images beamed from
back home of Floyd's daughter (played by Kubrick's own daughter Vivian) and
the mother of one of the astronauts, the rest of the women who fleetingly show
up in 2001 are mod Pan Am stewardesses, along with a receptionist and an
elevator attendant. That elevator attendant happens to speak the first words in
the film, some thirty minutes after it has begun: "Here you are, sir," she says
to Floyd. These latter female figures, all so fashionably outfitted, are really just
part of the film's futuristic furnishings. And come its second chapter, "The
Jupiter Mission," Kubrick's *Space Odyssey* turns into a *no women at all* in the
world of men scenario.

This part of the film is set on board the massive Discovery 1 spacecraft,
which looks like both a giant floating vertebra (more echoes in the bone) and
an astral spermatozoon. Manning the ship is a crew of Dave, Frank, and HAL:
such regular Joe names, especially after the grotesques of *Dr. Strangelove*, for
this trio of twenty-first-century spacemen, one of them a thinking, feeling
supercomputer (unctuously voiced by Canadian Shakespeare actor Douglas
Rain). The ship's contained all-male world also turns out to be an incubator
for another episode of Kubrickian male melodrama. With the three other male
astronauts on board (one of them Russian) in suspended animation in white
coffin-like hibernacula, Dave, Frank, and HAL are all alone with each other

in deep space—and of course one of them cracks up, goes "a little funny in the head," as President Merkin Muffley explains of General Ripper, in the film that I keep pairing with this one. Naturally, it's the touchy supercomputer HAL, endowed with more personality than the handsome Ken doll astronauts Dave and Frank combined. After a secretive meeting between them to talk about him, HAL comes to feel left out, and thus lashes out, killing Frank and murderously terminating the life functions of those three hibernators, before turning too on Dave. Dave winds up being this epic traveler's tale's Odysseus: the only man to survive (sort of) these adventures and come back home (sort of).

"I sense something strange about him," Frank earlier had said of HAL to Dave. What's so strange about the computer? "I'm half cra-zy, all for the love of you," he will poignantly sing to Dave as he lets go of consciousness, deactivated by the screwdriver-armed astronaut in an intense scene—"I can feel it. I can feel it. I can feel it"—full of heavy breathing, one that hovers between a lobotomy and some kind of AI sexual assault. Does all this suggest that HAL, who in an earlier version of the story was a female computer named after Athena, the Greek goddess of wisdom and war, might have turned out somewhat gay? That question, aired in none too few reviews of 2001, launches this study of Kubrick's men's films into its next dimension of consideration. Perhaps of background relevance is Clarke's startling reminiscence that while he and Kubrick were hashing out the story, the latter came up with "the wild idea of slightly fag robots who create a Victorian environment to put our heroes at their ease."[79]

3

Male Sexuality and Homosexuality I

Lolita, The Killing, Spartacus

In *Color Me Kubrick*, Stanley Kubrick comes in shades of lavender and hot pink. The 2005 film, directed by Brian Cook and written by longtime Kubrick assistant Anthony Frewin, presents a "semi-true" account of Englishman Alan Conway, who in the 1990s made his way around London bars, restaurants, and nightclubs posing as the very private expatriate American filmmaker. (Kubrick had left the United States to settle in the English countryside back in the early 1960s, never to return.) How the clean-shaven con artist was ever able to pull off this act is curious, since he didn't look or sound a thing like the bearded, New York–born director. Nor did he really know Kubrick's work. The impostor auteur preyed especially on young men. "He uses you," rues one such lad in the film, "for his own wicked purposes": namely, swindling cash, sponging drinks, and occasional casting-couch sex. Dolled up in the trappings of faggotry, John Malkovich renders the film's flamboyant faux-Kubrick in broadly swishy brushstrokes. "Call me Stan-*lay*," he drawls; but his scarves, cravats, and cigarette holder make him a low-rent Quentin Crisp, though one with an on-again, off-again awful American accent.

This rouge and pancake-makeup "Kubrick" may seem utterly farfetched. Not so, explains one fellow, an aspiring actor, to a friend over drinks in the movie's most didactic scene. The director, this fellow proclaims, "left his calling card in *2001: A Space Odyssey*. But none of us recognized it." "*2001*?" replies his mate uncertainly. "Yes. HAL, the computer. Camp as a row of tents. Positively Danny Debonair with that voice. That's why he killed the astronaut, wanted to be alone with the other beefcake." Intrigued, the friend asks: "What's he working on now?" "He's doing a remake of that Julie Christie film, *Darling*. She's a boy this time. They wouldn't let John Schlesinger get away with *that* in the 1960s!"

Color Me Kubrick's fantasy of a gay Kubrick is indicated as just that: a dishy, rainbowed pipe dream, which the film further infuses with the stupefying fog of celebrity desire. This scene appears to have been inspired in part by the *New York Times* theater critic Frank Rich's account of his and his dining companions' phantomlike encounter with this Kubrick impersonator in a West End restaurant in 1993:

> Then he was gone, leaving us to celebrate our chance encounter with the great man, a meeting as brief and disjointed as a dream. . . .
> "Kubrick is gay?" someone else asked, taking note of the director's entourage [which included, reports Rich, a guy who introduced himself as a playwright, "a hustler in black, older and muscle-bound," and a "white-haired" Tory MP].
> "Everyone always thought HAL the computer acted like a jealous gay lover in '2001,'" I said.
> "And 'Full Metal Jacket' was full of homoeroticism," Larry said.[1]

In *Color Me Kubrick*, however, the gay reading of Kubrick is assigned and confined to a silly twink, who then goes on to boast about how "Stanley" has promised him "a juicy part" in that male remake of Schlesinger's *Darling* (1965).

But unlike Schlesinger, who also directed the bisexually oriented *Midnight Cowboy* (1969) and *Sunday Bloody Sunday* (1971), Kubrick himself wasn't gay, and he never made a gay movie. On the contrary, Kubrick's films can come across (someone once pronounced to me) as "painfully straight." This is so in more ways than one. For there is little sweetness and light on offer in Kubrick's portrayals of men and women together. And the view of marriage, family, and home life here is more often than not ruinous. So yes, Kubrick's films can come across as terribly straight. Yet, as these paired Chapters 3 and 4 on male sexuality will tease out, hardly any Kubrick film goes uninformed by something homosexual somewhere around its story's edges.[2] I don't just mean Kubrick's all but all-male movies, *2001* and *Full Metal Jacket* (which Frank Rich and his friends also single out), along with *Fear and Desire*, *Paths of Glory*, and *Dr. Strangelove*. One would expect to find homoerotic (and homophobic) intimations in these intensely homosocial films.

But there are also fascinating gay touches in Kubrick's hetero-tragic works, including *The Killing*, *Lolita*, *Barry Lyndon*, *The Shining*, and *Eyes Wide Shut*. Readings of these films, along with a few others that I will relate to them, provide this study's vantage regarding the place and function of homosexuality in Kubrick's work: a peripheral topic, I know, but one that I hope will yield some fresh perspectives regarding both the larger question of male sexuality in Kubrick as well as our concern with him here as a filmmaker of men's films. This

chapter focuses on three movies Kubrick made while the Motion Picture Production Code, which sought to keep sexual perversion—including homosexuality—out of the movies, was in effect. The next chapter takes up four
movies that Kubrick made after the Code had been abandoned. Both chapters are concerned with, among other things, the tendency of Kubrick's films to
add homosexual material that isn't in the literary source texts that they adapt
for the screen.

Two Normal Guys

> It would be great for two normal guys like us to get together—and talk
> about world events, you know, in a normal sort of way. (Clare Quilty to
> Humbert Humbert in *Lolita* the film, not the novel)

Where and how does homosexuality impinge on Kubrick's movies? As I
have begun to suggest, it tends to be tangential, staged—typically quite theatrically—at the margins of the story. Homosexuality in Kubrick is a vignette, carefully framed or circumscribed and then glimpsed only fleetingly.
Take the sliver of a scene near the end of *The Shining*, a scene that this
film's fervid fandom rates among the weirdest, the most inexplicable in a
work pored over for its perceived hermetic symbolism.[3] Wendy, played perfectly by an underappreciated Shelley Duvall, has herself at last started to
"shine," to start "seeing things." When she does, she catches sight in one of
the haunted hotel's guestrooms of a man in some kind of dog or bear fursuit
kneeling at the foot of the bed with his head in the crotch of a man in dinner clothes. The shot is perfectly picture-framed in the molding of the open
hotel room doorway, heightening its staginess, before an ultra-fast zoom
wings us right into the room (Figure 26). But our look at these queer goings-
on lasts only seconds—Did we really just see that? See a male animal
plushy, with an exposed behind, going down on another man?—before the
film immediately cuts back to the horrified Wendy, who gasps and runs
away. And that's it. We never, alas, get another peek at this fascinating phantom male couple.

Here the film's homosexual content is rendered apparitional, spectral. This
scene is indeed more a sight than a scene. In the Production Code–era films
by Kubrick to which the rest of this chapter is devoted, it is even less than that.
It's notional, only insinuated: a mere suspicion of homosexuality. But—and this
is important—it always seems to be there, even if, as we shall see, it has to be
added. Consider thus the strange, and much more drawn-out scene midway
through *Lolita* (1962) in which Clare Quilty (Peter Sellers) impersonates a

Figure 26. Queer ghosts.

homosexual—a homosexual state police officer to boot—and propositions
Humbert Humbert at the Enchanted Hunters Hotel.

But before we get to that, let us first note that this is just one of Sellers's roles
within his role as the prolific playwright Quilty. Later in the film he will show up
at Humbert's rented house in Beardsley in disguise with a moustache, Coke-
bottle glasses, and a put-on German accent as Dr. Zempf, a prying high school
psychologist. His aim is to pressure the possessive Humbert (James Mason) to
allow Lolita (Sue Lyon) to perform in the Beardsley school play, *The Hunted
Enchanters,* that (unbeknown to Humbert) Quilty has written and is directing.
Lolita stars as some sort of a bewitching tween nymph in a tierra and heavy cat
eye makeup, with Quilty the leering backstage impresario pulling the strings.
The visit is also to get Humbert to relax his prohibition against her dating any
boys: "Docktor *Hombarts,* . . . *Ve* Americans," says Quilty as Zempf, "are pro-
gressively modern. *Ve* believe that it is equally important to prepare the pupils
for the mutually satisfactory mating and the successful child rearing. That is
what *ve* believe!" The eugenics-y national credo of Sellers's Dr. Zempf predicts
his Dr. Strangelove's mineshaft repropagation of the species speech in Kubrick's
next film, his reverie about women handpicked for their highly stimulating "sexual characteristics" and made available to men who could "breed prodigiously."

Quilty's multiple characterizations in *Lolita* set the stage for Sellers's multiple roles in *Dr. Strangelove*. In that film, the role offered but not taken by Sellers was, I noted in the previous chapter, the part of Major Kong. The role not taken by Sellers in *Lolita* is the part of Miss Pratt, Beardsley's headmistress. He was going to play her, too, in ladies' tweeds.[4] During filming, the role of school authority was altered, however, from female to male, from Headmistress Pratt, who is in Nabokov's novel, to Dr. Zempf, who isn't. The movie's recasting of her as him thickens and highlights the male vertices of its two men, one-girl erotic triangle. This is in keeping with the movie's—which is to say Kubrick's—considerable enlargement of Quilty's role well beyond what is in the novel. For although Nabokov was accorded sole credit for the screenplay (and earned the film's one Oscar nomination), Kubrick completely reworked the script, with Sellers improvising on set additional dialogue for himself.

Sellers incarnates a compendium of queer male types for Kubrick. He plays gay in *Lolita* when Humbert happens to turn up, Lolita in tow, at the same hotel as Quilty. The Enchanted Hunters also happens to be hosting the State Police Convention, which apparently inspires Quilty's gay cop ruse. In the novel, the hotel is host to a religious convention. Nabokov changes it to a convention of doctors in the screenplay that he wrote.[5] Changing it yet again to a state police convention was, I take it, Kubrick's idea. Quilty waits until he finds his quarry alone outside on the hotel's shadowy veranda to target him. He first engages him in some leading, stuttering small talk. Quilty: "Hello. H-h-hello." Humbert: "Are you addressing me? I, I thought perhaps there was someone with you." Quilty: "No, I'm not really with someone. I'm with you." Then he launches into a self-conscious (which is to say highly calculated) monologue in which the loaded terms "suspicious" and "normal" keep cropping up. "I look suspicious myself," he quickly acknowledges. "A lot of people think I'm suspicious—especially when I stand around on street corners." "One of our own boys picked me up the other week," Quilty continues, playing on the phrase's double meaning. "He thought that I looked a bit too suspicious standing on a street corner and everything." Bear in mind that none of this is in Nabokov. "I couldn't help noticing when you checked in tonight," this observant, cruisy "cop" continues. "I noticed your face, and I said to myself when I saw you, I said, 'That's a guy with the most normal-looking face I ever saw in my life.' It's great to see a normal face because I'm a normal guy, and it would be great for two normal guys like us to get together—and talk about world events, you know, in a normal sort of way."

So as, one supposes, to avoid being recognized, Quilty, the gay poseur, remarkably plays the whole scene *a tergo*, leaning over the terrace railing with his rear facing Humbert (Figure 27). Quilty's hindside-foremost position also

Figure 27. Quilty *a tergo*.

points backward to the film's opening scene, which in the novel comes near last. Like Billy Wilder's *Sunset Boulevard* (1950), another black comedy of age-disparate desire, Kubrick's *Lolita* leads with its end, with a death—with Humbert, assassin-like, finishing off Quilty, who has played/will play his tormentor throughout: a metamorphic male nemesis capable of assuming different personae to hound—let's say haunt—Humbert wherever he goes. And "Humbert has it coming," judges Pauline Kael (who happens to like this one Kubrick film and really nothing else by him), "*not* because he's having 'relations' with a minor, but because, in order to conceal his sexual predilections, he has put on the most obsequious and mealy-minded of masks." Kael, writing in 1962, the year of the film's release, then provides this startling analogy: "Like the homosexual professors who are rising fast in American academia because they are so cautious about protecting their unconventional sex lives that they can be trusted not to be troublesome to the college administrations on any important issues (a convoluted form of blackmail), Humbert is a worm and Quilty knows it."[6] Kael makes no secret that she relishes how this "mealy-minded" academic closet case—remember that Humbert the pedophile is a lecturer in French poetry—is squashed.

One wonders what actual "fast-rising" homosexual professors this influential critic had in mind at the time. A year after Kael's piece on *Lolita* ran in *The Partisan Review*, Newton Arvin, for one, was arrested on pornography possession charges and lost his tenured position at Smith College. In any case, one needn't be in the sway of Kael's condescending homophobia, expansive enough to include other "unconventional" sexualities, to apprehend the gay nimbus that hangs about the scene in which Humbert melodramatically comes to wreak his revenge on the man who has been/will be his bane.

This scene also curiously acts like a mini-Kubrick retrospective. "Are you Quilty?" Humbert demands when he enters Quilty's debauched manor house and finds him peeking out from underneath a protective sheet thrown over an armchair. An empty wine bottle, somehow balanced atop the form underneath, marks the body and crashes to the floor when it stirs to life. "No, I'm Spartacus," Quilty retorts, rising in his white shroud—another of Kubrick's weird male ghosts—as mock eerie music plays on the soundtrack. "Have ya come to free the slaves or sumthin'?" Quilty continues, camping it up about the film that Kubrick made right before this one, while twisting the sheet into a makeshift toga. Then he lispingly beckons Humbert over to the table for "a little lovely game of Roman ping-pong, like two civilized Roman senators." (Would one of them be, say, the bisexual Crassus of *Spartacus*, whose "civilized" tastes embrace both snails *and* oysters?) "Roman ping," Quilty calls out, as he swats a ball across the net toward Humbert, who has now solemnly donned his fingerprint-proof black leather gloves. "You're supposed to say Roman pong!" Quilty exhorts his foe, when the ball goes unreturned.

None of this table tennis parlor game is in Nabokov's novel, or in Nabokov's own screenplay adaptation of it. It is yet more of the film's brilliant invention, which in this case Nabokov himself is said to have admired. James Mason takes credit for the idea of placing a ping-pong table under the chandelier to add to the scene's decorative bizarreries; but he also says that he had no idea that his character would then be asked to actually play on it.[7] As for games, Kubrick's favorite game, chess, also shows up in this film, as it does, I noted earlier, in several of his other films. (Nabokov was fascinated by it too and liked to compose chess problems.) Humbert half-heartedly tries to teach the game to Lolita's mother, Charlotte. "You're going to take my queen?" she wonders aloud, haplessly. "That," he murmurs, "was my intention," looking away from her to Lolita, who passes by as she heads to bed and plants an unexpected kiss on his cheek.

Humbert's chess partner in the novel is the flamboyantly gay Gaston Godin, a fellow academic. GG plays the pederast—"he knew by name all the small boys in our vicinity"—to HH's "nympholept," as Humbert diagnostically terms himself at the beginning of the novel.[8] Gaston Godin is not a character in the film, but I see some of his gayness absorbed into the film's Quilty, who in the Roman ping-pong scene keeps peppering Humbert with serves and sly lines such as "I sorta like to have it up this end, you know." When that come-on meets no response, Quilty puts down his paddle and dons his own leather gloves: boxing gloves, which just so happen, like the ping-pong table, to be part of this surreally anthological mise-en-scène. They take us back indexically to Kubrick's early noir boxing film *Killer's Kiss* and, earlier than that, to his very first film, the boxing documentary *Day of the Fight*, with its twin brothers. The male rivals Humbert Humbert and Clare Quilty are doubles too: not just "partner[s] in crime" and each other's "mirror image,"[9] but also (evil) twins, doppelgängers, as well as a pair, a kind of couple. "Alright, put 'em up," the gloved Quilty mock-challenges Humbert and starts shadowboxing. That image also looks forward to 2001's Frank Poole, half of the movie's matched pair of lookalike astronauts, whom we first see shadowboxing as he seems to run in place around the revolving giant space wheel. Shadowboxing—boxing with yourself—is a figure for the scene that Humbert unknowingly finds himself here playing with Quilty, his shadowy double, whom he shoots right in the glove. Quilty then stumbles over to a piano and sputters, "Why don't you let me play you a little thing I-I wrote last week?" Liberace-like, he starts playing Chopin. "We could dream up some lyrics, maybe. You and I dream them up together, you know, share the profits." You and I. I-I. Humbert Humbert. Clare Quilty. Two normal guys. Clearly guilty.

Finally, Quilty takes cover behind a large oil portrait of an eighteenth-century lady. This imitation Gainsborough also looks forward and backward in the world of Kubrick: forward to all those period painterly cinematic compositions in *Barry Lyndon* and backward to the even larger canvases that decorate the eighteenth-century chateau turned field headquarters in *Paths of Glory*. Recall that the final scene staged there between its two male antagonists— Colonel Dax and General Broulard (foes in the same army, a Kubrick trope)— ends with its own "stuff-it" insinuation. "Sir, would you like me to suggest what you can do with that promotion?" retorts Dax, played by Kirk Douglas, whose next role for Kubrick will be as Spartacus, with whom this whole outrageous scene began. In Kubrick's *Lolita* we have it straight from the horse's mouth that Quilty prefers "to have it up this end." Now, with his own end in sight, the playwright who, as he says, knows "all about tragedy and comedy and fantasy," tries to deter Humbert by dangling different s/m scenarios in front of him. Quilty first proffers an encounter with human furniture: "I've got some nice friends, you know, who could come and keep you company here. You could use them as pieces of furniture. This one guy looks just like a bookcase." *A Clockwork Orange* famously turns this idea into fiberglass female nudes as tables and beverage taps at the Korova Milk Bar. But the first expression of forniphilia in Kubrick, we find here, is male. (There is also a glimpse of it in the orgy scene in *Eyes Wide Shut*, where a man in black serves as a table for a naked copulating heterosexual couple.) Next Quilty turns to snuff voyeurism. Claiming his father is a policeman (another inspiration for his cop impersonation back at the Enchanted Hunters Hotel?), he pleads, more desperate now, "I could fix things up for you to attend executions." (That, incidentally, is what Dax and Broulard had just done in *Paths of Glory*, before their hysterical flare-up). "How would you like that? Just you there, nobody else. Just watching, watching. You like watching, Captain?" Quilty, part-time pornographer, presses. (I say so because we learn later in the film—which is to say earlier in the story—that Quilty had tried to talk Lolita into "making some kind of art movie" with his "weird friends"—"painters, nudists, writers, weightlifters"—at a New Mexico dude ranch.)[10] Humbert replies to these propositions by reloading his gun and shooting Quilty—he whose given name is both male and female—right through the face of that portrait of a lady. Killing Clare Quilty in the movie's first act effectively turns him into a ghost, an apparition that takes on many guises for the rest of the film, whose events unwind from here in flashback.[11]

Time to return now to the nocturnal exchange at the Enchanted Hunters (Haunters) Hotel between Humbert and the bent-over, backward-facing Quilty that occurs afterward—which again is to say before—in this film's literally pre-posterous narrative. From that arsy-varsy position, Quilty proposes, "It would be great for two normal guys like us to get together." While we wonder just how far this male solicitation is going to go—remember the film came out when the highly restrictive Production Code was very much in effect ("How did they ever make a film of *Lolita*?" tantalizes the poster for the movie)—Quilty suddenly changes tack and brings up Lolita: "I noticed you had a lovely little girl with you." Is the hotel treating the two of them properly, he wants to know. "You could have a lovely room, a bridal suite, for you and your lovely little girl." One supposes—at least the entry on "Homosexual Subtexts" by Gene D. Phillips in *The Encyclopedia of Stanley Kubrick* does—that we have come at last to this drawn-out scene's purpose, narratively speaking.[12] That is, all the police talk about what is suspicious and what is normal is meant to warn Humbert off his perverse designs on the young girl in his charge, who is asleep back in the hotel room that they have been forced to share at the overbooked Overlook, crawling with cops.

Though this supposed cop's come-on spooks him, it hardly deters Humbert from trying that very night to crawl into the sheets with Lolita for the first time. It's Lolita herself who ultimately thwarts him by taking up the whole bed, relegating her stepfather, childlike, to the little rollaway. To Humbert's consternation, it became available at the last minute, when, intriguingly, "two of the cops agreed to double up." The next morning is a different matter. The girl turns the tables on the older man by seducing him. Foreplay starts with Lolita brushing Humbert's cheek, feeling the grain of his day-old whiskers. "Boy, you need a shave," she complains teasingly. Humbert replies obtusely that of course he does because he hasn't shaved since yesterday morning. I remarked in Chapter 2 how *Dr. Strangelove* has a thing for hair. In *Lolita*, it's beards. This pillow talk of shaving itself serves as a "beard," as a cover for the illicit, for what the Beardsley-bound Lolita and Humbert are now about to do for the first time and keep on doing, until she tires of him and runs away to be with Quilty. On to the game at last, Humbert apprises Lolita that "All the best people shave twice a day": more Production Code–era erotic innuendo to go with the film's cheerfully smutty cherry pie, cavity filling, "loaded with mayonnaise the way you like it," limp noodles, and "Frigid Queen" diner quips.

And what is Lolita's mother, Charlotte Haze (Shelley Winters), to Humbert but a beard? His marriage to the "brainless ba-ba," as he cruelly terms her, is a handy way for him to pass in the Haze household as something other than the pedophile in their midst. (Quilty, it appears, also slept with Charlotte on his way to bedding her daughter.) The film has Humbert perched on the edge of Lolita's rumpled bed when he reads the widow's forlorn confessional love letter/marriage proposal. (Quilty is there too in the form of a poster on the wall advertising "Drome" cigarettes.) Again we have come upon Humbert unshaven and still in his pajamas and robe, a small dark forest of chest hairs sprouting and curling underneath the silk. Indeed, apart from the epiphanic first sight of the luscious Lolita in her bloomy bikini, feathered sombrero sun hat, and cat-eye sunglasses, Kubrick's movie perversely puts more of the hirsute Humbert on display than it does the young female universal object of desire who gives this twisted sex comedy its title. Earlier in the film, right after Humbert has moved in with the Hazes, we see him outdoors in the yard in another dressing gown—that, and apparently nothing else: a potential pastoral flasher in a terrycloth trench coat, the snake in this garden of juvenile delights.[13] There the poetry scholar pretends to be reading his book but is really studying his landlady's daughter as she mechanically hula-hoops to bubblegum radio: Nelson Riddle's annoyingly catchy nonsense ditty, "Lolita Ya-Ya," which charted as a pop single. Sue Lyon herself provided the baby-doll vocals, which wordlessly go: "Ya-ya, wow-a wow, ya-ya."

Riddle also composed a "cha-cha" for the sexually hungry "ba-ba" Charlotte and her leopard-skin dance scene with the cold fish Humbert—which Lolita interrupts by returning home early from a party. "Cha, cha, cha," Lolita Ya-Ya archly mocks her mama. Female harmony may be in short supply in the Haze home, especially now that it has such a fascinating male lodger; but the mother's and daughter's tunes are nonetheless made to rhyme. Which is to say that Humbert and Quilty are not the only paired rivals here, Lolita not the only go-between object of desire. An outing to the drive-in places Humbert between Hazes, who stack their trembling hands on his (and thus each other's) at a conveniently scary moment in Hammer Film's *The Curse of Frankenstein*. So female desire too here turns out to be highly mimetic. And of course, as

Figure 28. Garden of delights.

these things go, the daughter will ultimately grow up to be a (let's face it, lesser) version of her mother. Charlotte cha-cha. Lolita Ya-Ya. I-I. Humbert Humbert. Clare Quilty. All clearly guilty, all monstrous creatures of desire.

But let us get back to the garden and the hula-hooping Lolita and Humbert the flasher. Notwithstanding (or perhaps because of) her mesmeric physical exertions, the girl remains buttoned up in a long-sleeve blouse and long pants, whereas the man is seen showing a lot of leg (Figure 28). And this time the killjoy is Charlotte, likewise in slacks, who suddenly appears—the skewed apex of a deep-focus backyard bizarre love triangle—to snap Humbert's picture. "See how relaxed you're becoming!" she shrieks. Kubrick's own camera, as I began to suggest, also likes to "man-gaze" at James Mason, a dark, debonair heartthrob in the day. In his beautifully turned out book on the film, Richard Corliss describes Mason as "Cary Grant in a broody mood," "almost a male Garbo."[14] Kubrick here keeps up his custom, going back to his first films, of showing off his leading man stripped to the waist. We first glimpse Humbert thus when he springs out of bed to catch a last longing look at Lolita before she is whisked away by her mother to "Camp Climax for Girls," and then again during a long, lounging scene (another of Kubrick's inventions) that Mason plays in the bathtub. There a phocine Humbert luxuriates after his good fortune of Charlotte's sudden death, a celebratory drink close at hand set atop his dark furred wet chest.

Humbert's shadow, the smooth-cheeked, pasty white Quilty, who harbors his own dark desires, also comes with a beard. She is Vivian Darkbloom: that is,

Vladimir Nabokov's name in anagrammatic drag. James Naremore sees her as "wildly Bohemian," while Thomas Allen Nelson finds her "darkly exotic and slightly lesbian."[15] Played by the wonderful English character actor Marianne Stone, Darkbloom does the jitterbug with Quilty at the Ramsdale summer dance. She turns up again with him in the lobby of the Enchanted Hunters in another scene there that has the feel of a hotel pick-up. "Since you're a professional playwright, maybe you could use me sometime, hmm?" George Swine (Bill Greene), the night manager and a former actor, proposes to Quilty. Sizing him up, the playwright agrees: "Maybe I could *use you*, sometime," he replies to this fellow who has just told him that he gets rid of his "excessive energy" by lifting weights. "What do you do with your excess energy?" Swine wants to know back. "One of the things we do," intimates Quilty, drawing Darkbloom back into it, "is judo." "What happens," he explains, "is she throws me all over the place. I lay there in pain but I love it. I really love it." Darkbloom, the stern-faced dominatrix, isn't given any lines in the movie—or at least none that we are privy to, though she whispers something in Quilty's ear at the hotel. One wonders what they are doing at the Enchanted Hunters in the first place. Is the cop convention a kinky draw? In any case, Quilty leaves Darkbloom—he sheds his beard—when he makes his cruisy move on Humbert alone out on the veranda.

As I have already indicated, the critical consensus on that scene—greatly expanded from the novel and utterly reconceived in the film—is that it's there to put the fear of the law into Humbert, to get him to ditch his plans to sleep with his "lovely little girl." But, as I have also already noted, it accomplishes nothing of the sort and makes no difference at all to Humbert's plans. Hum will still have his Lo. The film's preposterous gay interlude—mere innuendo, all a pose—is, then, a narrative dead end. "You don't have to go," Quilty insists as behind his back Humbert finally gets up to leave. And as he departs, Quilty continues to proposition him: "Before you go, I was wondering whether maybe in the morning, you know . . . me being lonely and normal . . . we could have breakfast. I can arrange it with George Swine." No, no, no, no, Humbert keeps replying. The scene goes on too long. And it doesn't go on long enough. It is as superfluous, plot-wise, even gratuitous, as it is provocative—and haunting.

Yes, Humbert will have his Lolita—Quilty will too—just as surely as Humbert will finally lose her and melodramatically dissolve into tears. This is when he sees Lolita for the last time. Married, pregnant, broke, and already tending toward dumpy, she has summoned him with a plea for money. "Life is short. . . . Come away with me now," Humbert beckons: a pitiful *carpe diem*, for the bloom is already off this rose. The swap of the fashionable shades that Lolita wears in her first scene in the garden for the ill-fitting public assistance spectacles that she wears here, in the unkempt hovel she shares with a husband simply called Dick, says it all. Even so, the love of Humbert's life laughs in his face—the film makes him more victim than villain—and he is twice reduced to tears in this shamelessly melodramatic scene. *Lolita*: another Kubrick male weepie in the end. "It's as if we were watching a Douglas Sirk picture," writes Naremore, "with the gender roles reversed, so that a 'feminised' man suffers for love."[16] Or, as I'd put it, Kubrick's *Lolita* masculinizes the women's picture. Humbert agonizes for love, endures an unhappy marriage, and becomes hysterical when he discovers that Lolita has thrown him over for someone else. And, worse, he later learns that she never loved him, that she only ever loved Quilty. Humbert suffers all this—and he does all the housework. "Who does the tidying up? I do. Who does the cooking? I do," he spits out during one of their domestic spats. And he is the one to die of a broken heart—or "coronary thrombosis," as both the novel and the film medicalize it, so as to save Humbert some shred of male dignity.

But before that, there is still one more scene for Humbert Humbert here to play, though it has already been screened for us. The film ends by doubling back on itself, by rewinding to where it began at Quilty's place. Framing the entire narrative this way, within the space of the encounter between its two showy male leads—rivals, enemies, doubles, "two normal guys" passing in the night—further augments the sense that Kubrick has subversively turned Nabokov's novel into a men's film. Who are these men? What is their relationship? What has happened between them to bring them to this point? What follows in the film thus presents itself as the answer to those questions.

At first everything about the end of the film's replay of its beginning looks to be the same. That is, until the shot takes in that shroud-covered armchair. When we observed it in the opening scene, a wine bottle lay on its side precariously atop it: detritus from the past night's or many nights' bacchanal. Like an overturned sepulchral statuette, the wine bottle is also a pointer that something lurks here beneath. But now it's not there on the chair. A continuity error? Or has the queer phantom whose hiding place it marked disappeared, like those costumed gay ghosts in *The Shining*, before we get a second look?

The first and last word of Nabokov's novel, its alpha and omega, is "Lolita." The end and beginning of Kubrick's film is Humbert Humbert calling out, "Quilty! Quilty?"[17]

Killing Time

I've got a peculiar weakness for criminals and artists. (Stanley Kubrick)

"I'm Spartacus," pretends Quilty, wrapped in his white shroud-cum-toga, before the homicidally vindictive Humbert makes a real ghost of him. And it is back to *Spartacus*, the swords, sandals, and muscles Roman epic Kubrick directed, where we are heading. But before that, a detour even further back in Kubrick's corpus to his third feature film, *The Killing* (1956), which stages a different kind of homosexual vanishing act.

The Killing is Kubrick's first studio film and his first movie adaptation of a novel, Lionel White's fatalist pulp parable, *Clean Break* (1955). Kubrick brought in the brutal, brilliant crime novelist Jim Thompson—nicknamed "the dime-store Dostoevsky"—to work with him on the script, though Thompson was given credit only for dialogue. (He also had a hand in the screenplay for Kubrick's next movie, *Paths of Glory*.) *The Killing* is typically praised as Kubrick's first significant film, his first mature work, after his apprentice pieces, *Fear and Desire* and *Killer's Kiss*. All three films, as the repetition of forms of the word "kill" in two of these titles signals, are about the eruption of deadly violence—mostly, though not only, men killing men. Crime, the backdrop of *Killer's Kiss*, becomes the main event in *The Killing*, with its audacious, multi-man, clockwork plot to steal $2 million from a racetrack. Ironically, the "killing" that is successfully made at the track ends up in a shootout slaughter—a real killing—when two rival hoods barge into the gang's meeting place to steal from them what they have just stolen. The sudden piling up of carnage here, near the film's end, is worthy of a Jacobean tragedy, though the way that the eerily backlit bodies here fall and crumple also evokes the grotesque expressionist geometry of male corpses in *Fear and Desire*.

After the one-on-one, mano-a-mano battles of *Killer's Kiss*, inside and outside the ring, *The Killing* represents a return to Kubrick's first feature in another formal respect. Like *Fear and Desire*, *The Killing* is a male ensemble piece—the film's own jaded figure for it is a jumbled jigsaw puzzle—though here the men are considerably more fleshed out than the male abstractions we encounter in *Fear and Desire*. Much of that has to do with the story, which is veined with the kind of particularized character sketches that would be out of place in the allegorical *Fear and Desire*. But it is also a function of the veteran actors whom the young director, now in partnership with producer James B. Harris, at last had the financial resources and backing to hire.

For the first time, Kubrick landed a Hollywood star, Sterling Hayden, though at this point in his career he was not especially in demand as a leading man. Hayden plays Johnny Clay, both the mastermind of the crime and the one who will perform the actual holdup concealed behind a sardonic clown mask (Figure 29). Think back to those scenes of Kubrick's boxers in *Day of the Fight* and *Killer's Kiss* manipulating in the mirror their handsome, putty-like faces, wondering what they will look like after the night's fight. Here the mug, the crime face, of the man named Clay is hardened into an overstated plastic

Figure 29. Johnny Clay's plastic face.

smirk. Think also ahead to *Full Metal Jacket*. "Let me see your war face!" Hartman demands of the fresh-faced recruits in his charge. The guise that the clowning Private Joker puts on for him is just one-part bellicosity, however, and three-parts sheer fear. "Work on it," Hartman spits back. "You don't scare me." The mien of Hayden's Johnny Clay, a charismatically gruff man's man, would appear to be more effective in *The Killing*, with that rapid-fire, basso voice rumbling from out of the deep of his 6′5″, former male print model body. Clay is able to enlist and mostly keep in line the supporting male cast he has assembled around himself. Each fellow is assigned a bit part in a series of precisely timed, interlocking actions that will allow Johnny access to the track's coffers during the marquee seventh race, "the $100,000 Added Lansdowne Stakes," when they are flush with the day's receipts.

Johnny Clay is a small-time thief, fresh out of Alcatraz. He spent his five years there perfecting his plan to pull off the ultimate score, after which he would leave the country with his long-suffering girlfriend, Fay (Coleen Gray). None of his accomplices, Johnny explains to her, "are criminals in the usual sense. They've all got jobs. They all live seemingly normal, decent lives." "But"—here comes the punch line—"they got their problems." Mike O'Reilly (Joe Sawyer) is a bartender at the track, who needs money to care for his bed-ridden, sedative-reliant wife. Randy Kennan (Ted de Corsia) is a cop in trouble with a loan shark. Then there is George Peatty, a track cashier. Peatty hopes that his big money payout will impress his castrating wife Sherry, whom he jealously adores. The scenes between them make for a mordant travesty of heterosexual love, marriage, and family: "You want me to call you poppa. Isn't that it? And you'd call me momma," she taunts him. George is played by Elisha Cook Jr., who had a long career portraying the little man fall guy, and Marie Windsor—"queen of the B's," that is, B-movies—is Sherry, who lords it over her husband while lounging about in their tiny apartment.

Speaking of Kubrick's women, the devoted, drab "I'm not pretty and I'm not very smart" girlfriend Fay and the sadistic, exciting wife Sherry are set up as a study in female contrasts. In that sense, *The Killing* departs from the repeating Kubrick scenario of one woman in a world of men. Fay, however, appears in only two scenes, whereas the movie is almost as much Sherry's as it is Johnny's. Through her manipulations of George, she worms her way into the gang's secret plot. And her disclosure of it to her dark and handsome younger boyfriend Val Cannon—played by Vince Edwards, later the heartthrob TV neurosurgeon Ben Casey—leads to its deadly ruins.

The fourth member of the gang and the first of this cast of characters to appear in the film is Marvin Unger (Jay C. Flippen), a bookkeeper. He fronts the money to set Johnny's scheme in motion. He also lets Johnny stay with him in his apartment. Marvin's "problem"? In contrast to the other members of Johnny's supporting cast, it's not named. Marvin himself simply says to Fay— this in front of Johnny—"There's nothing that I wouldn't do for Johnny."

These four fellows make up Johnny's unlikely inner circle (which is also a small hall of fame of noir character actors). The film's interest turns nearly as much on how this ad-hoc male assemblage is pieced together and then comes undone, as it does on the heist itself. Johnny also enlists gunman Nikki Arane and strongman Maurice Oboukhoff, figures each as strange, though in very different ways, as their strange names. Maurice—a character completely reimagined from the novel—is a philosophically minded former wrestler, who hangs out at a place called the Academy of Chess and Checkers. There he butts in on other players' matches, while dispensing such bracing maxims as "Individuality is a monster, and it must be strangled in its cradle to make our friends feel confident," and "I've often thought that the gangster and the artist are the same in the eyes of the masses." Kubrick cast the non-actor Kola Kwariani as Maurice. Kwariani looks the part with his hairy, barrel chest, and cauliflower ears. He was himself both a Greco-Roman, then professional, wrestler and a chess hustler, whom Kubrick knew from his own chess-hustling days back in New York. The one-man-riot Maurice's task is to draw the track security guards away from their posts by staging a ruckus at the bar. At a touch, his shirt bursts off him as though he were the Incredible Hulk. The odd-looking, even odder-acting Timothy Carey plays Nikki. Like Hayden, Carey would work again with Kubrick. He is one of the three condemned soldiers—the repellent one, the one that you almost don't mind being made a scapegoat—in Kubrick's next film, *Paths of Glory*. Here the equine-faced Carey's role as Nikki is to shoot the favored horse, Red Lightning, midway through the race. "You shot a horse. It isn't first-degree murder. In fact, it isn't even murder. In fact, I don't know what it is," Johnny persuades him. Cradling a puppy in his arms, Nikki mumbles his acceptance of the job.

Speaking of pets, the childless Peattys have a squawking parrot. Its cage is overturned when George, mortally wounded, stumbles home from the shoot-out to shoot Sherry too. But the animal world has its revenge. After rubbing out Red Lightning, Nikki's getaway is thwarted and he himself is shot and killed by a track security guard when he backs his convertible over a horseshoe and blows out a tire. It had been given to him for luck by a slightly disabled (he's a veteran) Black parking lot attendant played by James Edwards. The animal assassin Nikki finds the attendant overly friendly and inquisitive, dismissing him with an ugly racial slur and tossing away his gift of a good luck charm. The screenplay invents this encounter, adding a racialized dimension here to the dealings between men in Kubrick's film.

Johnny too is made to pay at the film's end at the airport by an animal, a poodle named Sebastian, whom we might think of as the return of Nikki's puppy in other form. The little lap dog bounds out of a woman's arms and sets in motion a rapid chain of events climaxing in Johnny's suitcase stuffed with stolen cash popping open on the tarmac, just as a plane has touched down, its propellers still spinning. The greenbacks go up swirling in the wind, and with that all Johnny's grand hopes and intricate plans turn to dust. This stunning, ill-fated climactic shot, which is also not in the novel, prefigures in small the billowing mushroom clouds to come at the end of *Dr. Strangelove*, Hayden's second movie with Kubrick. "Run," Fay urges Johnny. "Yeah?" he replies, his pallid face now as fixed as the clown mask that he had donned for the robbery. "What's the difference?"

"Oh Johnny, my friend," Maurice had said to him back in the chess club, "you never were very bright. But I love you anyway." That sentiment is a teaser for the male love scene, such as it is, to be played out later in the apartment that Johnny has been sharing with Marv. Johnny wakes him early on the morning of the robbery for a private farewell, without the other fellows around. "I just wanted to say goodbye," he tells the older man. "We'll probably never see each other again after we split the money and break up tonight. But, in my book, you'll always be a standup guy." In another of the film's desolating ironies,

Johnny says this to a guy who is prone alone in bed, one who will not be left standing at the end either. "Johnny," Marv replies, "I don't know how to say this, and I don't even know if I have the right." Then, after Johnny tells him that he can say anything that he wants, Marv ventures: "Wouldn't it be great if we could just go away, the two of us, and let the old world take a couple of turns and have a chance to take stock of things?" This is another proffer (to recall *Lolita*) that two normal guys get together to take in the world—though here Flippen's touching line reading, which mixes hopefulness with world-weariness, stands in sharp contrast to Sellers's wily gay cop impersonation.

Marv's attachment to the younger man is couched in paternal terms—"I've always thought that maybe you're like my own kid," he has just told Johnny—that recall George Peatty's fantasy of conjugal contentment in which his beloved Sherry would call him "poppa." Marv, however, means here to keep Johnny from going away with Fay: "It can be pretty serious and terrible, particularly if it's not the right person. Getting married, I mean." (This we know from those lovebirds, the Peattys.) The bedroom scene between the two men is at least as demonstrative as Johnny's one perfunctorily amorous scene with his girlfriend, which is also set in Marv's apartment and interrupted by his arrival home. This is when her older man rival lets Fay know that he would do anything for his boy Johnny.

A discarded early title for this movie was *Bed of Fear*. Fear in bed of what? And one wonders if Johnny, while sitting on the edge of Marv's bed, had decided to go off with him instead of Fay whether things might have turned out (to use a term of Johnny's) "differently." Of course, we will never know. "You'd better get back to sleep. . . . Keep away from the track. Go to a movie or something," Johnny tells his would-be poppa, gently brushing aside Marv's proposal and affectionately tussling the older man's thick gray mane: the male-to-male affectionate stand-in for the brief kiss at the beginning of the film with which Johnny dispatches Fay, who is likewise told to keep out of the way until everything is over.

In White's novel, the film's source text, Marvin is a misanthrope. Though he gives Johnny a place to stay, he feels no special bond with him, much less a paternal crush. In fact, the two men are fairly hostile to each other, with Johnny's own feelings for Marv eventually verging on hatred.[18] So the movie's homoerotic subtext is an added feature. We have encountered this before in Kubrick's adaptations, and we will do so again and again. But what is striking in *The Killing* is how what the film gives with one hand it takes away with the other. The scene in which Marv summons the courage to ask Johnny to go away with him, not Fay, occurs "at 7 that morning." We are told this by this film's authoritative male voiceover, whose principal function is to correlate the gang members' storylines for us and keep time in a multipronged plot where timing is every-thing. But in the very next scene the voiceover relays that Johnny arrives at the airport to check in one of his bags at "exactly 7 a.m." Another continuity error, this time a chronological one? Or is this film, famous for its nonlinear, frac-tured time loops, for replaying its temporalities from multiple subjective per-spectives, eliding one of the film's own narrative inventions—as though no such thing had ever taken place, as though Marv had never proposed what Johnny does not accept? To cover it over, to make all that disappear (though not really), the film rewinds and replays that precise interval of time to place Johnny elsewhere.[19] In *Lolita*, which runs on its own time loop, with its end as its begin-ning and its beginning as its end, the homosexual interlude at the Enchanted Hunters feels drawn out, gratuitously extended. In *The Killing* the scene that appears superfluous is, however, the one that doubles back in time to cancel out the expression of male/male desire. Does this tautly plotted narrative really need to take us on a preliminary excursion to the airport so early in the morn-ing? Or why couldn't the all but forgotten Fay, whom Johnny has instructed to make all the arrangements for their trip, check in Johnny's bag?

In any case, the day of the heist has just begun and already the time is out of joint. The weary, fatherly Marvin has yet to give up the ghost, though he will die that evening with the other members of Johnny's gang, caught in the crossfire of the shootout with Val and his henchman, just after 7 p.m. (All those unlucky 7s! Marvin's 7:00 a.m. spurned and then chronologically negated ro-mantic proposal. Red Lightning's and then Nikki's deaths during the seventh race. The 7:00 p.m. reconvening of the gang that ends in a slaughter.) But well before Marvin meets his end, what his character stands for begins to fade to a dead time—or a time in and out of time, where what transpired between him and Johnny early that morning is, like a passing dream, something, yet noth-ing. ("Go back to sleep," Johnny keeps telling him.)

Marvin emerges out of that dead time himself like an apparition. Though he has been told to stay out of sight, the old man shows up at the track, heart-broken and drunk, to silently haunt Johnny just as Johnny is about to steal downstairs to the office where the money is kept. When Johnny sees Marvin there, he shoots him a look that could kill. Like Hamlet's ghosted father, the old man, however, won't leave the younger one alone. And it's a good thing too, as Marvin's presence turns out to be a lifesaver. He will ever so slightly jostle a track cop—an action assigned to another character in the novel—just as the cop is about to apprehend Johnny, now returned from the holdup be-low. Marvin's intervention allows Johnny to punch out the guard and get away from the track safely. As Bill Krohn notes, this crucial sequence "plays without any narration."[20] It's as though the narrator now no longer notices Marvin.

Or sees right through him, as if he is there but no longer quite exists: another of Kubrick's apparitional homosexuals.

What I see, however, is Marvin, or a faint trace of him, appearing yet one more time, this time at the airport, via the poodle called Sebastian. That name has a long homoerotic pedigree that goes back to the early church martyr, Saint Sebastian, his attractive body stripped and penetrated by arrows. It continues through Shakespeare's Sebastian in *Twelfth Night*, the love object of Antonio, to the effete Sebastian Flyte of Evelyn Waugh's *Brideshead Revisited*. Tennessee Williams also uses Sebastian as the name of his homosexual character in *Suddenly, Last Summer*, which premiered a few years after *The Killing*. In *The Killing*, the poodle with the gay name and the pompadoured Marvin are further associated sartorially: both are collared in bowties. And it's this dog named Sebastian who is able to do what Marvin can't, which is to keep Johnny from going off at the film's end with his girlfriend.

At the Baths

They're arresting everyone. (Lentulus Batiatus)

In an interview with Kubrick published a few years after the release of *2001: A Space Odyssey*, Joseph Gelmis raises the question of homosexuality with reference to the supercomputer HAL: "Some critics have detected in HAL's wheedling voice an undertone of homosexuality. Was that intended?" he asks. Kubrick cuts off the discussion by insisting that HAL "was a 'straight' computer." There is no gay ghost in this machine. Kubrick also remarks rather dismissively how "it's become something of a parlor game for some people to read that kind of thing into everything they encounter."[21] Even as I resist the urge to question what *is* a straight computer, let me admit to indulging now and again—and why not?—in the "parlor game" to which Kubrick here refers: a parlor game that often feels more like a séance, given certain spectral qualities of Kubrick's homosexuals. But it should also be said that my endeavor has not been to read homosexuality into Kubrick's films, but instead to consider how their screenplays *write* "that kind of thing" into the story here and there, how they make it an element of their treatment of male sexuality. We have just seen this in both *The Killing* and *Lolita*. *Spartacus* (1960), which Kubrick directed as executive producer and star Kirk Douglas's hired hand, presents a different case, however. Here it was not a matter of adding a gay undertone or a trifle of homosexual interest to the film's literary source. It was instead about scaling back and rehandling the abundance of "that kind of thing" already there.

Spartacus is based on Howard Fast's best-seller of the same title about a slave revolt that threatened the decaying Roman Republic. Fast was a member of the Communist Party USA when he wrote the novel and self-published it in 1951. He reportedly came to the figure of Spartacus through the German radical thinker and activist Rosa Luxemburg, whose socialist organization was called the League of Spartacus and its members Spartacists.[22] Wanting to know where the name came from led Fast back to Plutarch, Appian of Alexandria, and other historical sources. He began working on his novel while serving a three-month prison term in 1950 for refusing to name names before the House Un-American Activities Committee. Fast renders the story of the rebellion and its gruesome suppression, which is set in 71 BCE, a polemic against capitalism, fascism, and McCarthyism as exemplified by the Roman patricians and a celebration of the rising tide of populist power as embodied by Spartacus and his multiethnic, multiracial army of slaves, who throw off their shackles and heroically rise up against their oppressors. "I began to see," Fast recounts in a note on his novel, "a wonderful continuity between that first great class war . . . and all the times that followed." Spartacus, he writes, "lived with me. He was no ghost that one could easily set aside—but rather did he more and more take on meaning and purpose for our own time."[23] A specter is haunting . . . postwar America: the specter of Spartacus.

The novel begins with Spartacus already dead—slain in battle—and the Appian Way now spectacularly lined with more than six thousand crosses, upon which hang the bodies of the men who followed him. The book unfolds Spartacus's story piecemeal, moving backward and forward in time, via the recollections and impressions of various characters, beginning with the powerful general Crassus, who ultimately led Rome's forces to victory. Though Fast's own storytelling purposes are politically preachy, he liberally exploits the legendary sexual decadence of ancient Rome to spice up his revolutionary socialist saga with kink: a hint of incest, rough sex, the lash, and of course rampant bisexuality and homosexuality. Thus he has Crassus recount what he came to know of Spartacus as pillow talk while "he lay abed with a boy," Caius Crassus, to whom he is distantly related. "And why not? he asked himself. Is it worse than other great men did?" As for the "boy" Caius, he belongs to a generation that "no longer felt a need to assuage guilt by rationalizing homosexuality. It was normal for him." "The *passion* of six thousand slaves who hung from the crosses by the roadside" was also, the novel adds, "normal for him."[24] Indeed, it excites him.

The general's story triggers Caius's own flashback while the two are still in bed together. Four years earlier, he got to see Spartacus in action for himself during a trip down from Rome to Batiatus's renowned school for gladiators in

Capua. Then Caius, "pretty as a girl," was in the company of another man, Bracus, described as "somewhat older, harder, playing the dominant role of the two" (102). This pair of "perfumed homosexuals" (272) picks out the combatants for two private exhibition matches. To Caius's delight, Bracus demands that the contests—one of which will pit Spartacus against the Ethiopian gladiator Draba, "a giant of a man, his dark skin glistening with a sheen of sweat" (107)—be to the death and conducted in the nude. Later in the novel, even Spartacus gets into the act, ordering "in a cold passion of rage and hate" two captive Roman commanders be "stripped naked" and forced to fight to the death like gladiators themselves (252). Though Kubrick made it clear when he was brought on board that he was interested in exploring a more morally ambiguous Spartacus (of which there are traces in the historical record), Douglas overruled him on all such accounts.[25] So in the movie no vengeful Spartacus ever gets to flip the script on the Roman ruling class and relish what the novel terms "a great orgy of reversed gladiatorial combat" (253). Nor does the film have patrician men handpicking the gladiators they want to see performing in the raw as we find in the novel. In the corresponding scene at Batiatus's school in the film, the selection of the fighters instead falls to two female spectators. "I want the most beautiful. Give me the Black one," demands the racy Claudia (Joanna Barnes). She also insists that the gladiators wear "just enough for modesty."

When Spartacus begins his training as a gladiator in the novel, he is so straitlaced that he recoils from "the knowing fingers" of the masseur in a spasm of what sounds like gay panic: "The first time this had happened to him, his feeling was that of . . . panic and terror . . . his own flesh invaded by these probing, writhing fingers" (115). However, he soon learns to like it, to "relax and take full advantage of what the masseur gave him": this to prime his brawny body for the ring, where he is the entertainment for "wealthy connoisseurs of slaughter . . . with their ladies or their male lovers." The novel makes the flagrant homosexuality of Crassus, Caius, and Bracus another pointer, like the institution of slavery itself, to the moral depravity of the Roman Republic in its death throes. Fast is also probably playing to a supposed correlation, operative then in both left- and right-wing circles, of fascism and male homosexuality. But his prose, especially the accounts of slaves and gladiators that he layers within this extended man/"boy" bedroom scene between Crassus and Caius, reads in stretches like soft-core gay historical porn, like Mary Renault on steroids. Thus we hear how a "delightful thrill of fear and excitement" shoots through Caius when, with Bracus, he first sees the whole troop of Batiatus's gladiators exercising in the yard: "There were about a hundred of them, clad in loin cloths and nothing else, clean-shaven, their hair cropped close to their heads, going through their paces with wooden sticks and staffs" (104–105). Out of this number, they select a sculpted Jewish fighter named David for closer physical assessment:

> "Tell him to shed his cloak, *lanista*," said Bracus.
> "Unclothe," Batiatus whispered.
> The Jew stood there for a little while; then, suddenly, he dropped his cloak and stood naked before them, his lean muscular body as motionless as it if were carved from bronze. Caius stared fascinated. (122–123)

After David wins his match, Bracus wants to inspect the fighter's body again: this time his backside, putatively to see how many punitive lashes have been laid upon it: "Bend over!" Bracus orders the gladiator, "still naked . . . his muscles still quivering," and forces him on his knees (131).

There are many such scenes here of nakedly objectified men, of athletic, aestheticized male bodies lined up, inspected, and handled, then singled out or coupled in contest—or hung bare upon a cross. David, who over time falls in love with Spartacus and will tell Spartacus's wife Varinia that he himself has no use for women (277), is the last of Spartacus's men to be crucified. He is led to the cross "naked . . . with his arms bound tightly behind his back," "his muscles . . . like leather and whipcord," and the "cuts . . . all over him . . . a veritable tapestry of scar tissue" (246). Once again Fast's doting prose on the male body in extremis gets erotically carried away with itself. This pulpy rendering of David's "passion," which the novel stretches over many pages, also apparently inspires the gratuitous s/m scene with which the novel all but ends: the imperious general Crassus taking a whip to the worshipful "young Caius," who had just been stroking his "beloved" older man's breast (360–361).

"Naked, completely naked" is, of course, how we here first come upon Spartacus himself, while he is toiling in the gold mines of the Nubian Desert (80). Like the other Thracian mineworkers, he wears nothing save a slave collar: "not even a loincloth hides their . . . sun-blackened organs of sex" (87). Our first impression of the book's hero manages to be both morally wrenching (how could they treat a man like this?) and titillating (what a man, what a male specimen for us to see thus exposed and so vulnerable!). Spartacus's collared "neck [is] thick and muscular," his "shoulders are padded with muscle," and his "hands are large and square and as beautiful as some hands can be" (78). This awful, exciting depiction of male bondage evokes the similarly clashing affective valences of a scene near the end of Quentin Tarantino's own slave-as-liberator movie *Django Unchained* (2012)—his *Spartacus*—where Django (a strapping Jamie Foxx) is shown nude and strung up upside down. Tarantino here may be quoting the scene in Kubrick's film when the bared corpse of the Ethiopian gladiator Draba, played by Woody Strode (Hollywood's first Black cowboy), is likewise hung upside down. Tarantino's recycling of that searing image in *Django Unchained* courts homoerotic interest, even desire, while at the same time, like Fast's novel, homophobically indicting it.

Spartacus in his slave collar and David on the cross may be the most copiously blazoned bodies in the novel. But there are also "tall, long-limbed black men from Ethiopia" (105), "big, blond Germans" (106), and "the huge, broad-shouldered, red-headed Gaul" (155) for readers, so inclined, to delectate over: something, that is, in Spartacus's inclusive band of brothers for just about every taste. As for the Romans, the man among men is certainly Crassus, with his "fine, strong manly features" (67)—"whose desires," we read, "operated differently" (91), who is more homosexual here than he is in the film, who "never looked more manly" than when he stands smiling before the young Caius awaiting him in bed for their more tender first sexual encounter (57). I return again to the virile Roman senator here because the novel provocatively makes him not just Spartacus's foe, but also his double of sorts. The film, we will see, also picks up on this relation.

This dark, handsome Thracian, Spartacus, is brought to life on screen by the good-looking, tough guy actor from New York—and champion of liberal causes—Kirk Douglas. Douglas had been a wrestler at St. Lawrence University, and one of his signature roles was a boxer in the 1949 noir sports drama *Champion*, directed by Mark Robson. In his autobiography *The Ragman's Son*, Douglas writes about how as a Jew he personally identified with Spartacus and the slaves: "As it says in the Torah: 'Slaves were we unto Egypt.' I come from a race of slaves. That would have been *my* family, *me*." "I came up with the idea," Douglas continues, "of combining [Spartacus's] character and the character of David the Jew," who in the novel, we saw, is not killed in battle but is instead crucified, which is how Spartacus's own end is recast in the film.[26] After giving Fast a shot at adapting his own novel, Douglas turned to the blacklisted writer Dalton Trumbo, one of the Hollywood Ten, to do the screenplay. Trumbo had refused to cooperate with the House Un-American Activities Committee's 1957 investigation into communist influence on the motion picture industry, and like Fast he went to jail because of it. Trumbo originally worked on *Spartacus* under a pseudonym—said at the time to be the worst-kept secret in Hollywood—but, at Douglas's insistence, he was ultimately credited as the film's writer. Though the movie tames the novel's strident socialism into '60s American liberalism, this didn't stop the right-wing columnist Hedda Hopper from denouncing *Spartacus* as a communist work. But when President Kennedy crossed the American Legion's picket line to view the film in

Washington and it turned out to be the year's top grossing movie, the Hollywood blacklist was effectively nullified, earning *Spartacus* its place in America movie history.

Just as Trumbo was not the first choice as the film's writer, Kubrick was not the first choice as director. The studio insisted upon Anthony Mann, best known for his westerns. But Douglas fired him two weeks into shooting and immediately offered the job to Kubrick, with whom he had done *Paths of Glory* a few years earlier. Kubrick had been working for Marlon Brando on *One-Eyed Jacks*, but he became available when Brando decided to direct the film himself. The $12 million budget for *Spartacus* dwarfed any production that Kubrick had worked on thus far and was then among the most expensive films ever made. Its cast was gigantic, including thousands of extras for the panoramic final battle scene added to the film at Kubrick's insistence.

The cast of *Spartacus* was also star-studded. In addition to Douglas, the movie showcased the English triumvirate of Laurence Olivier, who originally wanted the part of Spartacus for himself but agreed to play Crassus if the role were suitably enhanced for him; Peter Ustinov, who won the Oscar for best supporting actor as Batiatus; and Charles Laughton as the plebeian leader Gracchus. (All three actors were also accomplished film directors themselves.) Jean Simmons, who plays Varinia, the woman Spartacus loves, is an exception to Douglas's featuring American actors for the principal roles among the rebel slaves and English ones for most of the leading Romans. Tony Curtis was cast after he lobbied Douglas for a part in the movie. The role of Antoninus, the young household slave who flees Crassus to join with Spartacus, was created for the pretty boy actor, fresh from his cross-dressing role in Billy Wilder's *Some Like It Hot* (1959).

Kubrick would later remark that *Spartacus* "had everything but a good story."[27] For the first and last time in his career, he lacked control over the screenplay, casting, and editing. Naremore dubs *Spartacus* "the only alienated labour of Kubrick's film career" and omits it from his otherwise comprehensive treatment of Kubrick's feature films.[28] So do most other commentators on Kubrick, as Naremore himself points out. Here I part company. Though my approach is likewise auteurist, it's not purely so. Kubrick *did* direct most of *Spartacus* (the opening scenes in the mines are Mann's work), even if he didn't rule the movie from its inception to its final cut. Why such condescension and disregard in Kubrick critical circles for the collaborative and partial? And, in any case, what viewer concerned with male sexuality in Kubrick could overlook *Spartacus*, with its famous marble bathroom scene?

Those much-discussed bathroom scenes that recur throughout Kubrick's movies can be traced back to *Spartacus*, which takes three trips to the baths.

The first occurs at Batiatus's gladiatorial school. Kubrick's camera showily plunges through the stone floor of their slave quarters for our glimpse of the private, underground world of these warrior-athletes in training. There Spartacus tries to make friends with the other gladiators as they tend to their wounds and wash themselves in an atmospheric sauna-like grotto. "What's your name?" he asks, when Draba takes a place next to him. As I mentioned earlier, the Ethiopian gladiator is played by Woody Strode, former All-American UCLA football star, decathlete, and model. The 6'4" Strode, who earned a Golden Globe supporting actor nomination for this part, is a giant among men in this film well-stocked with lookers. "Gladiators don't make friends," Draba at first rebuffs Spartacus. "If we're ever matched in the arena together, I have to kill you." But when that happens, he doesn't. Draba defiantly spares Spartacus, whom he has just disarmed in the ring, and instead takes aim with his trident at spectators in the grandstand. The African gladiator targets the (white) Roman patricians, in a scene that surely bore an extradiegetic political charge at the time the movie played in American theaters. Just before Draba reaches them, an arena guard spears him from behind. Crassus supplies the coup de grâce with a knife as his face is sprayed with Draba's blood.[29]

The film's display of the gladiators in their subterranean sauna is cloaked in friendship and fraternity, in keeping with one of the film's principal humanist themes: the "brotherhood of all men." It is followed by an even more intimate bath scene between Crassus, the "commander of Italy," and his new, handpicked "body servant," Antoninus. (Like the pampered poodle Sebastian in *The Killing*, Antoninus's name has a homosexual tinge; it evokes the Roman emperor Hadrian's youthful male favorite Antinous.) The film grants us a view of this bath scene at a slight distance and with our gaze veiled by see-through curtains: a prurient visual effect that heightens the sense of voyeurism (Figure 30). Like those many passages featuring nude men in Fast's novel, this encounter has the ambiance of soft-core period porn. Alex North's shimmering exotic music soundtrack enhances that mood. "Do you eat oysters?" Crassus asks Antoninus, naked except for his skimpy square-cut slave trunks, once his body servant has joined him in the bathwater. "When I have them, master," replies Antoninus. "Do you eat snails?" "No, master." "Do you consider the eating of oysters to be moral and the eating of snails to be immoral?" Crassus further queries him. "No, master." "Of course not," Crassus affirms. "It is all matter of taste, isn't it?" "Yes, master." "And taste is not the same as appetite. And therefore not a question of morals, is it? Hmm?" After a pause, Antoninus hesitantly replies: "It could be argued so, master." The great Roman general then pronounces meaningfully: "My taste includes both snails *and* oysters."

Figure 30. Male tastes.

Crassus conveys his Socratic object lesson about male sexual tastes under the veil of metaphor and innuendo necessary at the time. But the analogy he implies between food and sex, along with the distinction he makes between taste and appetite, is historically apt. Michel Foucault considers the matter in *The Use of Pleasure*, the second volume of his *History of Sexuality*: "This association between the ethics of sex and the ethics of the table was a constant factor in ancient culture. . . . Foods, wines, and relations with women and boys constituted analogous ethical material; they brought forces into play that were natural, but that always tended to be excessive."[30]

Crassus's gustatory come-on to Antoninus is one of Trumbo's additions to the story. "It was just another way Romans abused the slaves," explains Douglas, who was so taken by the scene that he reprints it in its entirety from the screenplay in his autobiography.[31] We might also regard Crassus's coded talk of mollusks as a delicate stand-in for all the overt homosexuality and bisexuality in Fast's novel. But apparently it was not delicate enough. Like the film's most graphic images of violence, this bath scene wound up on the cutting room floor. In deference to the MPAA's Production Code's ban on the indication of any kind of "sexual perversion," Universal Studios removed it from the American version of the film between the film's preview and its premier. (It was suggested that the scene would be more palatable if the talk of snails and oysters were changed to artichokes and truffles, though that may be even more gay-seeming.). Kubrick would pretty much disavow *Spartacus*, but he cared enough about it to give his stamp of approval to the complicated and expensive restoration of the film, which was then rereleased in 1991, with this bath scene now back in its place. Since the original dialogue recording had been lost, an aged

Tony Curtis had to redo his "Yes, master; no, master" lines, while Anthony Hopkins was called upon to dub in those of the late Laurence Olivier.

The second half of this scene survived the studio's censors—oddly so, since the sexual subtext between this powerful older man and subservient younger one now becomes more pronounced. Everything is on the verge of being exposed when Antoninus pulls back those gauzy sheers that have veiled our view of the bath. As Crassus walks toward the camera through that opening into the courtyard, he summons Antoninus to follow. "Antoninus, look! Across the river. There is something you must see," he beckons from his vista overlooking the city. Gazing outward, Crassus rhapsodizes over a troop of Roman soldiers marching in the distance. "There, boy," he proclaims, "is Rome: the might, the majesty, the terror of Rome. There is the power that bestrides the known world like a Colossus." "No man," Crassus exults, "can withstand Rome. No nation can withstand her. How much less . . . a boy?"

On the word "boy," Crassus turns away from the sight of soldiers marching afar to regard the silent male slave at hand, submissively standing behind him. Rendered now in a half-body medium close-up, Antoninus's bare sculpted torso seems of a piece with the decorative nude statuary in the background: another of the film's images of male sexual objectification. ("Tony, where do you get arms like that?" Curtis reports Olivier asking him during the scene.[32]) Shifting his gaze from Antoninus back to the comparably exciting spectacle of the Roman legion on its way to another imperial conquest, Crassus continues his erotic tutelage: "There's only one way to deal with Rome, Antoninus. You must serve her. You must abase yourself before her. You must grovel at her feet. You must . . . *love* her. Isn't that so, Antoninus?" But when he turns back around again to see what effect his words have had, Crassus finds himself alone.

The "boy" got the point, even if the studio censors did not. Or was this segment of the scene allowed to pass (so to speak) whereas Crassus's bisexual innuendo of "snails *and* oysters" was not because here the homosexual come-on has a heterosexual front? "Boy, you must love her!" Rather than love "her" (him), Antoninus finds his way to Spartacus, whom (like the character of David in Fast's novel from whom he partly derives) he has come to love instead. Crassus has better luck during the film's third trip to the baths, another communal one like the gladiators' underground sauna. Here we find, as Kuberski wittily puts it, "the Roman senators, like mobsters in a *film noir* sauna, walking about in towels and talking *Realpolitik*."[33] Crassus succeeds in seducing the bronzed, buff Julius Caesar (John Gavin in his dark and handsome prime) to his side in the Roman political crisis occasioned by the slave revolt and its early victories in the field. "Is it me you want," Caesar asks Crassus—who, let it be said, is himself also quite a looker in this film—"or the garrison at Rome?" (Figure 31). How about both?

Figure 31. Crassus and Caesar at the baths.

But let us return to Antoninus, whom Spartacus first comes upon in a lineup of new arrivals—recruits, we might think of them—who have escaped from their masters to join his army of renegade gladiators. ("An army of gladiators," muses Spartacus; "there's never been an army like that!") He touches the new-comer's brocaded white toga, finery that sets Antoninus apart from the other men in their burlap tunics. Spartacus then asks him what work he did while still a slave. "Singer of songs," says the young man. Incredulous, the proletariat-minded Spartacus asks again, "But what *work* did you do?" Male lineups are a recurring feature of Kubrick's men's films, from *Paths of Glory* to *Full Metal Jacket*. This one in the sprawling rebel encampment on the slopes of Mount Vesuvius replays an earlier such scene in the courtyard of Crassus's villa. There, in a row of new household slaves presented for his approval, he singles out Antoninus for special attention, just as Spartacus will do. Whereas Spartacus fingers Antoninus's toga, Crassus takes in hand the placard that hangs around the slave's neck, reading from it his name, age (twenty-six), and birthplace (Sicily). Then Crassus, again just as Spartacus later does, interrogates Antoninus about what he can do. This time the young singer of songs volunteers that he is learned in the "classics." More classic code for homosexuality? Crassus appears to think so. "Classics, indeed," he replies. "What position have we, I wonder, for a boy of such varied gifts? Hmm?" Crassus asks himself aloud, before determining: "You shall be my body servant."

Through matched scenes like these, the film counterposes the populist Spartacus and the patrician Crassus, the earnest freedom fighter and the crafty would-be dictator. Spartacus is unlettered, but naturally kindhearted ("What's your name?" he asks everyone he meets), while Crassus, like the French generals in *Paths of Glory*, is debonair and heartless. Crassus is omnivorously bisexual, while Spartacus falls in love with the first woman he ever touches, the doe-eyed Varinia, whom Crassus also comes to desire and possess for a time as his slave.[34] The Roman general and the rebel gladiator are also drawn to Antoninus, whom both men take to calling "boy," even though he is twenty-six. It is here, around the young Antoninus, where the film stages the matching of Crassus and Spartacus that is suggested on other levels in Fast's novel—as though, in the Kubrickian world of male doubles and copies, they are the ancient "pederastic" antecedents of the pedophiliac pair Humbert Humbert and Clare Quilty of *Lolita*, which Kubrick started working on right after he finished with *Spartacus*. The Romans customarily addressed their male slaves as *pueri*—"boys"—no matter how old they were.[35] What are we to think of Spartacus using that term too, just for Antoninus? Kubrick himself gets into the act. In a personal letter to Trumbo, with whom he locked horns during the film's production, Kubrick describes the feeling of the end of the film as he would have it this way: "I think [Spartacus] is crushed by his defeat. Raised out of this by the love of Antoninus and his need to spare *the boy* the suffering of crucifixion. And finally given a merciful release by the sight of his wife and baby. Audience cries. $20,000,000 gross."[36]

Even though this Production Code–era film must perforce cut way back on all the homoeroticism and homosexuality spicing up Fast's novel, it finds its own ways to make different kinds of male love part of its plot. "You like him, don't you?" Varinia blurts out, after seeing Spartacus's enthralled response to the quasi-Homeric homecoming ode that Antoninus, singer of songs, performs at a campfire: "[When] twilight touches the shape of wandering earth, I turn home," he intones. "Through blue shadows and purple woods, I turn home." Against a painted sound stage pastoral backdrop of blue, pink, and purple that matches this purple poetry, the film renders one of its many scenes of looking. Varinia intently watches Spartacus raptly gazing at Antoninus. We then see a montage of scenes glimpsed around the camp illustrating the family values of which Antoninus sings: "I turn to the place that I was born. To the mother who bore me and the father who taught me long ago." On the word "mother," the film cuts, however, to the image of a hale father, feeding and dandling his young son in the open field (Figure 32). The bearded father and his rosy-cheeked son are flanked, one on either side, by a pair of adult, though beardless men, who are also sharing food and drink. "Where'd you learn that song?" Spartacus asks Antoninus. "My father taught it to me," he replies, of course.

The idealized picture of family that momentarily materializes in this scene shows no place for women (including a mother), even as it expands to take in more men. Is this Antoninus's fantasy? Spartacus's? Has the film's image-system

Figure 32. All-male family

itself momentarily turned queer? And who might those beardless fellows be? Younger brothers to the father and thus uncles to his boy? Two friends? Comrades in arms in Spartacus's new model army? Why not a couple themselves? That is, rebel fighters and lovers? (Bear these two in mind for when in the next chapter we turn next to *Barry Lyndon*, Kubrick's other historical costume drama and its bucolic scene of army officers in love.) Whoever these men are, they disappear from sight almost as soon as one notices and starts to wonder about them. For the film quickly "corrects" its visual miscue, replacing this all-male image with another, more familiar family scene. The same bearded father reappears in it, but now there is a mother at his side, and his boy has been replaced by an even younger child. They are surrounded by others, presumably more family members in the form of grandparents and yet more children. But those other two paired fellows are not among them. Like the spectral male couple about to have sex in *The Shining*, now you see them, now you don't.

The love that Crassus demands from Antoninus is the dreadful devotion of a slave or a subordinate for his master, which is also the predominant model for homosexuality in Fast's novel. The idyllic all-male tableau that illustrates the "boy's" pining Homeric homecoming ode transiently presents additional possibilities for how he might be loved by Spartacus, the other older man here: as comrades, as brothers, as "father" and "son"—all perfectly acceptable ways for Hollywood to domesticate male love. The nature of the love that has grown between Spartacus and Antoninus is not fully delivered (perhaps even unto them) until late in the movie in a melodramatic scene that is arguably its emotional climax. After Spartacus's army has been defeated, Crassus recognizes

Antoninus in a long file of captives being marched to their roadside crucifixions. Chained directly in front of Antoninus is Spartacus (slaves again), though Crassus does not yet know who he is. Here the movie stages another of its scenes of intense looking. While film criticism has developed much to say about the male gaze, *Spartacus* prioritizes the male-male gaze.[37] "Antoninus?" says Crassus. His recognition is followed by a shot of Spartacus looking back at Antoninus, followed by one of Crassus noticing him looking at Antoninus, and then a shot of Spartacus looking at Crassus. It's by means of this silent circuitry of male gazes that Crassus comes at last to know what his opponent and rival looks like (something, by the way, denied to him in the book).

Right before this scene, Crassus had offered to spare the lives of the surviving rebels on the condition that they identify to him their leader, dead or alive. In the film's most famous scene, all six thousand of Spartacus's men, starting with Antoninus (whose hand is manacled to Spartacus's), stand to their feet and declare, one by one and then in a booming male chorus: "I am Spartacus."[38] Kubrick, I suggested in Chapter 1, was, from the beginning, intrigued by forms of male replication, especially when it comes to fighting men: boxers, soldiers, and now gladiators. Here that interest is exponentiated several thousand times over. These six thousand Spartacuses are all to be lined up and crucified, save now for Spartacus himself and Antoninus. Crassus cruelly orders a gladiatorial fight to the death between them. The winner will then suffer the more painful prolonged death of crucifixion. "We shall test this myth of slave brotherhood," the Roman aristocrat declares contemptuously. (Crassus's cruel vindictiveness here has less force without the censored scene in the baths between him and the "boy.") "Don't give them the pleasure of a contest," Spartacus tells Antoninus. "Lower your guard. I'll kill you on the first rush." "I won't let them crucify you," Antoninus defiantly replies. "It's my last order. Obey it," Spartacus insists. After a fierce exchange of blows, he gains the advantage. Pinning the younger man beneath him, Spartacus tenderly whispers, "Forgive me Antoninus," before thrusting his sword deep into him. Looking up into his (mercy) killer's eyes, Antoninus, who has already taken the older man's name ("I am Spartacus!"), says with his last breath, "I love you, Spartacus . . . as I loved my own father." "I love you," Spartacus replies, "like my son that I'll never see." Spartacus and Antoninus thus consummate their relationship in death, while Varinia is granted her freedom as she flees Rome with that unnamed son. (Another Spartacus? Or perhaps another Antoninus?) "Here's your victory," Spartacus hisses to Crassus, after he has been forced to kill the one they both call "boy." "He'll come back," Spartacus warns him, "and he'll be millions."

Early in the film, Kirk Douglas, whom Kubrick had shown off shirtless in *Paths of Glory*, appears in a loincloth chained to a rock. Douglas completes his exhibitionist star turn here by going, Christ-like, to the cross at the end of the movie, though now he's less naked, perhaps so as not to make the Jesus parallel—*ecce homo*—too explicit. Still, it is hard not to see the hero's crucifixion as at least an associative emblem of the film's voiceover prologue's prophecy of the coming triumph of Christianity and with it a new society sans slavery. (Not that this new religion was itself in a hurry to do away with that particular form of inhumanity.) In contrast to other Roman epics—most famously *Ben-Hur*, the 1880 Lew Wallace novel subtitled *A Tale of the Christ*—Fast's left-wing political allegory scrupulously refuses to take any religious turn. There is not even anything about pagan religion here. Remember, more important, that in Fast's telling Spartacus is slain on the battlefield, where his body is chopped to pieces (17, 43), like the book's fragmentary recounting of his story. Plutarch and Appian of Alexandria also report that Spartacus died fighting, that he was not one of those crucified. But even as Hollywood's ahistorical Christianization via crucifixion of Spartacus—the man and the movie—dilutes the radical politics of this slave revolt story as Fast would allegorize it for us, it also opens onto other devotional possibilities for rendering male love. Here Spartacus goes to the cross in place of Antoninus. If that makes Spartacus a Christ figure, then Antoninus is surely his John, his Beloved Disciple. The film's forms for male devotion thus keep multiplying until the end: master/slave; commander/soldier; father/son; friends; brothers; Lord/votary.

Marx is said to have fancied Spartacus as a personal hero, terming him "one of the best characters in the whole of ancient history."[39] And Rosa Luxemburg named her German socialist organization after Spartacus, which, we saw, is what led the leftist American novelist Howard Fast to the rebel gladiator in the first place. But this charismatic revolutionary, this inspiring athlete-warrior, has turned out to be an icon for more than political liberation. Coincident with that status—and this in keeping, as I have meant to show here, with elements of both the novel that Fast wrote and the film of it that Kubrick directed—Spartacus has also become a symbol for sexual liberation: homosexual sexual liberation. *Spartacus*, for instance, is the title of a long-running gay international travel and sauna guide that lists numerous gay bars and baths that are themselves likewise named after Spartacus. "Spartacus" is also the pen name of a gay erotic illustrator who was active in the 1960s and a frequent contributor to Bob Mizer's *Physique Pictorial*.[40]

Speaking of gay artists, earlier in this book I juxtaposed some of Kubrick's male photography for *Look* magazine to the work of Robert Mapplethorpe.

Figure 33. *Spartacus*, Robert Mapplethorpe. (*Spartacus*, 1988
© Robert Mapplethorpe Foundation. Used by permission.)

One of Mapplethorpe's most compelling statuary portraits is of a massive
bronze of a bare, brawny *Spartacus* (1988), with a possessed, haunted look in
his eyes (Figure 33). He is clutching in one hand a segment of broken chain:
an emblem of self-liberation. In the other he brandishes an elongated version
of the *rudis*, the short wooden sword awarded a gladiator who through some
extraordinary feat in the ring had won his freedom from slavery. Spartacus, of
course, would have been given no such thing; so here the great first-century
BCE rebel—this is perfect for the bad boy classicist Mapplethorpe—is depicted
as having taken that token for himself. In other words, the symbolic sword that
Spartacus wields in this image of him is a pure fantasy object.

"Gladiator" comes from the Latin word for sword, *gladius*, which was also
used to refer to the penis. Mapplethorpe's gleaming silver gelatin photograph
highlights the enduring phallic glamor of the gladiator, this unclothed warrior of the ring. In Fast's novel, men no less than women are turned on by the
games. *Spartacus*, the popular Starz cable TV series that ran from 2010 to 2013,

brings the gladiators themselves, along with their spectators, out of the closet. Its storylines feature much gay male sex and even a gay gladiatorial love story. As Theresa Urbainczyk notes, Ridley Scott's 2000 blockbuster *Gladiator* also exploits the romance of this specially trained, highly prized classical exhibition fighter—though Scott's movie, I would add, shies away from anything too gay.[41] That is, this updated swords-and-sandals historical drama may have won five Oscars, including Best Picture and Best Actor for its hunky, bearded star, Russell Crowe; but *Gladiator* is no *Spartacus* (and not only because there's no Spartacus in it).

As for Kirk Douglas and Stanley Kubrick's classic gladiator movie, it has maintained an allusive, tracelike homosexual afterlife in recent movies.[42] In *Clueless* (dir. Amy Heckerling, 1995), Cher (Alicia Silverstone) and her male crush, Christian (Justin Walker), watch *Spartacus* together on TV, with him gushing over the "snails and oyster" scene: an indicator, not yet apparent to Cher herself, that Christian is gay. The flamboyant gay housekeeper in *The Birdcage* (dir. Mike Nichols, 1996) played by Hank Azaria is named Agador Spartacus. In *Cruel Intentions* (dir. Roger Kumble, 1999), Sebastian's (Ryan Phillippe) gay friend Blaine (Joshua Jackson) says, "I do believe that *Spartacus* is showing on television tonight": the password for the two going ahead with their plan to frame a male rival. And then there is *In and Out* (dir. Frank Oz, 1997). In it, supporters of a high school teacher played by Kevin Kline, who has just been fired for coming out, rise to their feet during a graduation ceremony to declare their solidarity with him. "I'm gay," they each say, their gay-friendly variation on Antoninus's and the other rebel slaves' faithful falsehood, "I am Spartacus."[43]

4

Male Sexuality and Homosexuality II

Barry Lyndon, A Clockwork Orange,
Eyes Wide Shut, The Shining

Spartacus makes the kinds of love that arise between men (and between men and "boys") germane to its plot. What is more, this 1960 movie sets the sexual element of male love and also lust in plain view, even as it is there, in plain view, kept under wraps in code and innuendo, or put forth behind a heterosexual front. "You must love *her!*" the imperial Crassus, conflating himself with Rome, demands of his young "body servant" Antoninus. Not, as we have seen, that this obligatory Production Code–era obscurantism provided much of an impediment to later homosexual appropriations of the film and its inspiring virile male hero. Kubrick himself, however, was no fan. He viewed the film in its final form as an epic missed opportunity. More than a decade would go by before he would again take to the genre of the historical drama. When *Barry Lyndon* came out in 1975, the Motion Picture Production Code, which forbade "sex perversion or any inference to it," was itself history. No longer bound by these prohibitions, this film, adapted by Kubrick from William Makepeace Thackeray's 1844 picaresque novel *The Memoirs of Barry Lyndon, Esq.*, can be more forthright about such things. And it is. An openly gay scene presents itself midway through the movie. But the homosexual is also more marginal to this rake's progress than it is to the Roman court and rebel slave camp cultures of the earlier, Production Code–era *Spartacus.* Kubrick himself, as we will consider, passes off the film's gay scene as merely incidental, as all but insignificant in its own terms: that is, as a gay scene. It may seem strange, then, to make *Barry Lyndon's* one brief homosexual interlude the pivot for a consideration of male sexuality in that long film, as I do here. But this particular scene conveys a depth of feeling that exceeds its sideshow status. More than that, I see it as indicative of Kubrick's way with homosexuality in his post–Production Codes movies.

Homosexuals in History

"Oh, Jonathan!" "Frederick!"

Barry's brush with homosexuality comes midpoint in Part I of the film, which is subtitled: "By What Means Redmond Barry Acquired the Style and Title of Barry Lyndon." It occurs—and this military setting is of interest even as it is to be expected—while Barry is unhappily indentured to the English army during the Seven Years' War. "But fate," the film's narrator (Michael Hordern) informs us in one of his velour voiceovers, "did not intend that he should long remain an English soldier, and an accident occurred which took him out of the service in a rather singular manner." So it is that Barry comes upon the unmanned horses of two English officers. The horses are tethered to a lakeside tree, from which hangs the uniform of one of the officers. Through a round opening in the greenery the camera then spies from a modest distance the officers themselves, Jonathan (Jonathan Cecil) and Frederick (Anthony Dawes), naked in the waist-deep water. The men are intently gazing at one other and holding both of each other's hands (Figure 34). Here we are back at the baths again, this time en plein air, to behold a private scene between lovers. A zoom shot through this pastoral peephole ushers us, voyeurs that we are for this kind of thing, in closer. Kubrick, we saw, repeats and intensifies this cinematic gesture—a visual calling card of the homosexual in his work—to startling effect in *The Shining*. There a "shock-zoom" through the frame of an open doorway vehiculates us into a hotel guestroom where two male ghosts appear to be about to get down to it with each other. A similar shot in *Barry Lyndon* puts us in the position to hear Jonathan deliver the unhappy news to his lover that he will have to go away again for a fortnight on another royal courier mission.

As Frederick vehemently protests—"You promised me last time it would be once and for all and never be again!"—we watch Barry (Ryan O'Neal) watching them. By means of another, slower zoom the camera eventually settles on his handsome vacant face. Held in close-up, it registers no feeling at all about the mini male melodrama that he is fated thus to observe: neither homophobic disdain, nor homoerotic arousal, nor plain voyeuristic curiosity. Nor a suggestion of comradely sympathy either, even though Barry has just suffered his own personal loss with the death in battle of his one friend in the army, the fatherly Captain Grogan's (Godfrey Quigley). This heartbreaking event turns Barry's thoughts, reports the narrator, "from those of military glory to those of finding a way to escape the service, to which he was now tied for another six years." Aspects of Barry and Captain Grogan's relationship evoke the unrealized younger man/older man-with-money romance in *The Killing*. "I've only

Figure 34. British army officers in love.

a hundred guineas left to give you. For I lost the rest at cards last night," Grogan chuckles weakly, as he lies dying in the small wooded grove to which Barry
has carried him on the sidelines of the battlefield, where rows of advancing
redcoats have fallen like duckpins under close-range stationary French fire.
The captain's last words are "Kiss me, my boy"—which Barry does, hard and
on the lips—"for we'll never meet again." "We'll probably never see each other
again," begins Johnny when he wakes Marv on the morning of the heist to
say his private farewell in *The Killing*. Recall that rather than say goodbye, the
older man more or less proposes to the younger one: "Wouldn't it be great if we
could just go away, the two of us?" Johnny wordlessly brushes Marv's proposal
aside with an affectionate head rub. The young Irishman Barry is not so stoi-
cal. He dissolves in tears over Grogan's body, another of those many scenes of
male weeping in Kubrick.

Ryan O'Neal was good at crying and came to fame in the preppy tearjerker
Love Story (1970), where he was a hunky font of sobs.[1] There are many more
of those in store for Barry. But let us return now to the blank reaction shot as
he takes in the intimate scene in the lake between these two lovers. The
voiceover storyteller must resume in supply of the cipher-like young man's
thoughts:

Here was the opportunity to escape from the army for which he had
been searching. It was only a few miles through the forest to the area

occupied by their Prussian allies, where this officer's uniform and papers should allow him to travel without suspicion and stay ahead of the news of his desertion, which would be sure to follow.

While Barry helps himself to Jonathan's uniform and horse, Jonathan and Frederick reappear in the film's frame in the distance. As he steals away in the foreground of the shot and then exits it, they remain in its background. The film, that is, lingers a moment more with this male couple even as Barry, and with him the story, head in another direction. And even then it makes sure that we can still hear them just as well from this distance as when the camera had voyeuristically zoomed in closer. "Oh, Jonathan!" says Frederick, "it's times like this that I realize how much I care for you. And how impossibly empty life would be without you." Overcome by emotion, all that Jonathan now can manage by way of reply is his lover's name: "Frederick!"

In the highly mannered world of *Barry Lyndon*, this touching exchange is no less affecting for being more than a touch affected—after a certain gay fashion. On its way to making that very point, the entry on "Homosexual Subtexts" in *The Encyclopedia of Stanley Kubrick*, which I cited before, terms these officers in love "two obvious homosexual types."[2] As dated as this sounds—though the book itself is not *that* dated: it's from 2002—such talk may still rankle. Nor does it make things much better when this entry takes a second stab at rendering the film's brief dalliance with homosexuality, affirming that, "Although the two men seem on the surface to be stereotypical movie homosexuals, they nevertheless display a devotion to each other that gives their characters some depth." One could write a book about that shorthand formulation: "stereotypical movie homosexuals," as Vito Russo did in his groundbreaking study *The Celluloid Closet*.[3] And the dialectic of surface and depth is one way to get at the essence of the entire film, and not just these "two obvious homosexual types." Leaving that aside, the *Kubrick Encyclopedia* does have a point here. It's that this short scene is well stocked with homosexual indices, as though the love that dares now speak its name has, more than that, taken to quietly broadcasting itself. Consider first the homosexuals-in-history pedigree of these gay military officers' names. The film couples a Jonathan, who has the same name as the man whose love, the Bible tells us, David found "wonderful, passing the love of women" (2 Samuel 1:26), with a Frederick, who shares his name with Frederick the Great, the homosexual Prussian king and an aggressor in the very war in which these two officers take part. Consider also the slightly queeny, which is here to say *very* English, inflections of their ardent declamations— "Jonathan, don't be such a silly ass!" "Oh my God, you're not serious!"—in voices akin to the intonations of the film's similarly *very* English narrator.

(Remember that our foray into "gay Kubrick" began with a queer voice: HAL's.) And then there are the visuals of Jonathan and Frederick's pale, stick-figure bodies—mirroring versions of each other in the mirroring lake—unadorned by the virile accoutrement of muscle or chest hair. Let me emphasize again that these are homosexual markers and gay stereotypes *of a certain kind*. This is not Tom of Finland, though other types of more macho male corporeal display, including BDSM ones—beatings, in particular—will crop up later in the movie.

Barry Lyndon's gay scene takes up less than two minutes of Kubrick's lavish period piece, which is more than three hours long, and it is rarely discussed at any length in accounts of the film.[4] But these "two homosexuals in the lake" did catch the eye of the French critic Michel Ciment, who published a valuable study of Kubrick with which the director himself cooperated. Ciment asked him about them in an interview that appears in that volume, noting— and this is key—that the scene "is not in the book." Ciment's query calls to mind the Kubrick interview a decade earlier when Gelmis brought up the gay rumors swirling around HAL, which Kubrick simply refused to engage. "HAL is a straight computer" was all he would say by way of changing the subject. This time Kubrick doesn't shut down the discussion when homosexuality comes up, and his response to Ciment is worth quoting in full:

> The problem here was how to get Barry out of the British Army. The section of the book dealing with this is also fairly lengthy and complicated. The function of the scene between the two gay officers was to provide a simpler way for Barry to escape. Again, it leads to the same end result as the novel but by a different route. Barry steals the papers and uniform of a British officer which allow him to make his way to freedom. *Since the scene is purely expositional, the comic situation helps to mask your intentions.*[5]

So *Barry Lyndon* is another of those Kubrick film adaptations that adds some minor homosexual incident or texture that is not part of its literary source. Kubrick, who wrote the screenplay, apparently came up with this scene himself.[6] There was a storytelling problem to be solved, and a splash of homosexuality turned out to be the answer to it. But then Kubrick further explains that the whole thing is "purely expositional," a mere contrivance of narrative convenience.

Let us return to that drawn-out encounter in Kubrick's *Lolita*, discussed in Chapter 3, when Quilty impersonates a cop who seems bent on picking up Humbert at the hotel. In terms of plot, that scene (also not in the book) leads nowhere, even as it goes stutteringly on and on for five minutes of screen time.

In contrast, the raison d'être of the gay scene Kubrick inserts into *Barry Lyndon* is, according to Kubrick himself, strictly narratological: no more than just a storyline shortcut to get Barry out of the English army—and, as it happens, alas, into the far more brutal Prussian army. A drawn-out scene of Barry leading the way for a shirtless muscular and mustached soldier forced to walk the gauntlet for desertion, his hands bound in front of him, provides our introduction to it. This is the martial BDSM scene referred to earlier. It also gives us a foretaste of the male corporal punishment that will play such a prominent role in Part II of the movie, when Barry tyrannically assumes control of the Lyndon estate.

Let's return to the interpolated homosexual scenes in *Lolita* and *Barry Lyndon*, one made during the regime of the Production Code and the other after the industry's liberation from it. These two scenes—Quilty mock-cruising Humbert at the Overlook and the gay English army officers in the lake—appear to be, with respect to their ends, opposites. The latter is "purely expositional" (whatever that means), the former expositionally extraneous. But that scene from *Lolita* and this scene from *Barry Lyndon* amount to much the same thing: *a homosexuality of apparent insignificance.* What D. A. Miller's alluring, ultra-auteur study of Fellini's 8½ reports in passing about the anonymous good-looking young men who keep popping up in that film's background might also be extended to the recurring homosexual presence in nearly all Kubrick's movies: "They are there and yet they don't seem to matter; they don't seem to matter and yet they are there; in a word, they merely *persist*."[7]

The way that Kubrick downplays his gay officers may come as a letdown. But the notion of a homosexuality that is merely incidental to Kubrick's *Barry Lyndon*, as well as to Kubrick's men's films more generally—and this persistently so—seems to me rather interesting. As if to maintain: What is a men's film without some homosexual presence, however marginal, some gay ambiance, however evanescent? But then we hardly need Kubrick's highly wrought cinematic case studies of men and male sexuality to tell us what we otherwise already know from the standard issue military movie, or sports film, or male road movie, or male coming-of-age story, or the male buddy movie turned "bromance"—where, as it happens, in the 2015 film *The D Train*, directed by Andrew Mogel and Jarrad Paul and starring Jack Black and James Marsden, the guys actually do it. Once.

But it's not only that. It's also that Kubrick's trivializing account of the gay scene he adds to *Barry Lyndon* doesn't really satisfy, narratively or affectively. The well-worn stolen clothes plot device to get Barry out of the army forthwith could conceivably work just as well with only one (straight) skinny-dipping officer. I take it as the film's own unconscious registration of this point that a

single uniform (Jonathan's) hangs there on the tree, noticeably ready for the
taking. One might even think that the film has forgotten about Frederick's
clothes; but they are there too, barely visible, draped over the back of his horse.
I fuss over these details because I think that they amount to something more
than mere plot functionality in the film presenting us (whatever Kubrick's
stated intention) with two men naked in the water, two naked men who are a
couple, a couple utterly, melodramatically absorbed with each other.

The gay melodrama of it: is that, then, what Kubrick means by the scene's
"comic situation," which, he further explains, is merely meant to serve as a dis-
traction from the scene's reliance on that cliché stolen clothes/stolen identity
ploy? Has the scandal of homosexuality here given way to the gays as a joke?[8]

But, then, what is really so funny here? "Every frame in the film is a fresco
of sadness," Andrew Sarris recounts of *Barry Lyndon*.[9] This scene in the lake
is no exception. Am I just a gay romantic stick in the mud for wondering what
is next for these two men, who display (to echo the Kubrick Encyclopedia) such
depth of devotion to each other? It isn't as though this kind of gay love scene
is standard fare in movies of the time—or even, for that matter, that this particular film offers many love scenes period. Yet expressions of affection, such
as they are, in *Barry Lyndon* are tendered mostly between men, or men and
boys. In addition to the lovers in arms Jonathan and Frederick, there is Barry
and the paternal Captain Grogan, whose death, we saw, left the young soldier
in tears. Then there is Barry and the macabrely made-up Chevalier de Balibari (Hammer Films alumnus Patrick Magee), his Irish countryman in disguise and a second (corrupting) father figure. Barry again bursts into tears—this
time of joy—at meeting the impostor nobleman, who will sneak him out of
Prussian territory. Or Barry and his adored and adoring young son, Bryan (David Morley), whose tragic death reduces Barry to tears for the third time. By
contrast, Barry's marriage to the wealthy Countess of Lyndon quickly turns
unfeeling, leaving her emotionally desolate. Former *Vogue* model Marisa
Berenson plays Lady Lyndon as perfectly lovely and inert as a painted waxwork or a Gainsborough or Reynolds oil. And that, imparts the narrator, is just
how her new husband regards her: "as not very much more important than
the elegant carpets and pictures which would form the pleasant background
of his existence." Those very terms come back to us from *Paths of Glory*, also
set in an eighteenth-century manor house. "I wish I had your taste in carpets.
And pictures," one despicable general flatters another.

Despite the interest that Jonathan and Frederick may have aroused in a
viewer—certainly this viewer—the film "forgets" them once they have served
their plot device purpose. We have considered versions of such narrative
amnesia around homosexuals before in *The Killing* and *The Shining*. Here the

final credits fail to single out by role the actors who play them. The full name in the novel of the officer whose stolen uniform and papers Barry uses to disguise himself is, aptly, Lt. Jonathan Fakenham. There we learn that he has died, and that his death leads to Barry being found out as an impostor and a deserter. But we never know what becomes of the film's Jonathan and his aggrieved lover Frederick. Like the two queer ghosts in *The Shining*, they remain suspended in their one sideshow scene. "Characters and situations are taken away from us even in the midst of their happening," Alan Spiegel writes movingly of Kubrick's way in *Barry Lyndon*; "the camera withdraws from that to which we would cleave close—and in this respect, our sorrow is collateral to Barry's: we too can never get what we want or keep what we get."[10] Left to my own devices, then, I fancy *Barry Lyndon*'s officers in love as the return—the gay reincarnation (now that the Production Code-era had ended)—of the pair of beardless rebel fighters, unattached to women, who appear and then disappear in that idyllic camp scene in *Spartacus*.

Although there are many contact points between *Spartacus* and *Barry Lyndon*—brawny leading men at the peak of their stardom; enormous casts; a martial milieu and sundry military character types; combat training sequences; highly patterned battle formations and intimate duels; father figures and son figures; ritual enactments of male discipline and punishment; and one fascinating gay vignette apiece—critics remain disinclined to consider Kubrick's two historical costume pictures together. No doubt Kubrick would not have wanted them to. His unmade epic Napoleon biopic is more likely to be the referent in accounts of why the director turned to the genre of the historical film after he had made such a name for himself with that dazzling sci-fi run of *Dr. Strangelove*, *2001*, and *A Clockwork Orange*: each of these movies a sensation upon release. *Barry Lyndon* did, in a way, wind up being Kubrick's *Napoleon*. The eighteenth-century setting of Thackeray's Victorian novel also gave him, as others have remarked, something to do with the heaps of Napoleonic-era research that he had amassed. But one senses that *Barry Lyndon* is also meant to dispel, all these years later, the disappointment for him that was *Spartacus*. And yet as Kubrick here exorcizes the ghost of the latter film, the haunting, yellowed candlelit scenes for which *Barry Lyndon* is famous wind up making all its characters look like specters, not just the homosexual ones. In any case, the perfectionist Kubrick—researcher, writer, director, producer—had now made a historical film entirely his way. Among the many things that he had unsuccessfully lobbied for when he was brought on board by Kirk Douglas to direct *Spartacus* was a more morally ambiguous male protagonist. Kubrick clearly found that in Thackeray's Barry Lyndon, who likewise is something of a slave—at least to fate, if not also his own appetites and ambitions.

Even so, *Barry Lyndon* may be thought an eccentric choice for Kubrick. The film certainly bewildered, as well as bored, many critics at the time. It also rather flopped at the American box office. (However, like *Spartacus*, it won four Oscars, though yet again none for the writer/director himself.) Why would Kubrick have taken to this of all historical novels, Thackeray's first major work of fiction, though not among his most famous? Kubrick said he briefly considered doing *Vanity Fair*, then determined that it was too long even for a long movie. One wonders what he would have made of a story with female, not male, protagonists. That would have been a first—and only—for him. Kubrick told Ciment that he had a complete set of Thackeray on his bookshelf at home, but he demurred as to why he picked *Barry Lyndon* in particular. It is "a bit like trying to explain why you fell in love with your wife," he said and left it at that.[11]

Far be it from me, then, to set about explaining away the curiousness of Kubrick's falling in love with *Barry Lyndon*, especially when that element of strangeness is one of the things here to relish. While the film's reputation has grown enormously over time, there is still not all that much scholarly work on it. *Barry Lyndon* may now have the status of a Kubrick masterpiece, but it remains a somewhat unassimilated one. Let me suggest, however, that certain aspects of what may have been this story's appeal for Kubrick can be illuminated from the perspective of him as a men's film filmmaker.

"Gentlemen, cock your pistols." Those are the opening words spoken in this movie known for its duels. (Barry's father is summarily dispatched in the first one, which begins the story.) The line isn't in Thackeray. It's Kubrick, à la *Strangelove*, a movie famous for its dick jokes, which also brandishes its own twisted eighteenth-century satiric sensibility. The line isn't in Thackeray, but it could be. Whereas Kubrick's film version has to draw out and accentuate certain elements in Nabokov's *Lolita* to make his adaptation of it a men's film, Thackeray's *The Memoirs of Barry Lyndon, Esq.* already comes very much a men's novel, a masculinist satire, a deliciously unselfconscious (faux) self-portrait of male vanity and flair. That signal Kubrick question of what makes the man—here specifically a gentleman—is among the novel's chief preoccupations, a subject that it treats (as Kubrick does in *Dr. Strangelove*) in exaggerated terms as a form of male vaudeville. "I'm a man," roars the young Redmond Barry early in its pages, "and will prove it" (32): an exertion from which he never relaxes, even when he is irrevocably humbled by fortune and forced to live out the last eighteen years of his life as "an inmate of the Fleet Prison, where. . . . he died of delirium tremens" (307).

Deriving from petty Irish gentry stock, Barry is an adventurer and a trickster, who is not without talents, especially (as he boasts) of the "manly" sort (16). Set on rising as high as he can in the world, Barry's various schemes and strivings may seem like a naked grab for power, wealth, and a peerage. But his recounting of those exploits comes elaborately decorated with authoritative perorations on male style, taste, comportment, and manners—such matters with which Kubrick's films have been concerned all along. Here is a representative passage from midway through Thackeray's novel, in which Barry holds forth on how naturally he took to playing the part of gentleman:

> I came into it at once, and as if I had never done anything else all my life. I had a gentleman to wait upon me, a French *friseur* to dress my hair of a morning: I knew the taste of chocolate as by intuition almost, and could distinguish between the right Spanish and the French before I had been a week in my new position; I had rings on all my fingers, watches in both my fobs, canes, trinkets, and snuff-boxes of all sorts, and each outvying the other in elegance; I had the finest natural taste for lace and china of any man I ever knew. I could judge a horse as well as any Jew dealer in Germany; in shooting and athletic exercises I was unrivaled; I could not spell, but I could speak German and French cleverly; I had at the least twelve suits of clothes; three richly embroidered with gold, two laced with silver, a garnet-coloured velvet pelisse lined with sable; one of French grey, sliver-laced and lined with chinchilla. I had damask morning-robes. I took lessons on the guitar, and sang French catches exquisitely. Where, in fact, was there a more accomplished gentleman than Redmond de Balibari? (127–128)

Or more simply, as Barry is wont here to say, "such was the taste of the times" (238).

"Is there something 'inherently gay' about the role of arbiter of taste?" Joseph Litvak asks in a piquant essay on sophistication in Thackeray's *Vanity Fair* and *The Book of Snobs*.[12] There are reasons—historical ones (as Litvak also notes with respect to other male figures in Thackeray, as well as Thackeray himself)— why Barry Lyndon cannot be claimed as gay. What Thackeray's Barry is is a dandy, a male clotheshorse, a self-made connoisseur, an haute monde style queen, puffed up on his own gentlemanly ways. "Among the ladies I was always an especial favourite" (105), he has us know, right after recalling how "I won [Captain de Potzdorff's] heart in the first place by my manner of tying my hair in queue (indeed it was more neatly dressed than that of any man in the regiment)" (104). "There was," he concludes, "no man in Europe more gay in spirits, more splendid in personal accomplishment, than young Redmond Barry" (134).

Figure 35. Barry at his toilet.

Thackeray denies his pigtailed male peacock nothing in the way of flamboyance, especially once he becomes "the famous and fashionable Barry Lyndon" (307). Kubrick butches him up—as butch, at any rate, as a man can be in period wigs, powder, and beauty marks.[13] The movie also recreates Barry as a blond; in the novel he is notably "very dark and swarthy in complexion" (103), "black Irish," as they say. I have already remarked the lovers Jonathan and Frederick's pale, reedy bodies on display in the lake. The film also shows off its 6'1" leading man's buff physique in several scenes. One puts to use Ryan O'Neal's own training as a Golden Gloves fighter: an army boxing match in which the fresh-faced new recruit Redmond strips shirtless and pummels a towering red bearded older soldier named Toole, played by Pat Roach, a champion heavyweight wrestler himself. The film's low-angle, handheld camerawork here brings us back to those joltingly kinetic fight scenes in Kubrick's early boxing films. It's also worth noting that boxing—this combat sport that so captivated the director—began to take on its modern form around the time when *Barry Lyndon* is set, with the introduction of rules conceived by John "Jack" Broughton, the "father of English boxing." The film puts O'Neal's body on display again in a historical pictorial rendering at Castle Hackton, the extravagant Lyndon manor house. There we come upon Barry in period underdrawers as he makes his toilet, flanked in a striking visual composition by a matching pair of valets and wielding a period replica straight razor (Figure 35).

Kubrick makes Barry a man's man even while he is a boy—as when, early in the story, he challenges the high-strung Captain Quin (Leonard Rossiter, in his second Kubrick role) to a duel and wins. Later, Barry provides the muscle when needed to collect on the earnings that he and his cardsharp partner, the Chevalier, have swindled across Europe. This is also when Barry becomes a playboy, which he remains even after marriage. We discover him in a brothel, this time flanked by two topless women. Later his long-suffering wife sees him wooing one of her maids. But Barry is also shown to be a tender father to his own son, Bryan, whom he lulls to sleep with swashbuckling stories of his purported battle heroics involving decapitating French soldiers. (Then again, this may be thought a peculiar kind of story for an imposing father to tell his young son.) Regardless (or just because), Kubrick's Barry is, in sum, "a strong, handsome, vigorously heterosexual male . . . a romantic young swain of considerable glamour and phallic power."

I cite those adulatory terms from Naremore, who comes across as having something of a critic's man crush on Kubrick's studly cad.[14] But it is not as though the movie has nothing to do with the effeteness that is flaunted throughout Thackeray's novel. Rather the film redistributes it from Barry to other male characters: Jonathan and Frederick, to be sure, but also the coiffed and painted Chevalier de Balibari; Sir Charles Lyndon (Frank Middlemass), "aged and emasculated" in his wheelchair; the "sly, effeminate cleric," the Reverend Runt (Murray Melvin, who played fey gay in Tony Richardson's 1961 film A Taste of Honey), Lady Lyndon's spiritual advisor and tutor to her son; and perhaps even the "lofty, cosmopolitan" narrator.[15] The most important new male character for the second part of the movie—"Containing an Account of the Misfortunes and Disasters Which Befell Barry Lyndon"—is Sir Charles's son, Lord Bullingdon (Leon Vitali): a "melancholy . . . slight, 'feminine' young man," whose excessive devotion to his mother (posits Naremore) "thwarts his ability to achieve normative heterosexuality." Barry, "a 'manly' figure . . . [with] a castrating power,"[16] lords it over Bullingdon, his rival not only for the Lyndon estate but also for Lady Lyndon herself, by bending the young man over a desk and caning him, a scene the film ritually repeats for effect. The first time was for refusing to kiss his stepfather; the second time was for whipping his younger brother Bryan the way that he has been whipped. Like (step)father, like son.

Barry is the movie's he-man about whom various effeminized male figures carry on with or more often against him. We have been considering how Kubrick's films put on display and into conflict sharply contrasting gender styles, like the true grit Colonel Dax versus the affected Generals Mireau and Broulard in Paths of Glory. We have also seen how these iterations of warring ways of acting male often turn out to be not so different from each other, how these volatile creatures are really birds of a feather in many respects. And they all come—think back to *Dr. Strangelove* and its array of caricatured male types—to the same end. *Barry Lyndon* is the most philosophical of Kubrick's movies on that last point. "It was in the reign of George III that the aforesaid personages lived and quarreled," the film's memento mori final title card declares. "Good or bad, handsome or ugly, rich or poor they are all equal now."[17] The grave is the great leveler of mankind—of every kind of man. But well before Barry meets that end, Kubrick's film—for all its infatuation with its protagonist's golden boy, athletic good looks and virile charisma—brutally turns on him and reduces him to a version of those whom he sought to displace. In another important scene not found in the novel, the castrated turns castrator when, during the film's last duel, the young Bullingdon wounds his stepfather in the leg, which then has to be amputated. Barry with his crutch thus becomes a double of Lord Lyndon in his chair. The "feminine," failed heterosexual Bullingdon, who indeed never marries, thus prevails in the end, winning back his estate and his mother. The film's final scene shows them together, now a graying couple. The prissy Rev. Runt, his boyhood tutor and her spiritual advisor, is there with them too, leaving us with the faded Lady Lyndon and two jaded queens.

What about Barry? Our final, freeze-frame view of him, shot from behind as his own faithful mother helps him into the carriage that will return them together to Ireland, impresses upon us that Kubrick's disabled debauchee was likewise himself a momma's boy all along.

Resucked

"Are you now or have you ever been a homosexual?" Chief Guard Barnes (Michael Bates) demands of Alex (Malcolm McDowell), who stands buck-naked before him in *A Clockwork Orange* (1971). The scene is prison. The new prisoner "reception center," more specifically. This is the first and only time that the word "homosexual" is uttered in a Kubrick movie. Without missing a beat, though perhaps catching (as we do) the Chief Guard copping a glance at his crotch, Alexander DeLarge—to give his full name in the film—fires back, "No, sir." A quick reverse shot allots us, too, a glance at the full-frontal male nudity— another first in Kubrick—before the new inmate is ordered (you know the drill) to "Face the wall, bend over, and touch your toes."[18] Once the young man does so, his interrogator, now brandishing a pen-size flashlight—this (small) dick joke is on him—takes an official peek between the cheeks (Figure 36). From here, Alex is sent off (where else?) to the tubs. "One for a bath, one for a bath, one for a bath," we hear the other prison warders clucking offscreen like windup mechanical English hens.

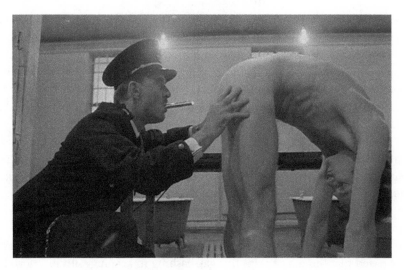

Figure 36. Induction inspection.

It will also not come as a surprise by now that none of this is in Anthony Burgess's dystopic, near-future futuristic novel from 1962, which Kubrick's screenplay—his first solo writing effort—otherwise follows quite closely. This inserted scene is among the most overtly homoerotic in all Kubrick's movies. No coded talk here of having a taste for both snails and oysters as in the famous censored Roman bath scene of *Spartacus*, or of liking "to have it up this end, you know," as Quilty volunteers in *Lolita*. A *Clockwork Orange* shoves the possibility of homosexuality right in our face.

Kubrick claims to have done extensive research on how new prisoners are processed for incarceration. Yet notwithstanding this characteristic attention to detail, he undercuts the new scene's significance when asked about it. As we have been considering, this is just what the director does when questioned about the brief "comic" interlude of those army officers in love interjected into his next film, *Barry Lyndon*. Here is Kubrick in a 1972 interview explaining why he added the prisoner induction scene to *A Clockwork Orange*, which, unlike *Barry Lyndon*'s two-minute gay intermezzo, is, he concedes, rather long:

It may be the [film's] longest scene but I would not think it is the most important. It was a necessary addition because the prison sequence is compressed, in comparison with the novel, and one had to have something in it which gave sufficient weight to the idea that Alex was actually imprisoned. The routine of checking into prison which, in fact, is quite accurately presented in the film, seemed to provide this necessary weight.[19]

Necessarily weighty; quite accurate. Nothing, apparently, telegraphs "welcome to prison" like a cavity search. The point is that whether his supplemental gay scenes are short or long, inserted for comic effect or instead for added dramatic gravity, Kubrick's tendency when speaking about them is to restrict their import to some very limited narratological function. Homosexuality turns out to be always part of the story in Kubrick's men's films, but it isn't allowed to be much of a story in itself.

Kubrick's screenplay augments what is already an abundance of homosexual material in Burgess's novel. But it also omits an episode in which the recently jailed Alex wakes up in the night to find himself being fondled in his bunk by a new inmate crammed that day into an already inhumanely overcrowded cell: "he was govoreeting dirty like love-slovos [words] and stroke stroke stroking away." Egged on by his cellmates, Alex beats this "horrible vonny stinking perverted prestoopnicks [degenerate]" to death.[20] Some have suggested that the movie skips this gay bashing in keeping with its effort, in this second part of the story, to make Alex a more sympathetic character, now suddenly the abused rather than the abuser. In another interview, however, Kubrick brushes aside that explanation, maintaining instead that the scene was not included in the film simply because it struck him as unnecessary to the story.[21]

As notable as these additions and omissions is the film's redistribution of homosexual interests and desires. In Burgess's novel, nearly all of this is confined to the other convicts, "some of them real perverts and ready to dribble," reports Alex boastfully, "all over a luscious young malchick [boy] like your story-teller" (86). Those words are repeated in the film after another added scene in which a fellow inmate blows menacing, mocking kisses at Alex during a prison chapel service. But Kubrick mostly transfers the story's homosexual features from the jailbirds who flock around Alex in the novel—such as, in addition to the cellmate he kills, the "two like queer ones who both took a fancy to me," one of whom "made a jump on to my back" (78)—to various male authority figures in Alex's life, beginning with P. R. Deltoid (a memorably unsavory Aubrey Morris), his pervy "post-corrective advisor."

The dialogue for the scene in which Mr. Deltoid catches Alex at home, skipping school, again closely follows the novel. But Kubrick makes the setting and action predatorily sexual. The devil is in the details, so I want to compare the novel and the movie closely here. In the novel, Deltoid's "ringringringing" (41) at the door painfully awakens Alex, "shagged and fagged" (39) from the previous night's "ultra-violence": the brutal attack by him and his "droogs" on the writer (and Alex's strange double of sorts) Mr. F. Alexander (a tremulous Patrick Magee in his first Kubrick role) and his wife (Adrienne Corri) in their

mod suburban house that a neon roadside sign names "HOME." Before letting Deltoid in, Alex—another male peacock like Thackeray's Redmond
Barry—dons "a very lovely over-gown of like silk, with designs of like great cit-
ies all over" it (41). In the film, however, the marauding Alex appears naked
except for his tighty whities, and he is rather startled to find Deltoid already
waiting for him in his parents' bedroom. He quickly recovers, however, and
strikes a fetching "ta da" pose for him in the doorway. Summoning "Little
Alex" to sit down right next to him on the bed, Deltoid questions him about
"some extreme nastiness" the night before, while the boy feigns innocence.
As with the prison induction scene, the last laugh here comes at the expense
of the older male authority. In a grotesque touch the film adds, Mr. Deltoid
sees too late that the glass of water left bedside to which he has just helped
himself is the repository for a set of parental false teeth.

The intimate older man/younger man encounters are a staple of Kubrick.
This one is a creepy, campy reprise of that tender bedroom scene between
Johnny and the older man Marv on the morning of the heist in *The Killing*.
Over the course of this impromptu interrogation, Deltoid strokes, then pulls
Alex's hair, drapes an arm around his bare shoulders, and clamps a hand down
on his bare knee. Eventually he pulls him backward onto the bed. In this su-
pine position, Alex, his legs invitingly spread, looks like a living male version
of the nude female-form, fiberglass mannequin tables by sculptor Liz Moore
in the movie's first scene in the Korova Milk Bar. The trench-coat-clothed man
and nearly naked boy lie there, in this unidirectional clasp, until Deltoid suddenly grabs Alex hard by the crotch, while declaring himself to be "the one
man in this sore and sick community who wants to save you from yourself!"
Again, none of this is in the novel, where the probation officer instead questions the boy while ensconced in Alex's father's rocking chair. (So take your
pick for the more perverse oedipal setting: the parental bed or paternal—note
not maternal—rocker.) Another notable difference: Burgess's Deltoid gets his
jollies here not by petting and pulling on the male youth in his charge, but by
leering at a newspaper ad featuring "a lovely smecking young ptitsa [girl] with
her groodies hanging out" (42).

The nasty gay vibes that Kubrick's Mr. Deltoid here gives off carry over into
his second scene in the film, when Alex is in custody at the police station after
his assault on the Cat Lady. Before Deltoid arrives with word that she has just
died, Alex is worked over by Detective Constable Tom (Steven Berkoff), with
his macho *Mod Squad* '70s sideburns. A *Clockwork Orange*—the film and the
novel—has a programmatic, fable-like quality, in which scenes are played over
twice, the second time with a twist. Most involve the violence Alex visits upon
others in the story's anarchic first act revisited upon him in its retributive

second and third acts: "the real weepy and like tragic part of the story," as he puts it, turning the film, at least for this stretch, into another Kubrick male weepy, a warped one. Its emotional climax comes when Alex starts to tear up himself after he returns home from prison to find that his parents have rented his bedroom to Joe the Lodger (Clive Francis), who declares that he has become a (better) son to them.

But let's return for a moment to the scene in the police station, which is a variation on the one in the parents' bedroom. Instead of pulling Alex backward with him on the bed as Mr. Deltoid did, Constable Tom pushes him up against a wall and leans in close, as though to kiss him. He too runs his hand through the boy's dirty blond locks, before pressing his finger on Alex's bandaged nose. (Back in the bedroom, Deltoid had warned Alex to "keep [his] handsome young proboscis out of the dirt.") "Nasty cut you've got there, Little Alex. Shame," the detective coos, "spoils all your beauty." This time Alex is the one to go for the balls or "yarbles," as he calls them in the Nadsat teen argot that Burgess invents for his male teen delinquents. The detective responds by beating Alex to a pulp. When Deltoid at last arrives, Constable Tom cocks his head on the probation officer's shoulder, lover-like, while Deltoid spits on Alex's face: the deferred climax from their earlier bedroom scene together.

The groovy bruiser detective and the hissy probation officer (who ends every sentence with an insinuating "yesss?") make for a butch/femme sadist duo. They recall *Lolita*'s Vivian Darkbloom and rich hipster playwright Claire Quilty, whom he says she likes to throw around. "I lay there in pain but I love it," Quilty explains masochistically to another man they may be trying to pick up, "I really love it." In *A Clockwork Orange*, however, the s/m pairing turns same-sex and all sadist. The homosexual touches added to characters of Mr. Deltoid and Constable Tom, as with the Chief Guard, are part of the film's male satirism. *Dr. Strangelove*, where the various caricatured male characters and acting styles are even more overdrawn, also works something like this. This especially so, as we saw, in the way that President Merkin Muffley and General Jack D. Ripper parodically figure the stereotypical homosexual polarities of effeminacy and hypermasculinity.

But just when you think that you've caught a homophobic drift in *A Clockwork Orange*, the movie throws a curve ball in the form of the burly, bellowing prison chaplain, played by Godfrey Quigley, later the rascally father figure Captain Grogan, beloved by Barry himself in *Barry Lyndon*. The chaplain, too, of course, finds Alex irresistible—"my being," says Alex, "very young, and also now very interested in the big book." What Alex likes about the Bible is all the sex and violence, which he pictures in terms of baroque Hollywood historical epics, all starring himself. In one of his biblically inspired fantasies, he imagines himself a Roman centurion—another ghost come back from the scorned *Spartacus?*—whipping a cross-carrying Christ onward to Calvary. Alex is also a favorite of the prison chaplain in the novel; but Kubrick's film makes his interest in the young inmate a hint more sexual than it is in its literary source. "Remember," he counsels Alex in a scene not in the book, "I know of the urges that can trouble young men deprived of the society of women." The chaplain's preaching in both the novel and the film is all fire and brimstone. Kubrick explains this as just "a satirical disguise," the chaplain being, as he sees it, "the moral voice of the film," "the only decent man in the story."[22] That's because the chaplain stands out as the lone voice against the Ludovico Technique: the coercive behavior modification program that the State determines is the answer to crime and Alex sees as an expedited ticket out of jail.[23]

One expects the story's religious authority to be its spokesman for the precept of God-given free will, the moral touchstone of Burgess's ultimately conservative twentieth-century fable. (More on that later.) "Goodness comes from within," the chaplain instructs Alex. "When a man cannot choose, he ceases to be a man." But Kubrick's subtle reworking of the chaplain's character acquires another charge when we bear in mind that aversion therapy was then still in use to "cure" homosexuality. Fascinating, then, that the film puts its polemic against shock treatments for modifying transgressive desires and perceived antisocial behaviors in the mouth of a confessor who himself confesses that he knows all about the urges of men when women aren't around: this presumably gay prison padre, "the only decent man in the story" in Kubrick's own estimation.

The demonstration of Alex's cure from violence, including sexualized violence, is staged cabaret-style. A select audience of government officials, prison personnel (including Chief Guard Barnes), and doctors is assembled in a small theater to watch a male actor verbally, then physically abuse the test subject, who is now completely unable to respond in kind. Instead, Alex lies on the floor face up to lick the sole of his tormentor's buckle-strap black leather shoe. The actor takes his bows, and a topless young woman with lavender hair replaces him under the lights. Alex automatically goes right for her breasts, but he quickly recoils, overcome by nausea. She exits the stage bowing like a peepshow ballerina, harking back to that strange solo ballet cameo stuck into the middle of *Killer's Kiss*. The first scene demonstrates that Alex's violent impulses have now been completely conditioned out of him; the second scene shows the same for his sexual impulses. Or that is how this sequence is always interpreted—and perhaps how it was intended too. But while the Ludovico Technique has clearly deprived Alex of the ability to respond heterosexually, we might regard the spectacle of him submissively tonguing another man's leather footwear—a man whom Walker calls "a curly-haired queer"—as in keeping with the movie's male s/m erotics.[24] Apparently, A *Clockwork Orange*'s brand of aversion therapy hasn't purged Alex of his capacity for homoerotic responsiveness. Rather, we see him here more deeply initiated into such possibilities.

It is the film's decorative features, however, that make A *Clockwork Orange* Kubrick's most flamboyant work, beginning with Alex's fright-drag false eyelashes applied to just one eye. As I have implied, Alex has a diva's sense of his own wicked charms. He puts them on display early in the film in an impromptu song and dance routine as he beats Mr. Alexander and prepares to rape his wife: "I'm singin' in the rain / Just singin' in the rain / And I'm ready for love." This is one of those camp renditions that forever revalences—I won't say ruins—the classic saccharine original. (Gene Kelly, for one, was not amused.) Alex's partners in crime share his taste for makeup. Georgie (James Marcus) and Pete (Michael Tarn) both wear eye shadow, while Dim (Warren Clarke), who supplies the chorus for Alex's Gene Kelly impersonation—"Ready for love," he keeps chiming in—likes his lipstick. The Teddy Boys, in their dandyish Edwardian getups, are considered an inspiration for the fashion-conscious young thugs of Burgess's novel. Peter Krämer finds the movie also drawing on elements of skinhead style (combat boots, suspenders) as well as the androgynous look then coming into fashion through glam rock (heavy makeup, unisex shag haircuts). Kubrick's A *Clockwork Orange* itself then became a glam culture touchstone, with David Bowie, for instance, drawing upon it for his Ziggy Stardust character.[25]

The film's quasi-gay decorative elements do not only accrue around Alex and his toughs. A hulking bodybuilder named Julian, who moves in with Mr. Alexander after his wife's death, supplies the beefcake that we have come to expect of a Kubrick film (Figure 37). Is this Julian simply a strongman caretaker, now that Mr. Alexander is in a wheelchair (more male disability in Kubrick, like Dr. Strangelove before and the two Lord Lyndons to come)—or that and something more? Kubrick never explained the nature of their relation to the actors in these roles. I think of Julian the bodybuilder, who is not in the novel, as semiotically related to Mr. Deltoid, a homosexually oriented character (though again just in the film) named after a muscle. Kubrick discovered David Prowse, the actor who plays Julian—later the towering physical form, though not the voice, of Darth Vader in *Star Wars*—in Harrods demonstrating home workout equipment, like what we now find in Mr. Alexander's so-named "HOME," as well as in the Cat Lady's manse. As though he were cut out of Richard Hamilton's iconic collage *Just what is it that makes today's homes so different, so appealing?* (1956) and dressed to match the modish décor of

Figure 37. Pop Art bodybuilder.

"HOME," the film makes a fabulous Pop Art spectacle of Julian's bulging pin-up physique in a pink muscle shirt, bright red posing trunks, and heavy black frame eyeglasses.[26]

Even Jesus gets the queer treatment here. Among the pieces in Alex's art-filled, padlocked bedroom is the Dutch sculptor Herman Makkink's *Christ Unlimited* (1970): a fist-pumping, fiberglass chorus line of four naked, anatomically detailed Jesuses, whose ginger pubic hair matches what's atop their crown of thorns adorned heads (Figure 38). (Alex will wear his own crown of thorns, an experimental electrode and wire version, when he is forced to watch an onslaught of horrific movie violence as part of his reconditioning treatment.) A rhythmically cut montage of Makkink's sculpture sets its serially repeated Christ clones—was Kubrick drawn to the piece because of his interest in male doubles, here squared?—cinematically dancing, while Alex "slooshies" (listens) to Beethoven's *Ninth* and jerks off to mental pictures of cinematic sex and violence. "O, it was gorgeousness and gorgeosity made flesh," he exclaims, orgasmically compounding incarnation and masturbation, image and sound, eros and thanatos. "It was," our ecstatic narrator continues in his most lyrical flight, "like a bird of rarest-spun heaven metal or like silvery wine flowing in a spaceship, gravity all nonsense now."

Speaking of masturbation, *A Clockwork Orange* rivals *Dr. Strangelove* in the ostentation of its phallic signifiers. Kubrick is the cinematic master of such imagery because he is so brazen about it. Here it's the jockstrap-like codpieces and the penis-nose masks that Alex and his gang wear, and the canes that they

Figure 38. A chorus line.

like to stick between each other's legs or wield as weapons. Alex's conceals a knife that he unsheathes and uses when his subordinates step out of line. Then there's his pet boa, Basil, whose perch is set up in front of the splayed legs of a female nude on his bedroom wall. (There is no snake in the novel.) And the popsicles that the two teen girls seductively suck on in the record boutique where Alex picks them up for an afternoon orgy back at his place. And also the red rubber dildo lever that operates the female mannequin drink dispenser in the Korova Milk Bar. Of course the most spectacular phallus in the film is the Cat Lady's supersized penis, plus curvy female buttocks, kinetic sculpture.[27] Titled *Rocking Machine* (1970), it's also by Makkink; indeed, it is his most famous work. "Naughty, naughty, naughty," Alex says when he sees it and sets it in herky-jerky motion. "Don't touch it!" the Cat Lady forbids, adding pretentiously, "It's a very important work of art!" So he picks it up to fend her off and ultimately murders her with it.

I have been treating *A Clockwork Orange*, made a few years after the demise of the censorious Production Code and its prohibition of depictions of "sexual perversion," as homosexuality's long time in coming full coming out in Kubrick, the film in which the word "homosexual" actually gets said. Let me now note that this movie's few expressions of female desire intriguingly come with their own same-sex aspects. This is another thing—female homoeroticism—that we have not observed before in Kubrick. The two girls who go to bed with Alex in that midday three-way are also thus in bed with each other. Here the film turns what is in the novel a brutal rape of two drugged

twelve-year-old girls into a free love teen romp filmed in skip-frame high-speed
motion and set to electronic music innovator Wendy Carlos's galloping Moog
synthesizer translation of Rossini's overture to *Guillaume Tell.* Kubrick said that
he rendered the scene this way to keep it from seeming "solemn."[28]

A *Clockwork Orange* also features the closest thing to a lesbian character in
Kubrick in the form of the gravelly voiced, unmarried Cat Lady (Miriam
Karlin) herself. Her actual name is Miss Weathers—though this is only in the
film, an added little detail that subtly makes the point that there is no husband. She is also younger here than in the book. Alex finds this female eccentric alone at home with her many cats. She's doing strange contortionist
exercises in a salon-size parlor large enough to double as a fitness studio.
(Mr. Alexander's personal bodybuilder Julian isn't the only workout enthusiast in the movie.) In addition to Makkink's doubly sexed *Rocking Machine*,
the room is decorated with Pop Art female erotic artwork, including one painting of a woman masturbating and another of a woman touching her tongue
to a female nipple. Nelson views these images as "lesbian self-portraits" of a
character who "colors herself like an art object (heavy lipstick on a large
mouth, red-tinted hair, green and white leotards), and twists her body into
contortions as if to replicate an abstract piece of sculpture or her own 'health
farm' exercise equipment"—the stuff of what he calls "a female masturbatory
nightmare."[29]

Clearly turned off by Kubrick's Cat Lady, Nelson celebrates Kubrick's Alex
DeLarge as, by contrast, a modern incarnation of that inspirational daemon
force revered by the Romantics. Young Alex, he enthuses, "is a child of darkness, a satiric spirit of life, who awakens from the sleep of the dead to act out
his worst dreams and bring a renewed vitality and function to the people and
things of his world."[30] By contrast, Nelson links the old maid Cat Lady's "de-
cadent aberrations"—her art, herself—to barrenness. "The Cat Lady," he cas-
tigates, "totally denies her procreative function."[31] This mechanistic biological
terminology evokes Dr. Strangelove's survivalist sex fantasy of women chosen
on the basis of their ability to "breed prodigiously." The Cat Lady, as Nelson
sees her, is on that account dysfunctional and the only milk that she dishes
out (one has to say it) is for her pussies.

Nelson has company in holding such views. Most commentators find Kubrick's Cat Lady to be a grotesque and altogether unsympathetic. Christopher
Ricks terms her "a professionally athletic virago," while Naremore regards her
"an upper-class anorexic."[32] My own sense is that sympathy for the Cat Lady
has something to do with whether you are a cat lover or not. (Kubrick, in case
you are wondering, was one himself. A great dog lover too.) In Nelson's so described "cultural" interpretation of the faceoff between the life force that is

Alex and the nonprocreative Miss Weathers, she (symbolically) gets what she deserves when Alex "crashes the bone-white phallus into the Cat Lady's mouth": a formulation that aligns Alex's weapon with the bone heaved skyward in 2001's famous match cut, figuring the evolution from hominid to man. Alex, Nelson continues, "symbolically . . . actualizes his culture's almost extinct unconscious . . . , gives its artifacts a renewed function (albeit a violent one), and increasingly assumes the role of life-force as well as scourge."[33]

A scourge for the lesbian, that is. For though Kubrick's Miss Weathers is no fleeting apparition like the gay figures I have been ghost-chasing in other of his movies, she does not survive her one scene. And we have to wait until *Eyes Wide Shut*, Kubrick's last movie, for anything like her, or those bisexually adventuresome "little sisters" Alex picked up in the record store, to come back.

Kubrick said that he saw the makings of a movie for him in Burgess's book as soon as he got around to reading it. The novel's compact, symmetrical three-act structure was screenplay-ready. Kubrick also liked how the story had the feeling of a fairytale, with its purposefully heavy-handed use of repetition and coincidence.[34] He was not the only one who thought that *A Clockwork Orange* would make a good film, especially in view of the late '60s/early '70s vogue for tabooflouting material that pushed the boundaries for showing sex and violence on the screen. Kubrick first learned of *A Clockwork Orange* from Terry Southern, his collaborator on the screenplay for *Dr. Strangelove*, who gave him a copy of Burgess's novel. While it sat unread on Kubrick's bookshelf for a few years, Southern optioned the film rights himself and wrote a screenplay, which was rejected out of hand by the British film censor. There was some buzz around Mick Jagger playing Alex and the other Rolling Stones playing the droogs—this after Jagger's 1970 acting debut in Nicolas Roeg's bisexual-themed film *Performance*. Burgess himself was keen about this casting. Nothing came of it, however.[35] Ken Russell seemed interested for a time in directing a movie version of *A Clockwork Orange*, but then he decided instead to make his religious horror film *The Devils* (1971), with its crazed writhing nuns. Burgess also wrote his own screenplay, which Roeg was supposed to direct, but that didn't amount to anything either. Years later Burgess adapted his novel for the stage as *A Clockwork Orange: A Play with Music*. By then, he had come to resent Kubrick and the movie, which bills itself as *Stanley Kubrick's A Clockwork Orange*. "Kubrick's achievement," complained Burgess, "swallowed mine whole."[36] At the conclusion of his stage version of his novel, "A *man bearded like Stanley Kubrick comes on playing* . . . '*Singin' in the Rain' on a trumpet*." He's kicked off the stage, while the cast sings: "Do not be a clockwork orange, / Freedom has a lovely voice. / . . . / Let's not be changed to fruit machines."[37]

Speaking of fruit machines, Andy Warhol was also drawn to *A Clockwork Orange*. He reportedly liked all the male rough stuff and made his own movie version of it at the Factory in 1965. Warhol's take on Burgess's book is titled *Vinyl*, perhaps after the vinyl leather jacket worn by its Alex figure, here renamed Victor and played by Gerard Malanga. This four-shot, black-and-white, 66-minute film involves two BDSM tableaux, with sporadic go-go dancing mixed in. The erotic abuse depicted in Warhol's film—beginning with a young fellow bound to a pole and worked over with various s/m contrivances ("Anything but the 'old up-yours,'" he pleads), is all male-on-male. But a chain-smoking Edie Sedgwick, perched on the edge of a steamer trunk, is present throughout to watch—or not. (Malanga said he was peeved at her disruption of the original idea of an all-male setting. "It's okay," Warhol replied, "she looks like a boy." Indeed, Malanga and Sedgwick here rather resemble each other.) Kubrick's movie runs on amphetamine-spiked "Milk-Plus"; the rhythms of Warhol's version seem more downer-induced. *Vinyl* is a piece of queer art porn, but of a torpid, dreamy kind, a slow burn to ecstasy.

Who knows if Kubrick ever saw Warhol's version, which came out six years before his did. But both movies strikingly begin the same way with a tight close-up of the protagonist's made-up face as he stares directly into the camera, followed by a slow pullback. In Kubrick's movie, this famous shot reveals Alex and his droogs lounging at the Korova and sipping some of that "Milk-Plus," before hitting the road for "a bit of the ultraviolence." In the Warhol movie, the analogous shot shows Victor curling dumbbells, which is just what Julian the Pop Art bodybuilder is doing when we first lay eyes on him in the Kubrick film. "I do what I like because I like it," Victor declares in a line lifted right from the book. Eventually, he's tied up and stripped of his shirt. His bared torso is crisscrossed with electrical tape in preparation for his "reconditioning." "We're doing this for your own good," a guy informs him. "I trust you, doctor," Victor replies. Hot wax is dripped on him. He screams. And then a black submission hood with studs is pulled over his head.

Warhol's art film is just about all sex and violence. The Warhol version of *A Clockwork Orange* has no interest in Burgess's humanist lesson about free will and goodness needing to come from within. Kubrick's film isn't really all that interested in such things either, notwithstanding what he said at the time in some fairly defensive interviews when his movie was being denounced for triggering copycat crimes. The film pays lip service to Burgess's socioreligious theme, as noted earlier, in a few utterances made by the prison chaplain, who has a thing for Alex and is probably in no hurry, in any case, to see him paroled. But the movie's real interests and energies lie elsewhere. Kubrick's *A Clockwork Orange* is ultimately much more an exercise in style than it is about the exercise of moral choice. After all, it was the style as much as the story that drew Kubrick to Burgess's novel in the first place. "The violence in the film is stylized," Kubrick remarks in another interview, "just as it is in the book." "My problem, of course," the director describes with relish, "was to find a way of presenting it in the film without benefit of the writing style."[38]

Not that Kubrick's own art film is devoid of ideas. Its principal one appears to be that loving art or being aesthetical doesn't make you good. Alex collects art and thrills to his Ludwig van, whose music stimulates the lyrical young thug's violent fantasies.[39] Again: art is not necessarily good for you—including Kubrick's art. In the movie's most meta moment, Alex, strapped tight to his auditorium seat and his eyes clamped wide open, praises the first film of beatings and rape that he watches as part of his reconditioning treatment as (in Burgess's brilliant pun) "a very good professional piece of sinny, like it was done in Hollywood." "It's funny," he further reflects, "how the colours of the real world only seem really real when you viddy them on the screen." William Blake explained that Satan turned out to be the most compelling character in *Paradise Lost*, another work about man's free choice, because Milton was "a true poet, and of the devil's party without knowing it." Kubrick is of the devil's party here, and he knows it.[40] The same goes, I venture, for most of us. If you're drawn to Kubrick's A *Clockwork Orange*, it's for its style—including all the stylized "sinny-matic" sex and violence—not really for any message.

The message, as Burgess sets it out in his Introduction to the novel's 1986 reissue, is that a man deprived of free will is a clockwork orange: "he has the appearance of an organism lovely with colour and juice but is in fact only a clockwork toy to be wound up by God or the Devil or (since this is increasingly replacing both) the Almighty State" (xiii). This reedition includes a final chapter that had been omitted from the book's first American printing. In that chapter—chapter 21, 21 being "the symbol of human maturity," expounds Burgess (x)—young Alex decides that he has had enough of his sociopathic pursuits. He also suddenly starts picturing himself as a family man with a wife and son. "O my brothers. I was growing up . . . a new like chapter beginning," he announces (211–212). Kubrick claims that he knew nothing of this alternative ending until he had nearly finished his screenplay. And even then he says that he never considered including this denouement, which turns the story into a moral progress narrative of the most domesticating kind. "The twenty-first chapter," asserts Burgess, "gives the novel the quality of genuine fiction, an art founded on the principle that human beings change" (xii). Kubrick, of course, had other ideas and instead completely makes up his own ending: a kinky fantasy or sex dream that reprises arty exhibitionist elements from other sexual vignettes in the movie. A woman dressed only in fetish wear elbow-length black gloves, knee-length black stockings, and black neck choker straddles a completely unclothed Alex. They rollick about in slow motion in a bed of faux snow, while an audience in high Victorian drag looks on approvingly and applauds. "I was cured all right," chortles our hero in a voiceover. Alex's ability to perform heterosexually has thus apparently been reprogrammed back into him per the instructions of the squirrelly, fascistic "Minister of the Inferior," as Alex calls him. This accords with the novel. But in the film that cure comes without any thought at all of goodness, marriage, or children—which is another thing the resentful Burgess had against it.

Burgess also uses this 1986 Introduction, which he titles A *Clockwork Orange Resucked*, to address his novel's curious title. "Clockwork oranges don't exist," he notes, "except in the speech of old Londoners. The image was a bizarre one, always used for a bizarre thing" (xiv). The title phrase is lifted from a Cockney expression that itself requires further explanation: "'He's as queer as a clockwork orange' meant he was queer to the limit of queerness. It did not primarily denote homosexuality, though a queer, before restrictive legislation came in, was the term used for a member of the inverted fraternity" (xiv–xv). The more that Burgess explicates the relation between the "queer" and queers here the mushier this fruit gets. In one breath he differentiates male homosexuality from the "bizarre," from "the limit of queerness," and in the next he reassociates them. It should also be noted that Burgess uses "queer" in the novel to mean homosexual, as we saw with, for instance, the "two like queer ones who both took a fancy" to Alex in prison (78).

Burgess's evocation of a fraternity of inverts, a brotherhood of buggery leads me, in conclusion, to a work of art in this film full of art that I have yet to touch upon. It's a large mural in the trashed elevator lobby of the brutalist council flat where Alex lives with his parents. This piece of public art, according to the novel, is meant to celebrate "the dignity of labour" (35), this as part of the story's vaguely socialist milieu. In both the novel and the film the well-developed bodies of the noble workers on display here are proudly unclothed. And in both the novel and the film the mural is covered with puerile pornographic graffiti. But there is a notable difference between the mural as the novel describes it and the mural as it appears in the film. In Burgess, the painting portrays both male and female laborers, "bare vecks [men] and cheenas [women] stern at the wheels of industry . . . with all this dirt penciled from their rots [mouths] by naughty malchicks [boys]" (54–55). But in Kubrick, all the figures, save for one woman in the background with a flat chest and short-cropped hair, are indicatively male: an industrious fraternity comprising several men in their hulking prime, a graybeard, and a couple of boys (Figure 39). The intergenerational component added to the painting in the film

Figure 39. Spectral gay graffiti.

takes me back once again to that rebel slave campfire scene in *Spartacus*, considered in the last chapter, and its idyllic image of an all-male clan.

As chaste as that campfire scene in *Spartacus* is, the public art mural in *A Clockwork Orange* is X-rated, just like the film itself upon its initial American release. Attention-getting genitalia have been superimposed in white on the male forms here depicted. An especially large cock and balls is pointed like an arrow at the muscular ass cheeks of a fellow sporting his own, even larger graffito erection. "OUCH! THAT'S A TREAT," exclaims the comic book speech balloon drawn in by his head. A gargantuan tongue is added to another worker-hero hunk so that he can have at his own bulging equipment. "SUCK IT AND SEE" is written near him. Other orgiastic encouragements are scrawled all over the mural: "IF IT MOVES KISS IT," "OOH LUVLY!" "HMM, SOMEBODY'S YARBLES," "IT HAS COME," and (next to one of the boys) "HARD LUV SUN."[41]

The homosexual interests and desires that circulate throughout *A Clockwork Orange* are abstracted into the movie's graffiti-embellished painting. This larger-than-life piece of background art represents (to take up again Burgess's tantalizing phrase) "the limit of queerness," or let's say, the limit of male homosexual sexual expression in Kubrick. It does not get any gayer here, or in any Kubrick film, than this—than these somewhat hard to read in places sodomitical sayings and these chalk-drawn mega phalluses, whose white outlines convey their Kubrickian spectrality.

Where the Rainbow Ends

DR. BILL HARFORD: Now, where exactly are we going . . . exactly?
GAYLE: Where the rainbow ends.
BILL: Where the rainbow ends?
NUALA: Don't you want to go where the rainbow ends?
BILL: Well, now that depends where that is.
GAYLE: Well, let's find out.

"Now get undressed." That's what doctors say, not what's said to them. But the tables are turned on Dr. Bill Harford (Tom Cruise) when he crashes the solemn, mildly bisexual orgy that is the centerpiece of what turned out to be Kubrick's final film, *Eyes Wide Shut* (1999): a waking-dream case study of desire's waywardness within marriage. We have heard this line before in Kubrick, this command from one man to another to strip. "Get undressed," Alex is ordered when he's checked into prison in *A Clockwork Orange*, the Kubrick film from the sexual revolutionizing '70s that we have just been considering. The young man out of his clothes and bending over to touch his toes leads, we saw, to one of the most blatant bits of homosexual imagery in all of Kubrick.

"Remove your clothes," the red-cloaked high priest of the film's ritual orgy again orders the interloper.[42] "Or would you like to have us do it for you?" "Gentlemen, please . . ." stammers Bill. Why do the other orgiasts insist that the doctor disrobe—and what do they have in mind for him once he has? Bill has already been shown shirtless in the bedroom with his beautiful wife, Alice (Nicole Kidman). A viewer might wonder if now, at the orgy, he will get to see even more of the handsome young doctor. After all, who gets all dolled up for a sex party—here in a gilt volto carnival mask and a monkish hooded cloak—and intends to stay fully dressed, cap-a-pie, the whole time?

Eyes Wide Shut was promoted as the sexiest big studio film ever made. That the husband and wife in it were played by an actual husband and wife—said to be Hollywood's hottest couple—amplified the film's erotic charge. "Cruise and Kidman Like You Have Never Seen Them," heralds *Time* magazine's July 5, 1999, cover, showing the married movie stars (who would divorce two years later) in an awkward, semi-nude embrace, shot by Herb Ritts. Earlier in his career, Kubrick may have toyed with the idea of doing an "adult" film in studio conditions with a serious budget. This was back in the days of "porn chic," when films like Gerard Damiano's *Deep Throat* (1972) and *The Devil in Miss Jones* (1973) enjoyed wide theatrical release and vied with major mainstream movies in terms of greatest profit margins. The notion of a top director making Hollywood's first highbrow hard-core sex film can be traced through Kubrick-collaborator Terry Southern, who spoke in interviews of watching a stag film at a party at Kubrick's house in 1964, just after the release of *Strange-love*. "Wouldn't it be interesting," he recalls Kubrick then musing, "if one day someone who was an artist would do that—using really beautiful actors and good equipment?"[43] Southern wrote a 1970 satiric novel about the making of just such a film as "the work . . . of an artist," "the best in the biz."[44] He generically titled the novel *Blue Movie* and dedicated it: "*for the great* Stanley K." "Congratulations," Kubrick complimented Southern in return; "you've written the definitive blow job."[45]

Eyes Wide Shut, made all those years later, can be taken for Kubrick's artistic, star-studded "blue movie," such as it is. Hitchcock films feature chilly female beauties: Grace Kelly, Ingrid Bergman, Eva Marie Saint, Kim Novak, Janet Leigh, Tippi Hedren. Save for the frozen-face Marisa Berenson in *Barry Lyndon*, there is nothing like them to look at in Kubrick—until we get to *Eyes Wide Shut*. (Kubrick's other female leads, of which there are so very few in all his work, tend to be, as I noted earlier, character actors. The fabulously mercurial, plus-size Shelley Winters. The quirky, sad sack, bean-pole Shelley Duvall. The waspish Marie Windsor. And that's about it.) Within the film's opening seconds, immediately after the title card announcing "A Film by Stanley Kubrick," Alice/Nicole Kidman steps out of a slinky black dress, naked but for her black high heels. Then comes the final title card: *Eyes Wide Shut*. The quick nude scene inserted between the intertitles serves no real narrative purpose. It's just there, classically, to look at. Kubrick showily frames Kidman's tall, elegant, alabaster body, shot from behind, between Doric columns.

The next time we see the one screen goddess to appear in his films Kubrick has Kidman seated on the toilet, wiping herself underneath a different black dress, the one that she wears to Victor Ziegler's (Sydney Pollack) glamorous high-society Christmas party. There the film promptly returns her to the john: "Honey, I desperately need to go to the bathroom," Alice (who has been quaffing champagne) excuses herself from her husband. Prior to this, the bathroom in Kubrick had principally been the men's room. "How do I look?" Alice asks, when she gets off the toilet in the earlier scene at home. It would be a mistake, I think, to consider this sight as deflationary or prurient, much less misogynist. I take it instead as a signal that this film cares more than Kubrick's others about a female character's inner life, her desires. Also bear in mind that Alice will be given the film's memorable one-word final line: "Fuck," which also wound up being Kubrick's own exit line.

Alice is also the one who first gets us thinking about Bill out of his clothes, though not so at home with her. The night after that party, where they both have been hit on—she by a suave European lothario who wants to take her upstairs to see Ziegler's collection of Renaissance bronzes; he by two sinuous

female models on a quest for a three-way to "where the rainbow ends"—Alice
and Bill get high and perilously start talking about marital fidelity, sexual fantasy, and "the way" men and women are. "Let's say," supposes Alice, "you
have some gorgeous woman standing in your office naked, and you're feeling
her fucking tits." (The film shows us just such a scene earlier that day when
Bill is seeing patients.) "Now, when she is having her little titties squeezed,"
Alice presses on, "do you think she ever has any little fantasies about what
handsome Dr. Bill's dickie might be like?" This part-jealous, part-belittling
("dickie") challenge is just a prelude to the bruising personal lesson on female
sexuality—"If you men only knew . . ."—this lit wife is going to inflict on her
too sure of himself husband. For Alice then lets him know that she was ready
to give up everything—their marriage and their daughter—for a naval officer
she'd glimpsed while they were vacation the year before—"if he wanted me,
even if it was only one night." Then, in another turn of the screw, she adds:
"And yet it was weird because at the same time you were dearer to me than
ever . . . and at that moment my love for you was both tender and sad." No wonder, though Alice says she and this captivating stranger exchanged but a single glance, that Bill can't stop thinking about them having sex. Kubrick pictures
Bill's fantasy of the adulterous Alice together with her lover as a blue movie
continually playing in his mind: wittily, an actual *blue* movie, with its black-
and-white grainy film stock tinged blue-gray. This military stag film, starring
a naked Alice and a blond naval officer (Gary Goba), who fetishistically keeps
on his dress white uniform for much of it, winds up being the sexiest footage
in *Eyes Wide Shut*.

Like all the Kubrick films considered in this chapter, *Eyes Wide Shut* is an
adaptation. Its literary source is the Austrian writer Arthur Schnitzler's 1926
novella *Traumnovelle*, or *Dream Story*. Schnitzler's best-known work is the play
Der Reigen (1897), an interclass sexual roundelay of ten intersecting scenes.
Ophüls made a 1950 movie of it titled *La Ronde*. In 1998, Nicole Kidman starred
in a reworked London stage version by David Hare, retitled *The Blue Room*,
which also had her briefly out of clothes. Freud was an admirer of Schnitzler
and famously termed him his doppelgänger.[46] Others at the time called Schnitzler a pornographer for his unblinkered literary exploration of dreams, sexual
desire, and fantasy. Kubrick bought the rights to *Traumnovelle* in the early
1970s, around the time when Southern was trying to interest him in making a
big-budget, Hollywood art sex film. Although *Eyes Wide Shut* updates Schnitzler's fin-de-siècle Vienna to late twentieth-century New York—so that, for instance, a prostitute with syphilis in the novella becomes a streetwalker who
turns out to be HIV-positive in the film—it remains quite faithful to its source
text, absorbing key passages of dialogue from it translated nearly word for word.

But there are some other notable alterations, including the movie's effacement of the Jewishness of Schnitzler's protagonist—who in the novella is named Fridolin—a matter we will return to shortly. The movie also changes the story's seasonal setting. In the novella, it's "just before the end of the carnival season."[47] In the movie, it's Christmas—though the Carnival backdrop in Schnitzler informs the Venetian costumes worn by Kubrick's orgiasts. And at that orgy, in both the novella and the film, the young doctor is ordered to remove his mask when he is discovered as an interloper. But it's only in the film that he is told to strip naked.

And then what?

Indulge me in once again deferring that question in order to note some other of the film's alterations and additions relating to our concern here with male sexuality. The first appear when Bill is wandering the streets of Greenwich Village alone at night and is taken for gay by a pack of rowdy college guys. "Hey, hey, hey! What team is this switch hitter on?" one of them taunts him. "Looks like the pink team," answers another, who elbows Bill into a parked car. The homophobic slurs keep coming as the group passes the other way down the street. "Faggot." "Merry Christmas, Mary." "C'mon, macho man!" "Go back to San Francisco, where you belong." "I got dumps that are bigger than you." "You want a piece of this thing, baby?" a guy calls out, theatrically pointing to his behind; "Exit only, honey."

That "Hey, hey, hey!" sounds like Alex's "Ho, ho, ho!" and his "Hi, hi, hi!" refrains in A Clockwork Orange. These college ruffians are the droogs reincarnated, but gentrified. They are also the film's contemporizing translation of "the small troop of fraternity students"—a fencing fraternity—that Fridolin has a run-in with in the novella: "he thought he recognized a few members of the Alemannia fraternity, dressed in their blue, among them" (215). The movie keeps one small linking detail in place as the blue of this Germanic corps is picked up in the Yale blue of the varsity jacket worn by one of Bill's assailants.[48]

But Eyes Wide Shut also makes a notable alteration by turning the suggestion of anti-Semitism in Schnitzler into pronounced homophobia. Kubrick's is not the first film adaptation of a literary source text to change out one for the other. The 1947 noir drama Crossfire (dir. Edward Dmytryk) provides a classic example of such transmutation, though there it works the other way around. The problem of homophobia and (in Vito Russo's phrase) "obsessive masculinity in the military" from the literary source—Richard Brooks's 1945 novel The Brick Foxhole—are converted to an indictment of anti-Semitism in the movie version.[49] The substitution was due to the Production Code's ban on any mention of homosexuality; but it also provided Hollywood a platform on which to come out as enlightened with respect to another form of bigotry.

Brooks himself did not seem to mind the movie's switching a Jewish victim for his novel's homosexual one. "They got the same problems," he remarked.[50] As for *Eyes Wide Shut*, Frederic Raphael reports in *Eyes Wide Open*, his sour memoir of the thrills and chills of working as Kubrick's hired-hand screenwriter, that his (Jewish) boss "forbade any reference to Jews" and "wanted Fridolin to be a Harrison Fordish goy."[51] The gang of preppy Yalies who appear out of nowhere and then just as quickly vanish raise the specter, if only momentarily, that this goy might also be gay. That said, one can't help but wonder whether *Eyes Wide Shut* is also playing on rumors then that Cruise himself was in the closet, which makes the gay bashing scene quite an act of artistic submission on the actor's part.

In the novel, Fridolin's wounded male honor sets him fantasizing about challenging the student who "seemed deliberately to lag behind, and bumped into him with a raised eyebrow" (215) to a duel. In the movie, Bill remarkably has no reaction to being called a faggot. (Compare Barry's blank response in *Barry Lyndon*, a movie of duels, to the demonstrative farewell scene he voyeuristically takes in between the two army officers.) The gay bashing of Bill while he is roaming the Village after dark might also raise eyebrows: Could he be? Even a little? Once activated, however, such suspicions are not so much allayed as simply set aside. Blink, and the next thing you know Bill—another Kubrick profile in male passivity—is picked up by a sweet-natured streetwalker (Vinessa Shaw), whose unusual name, Domino, is a further evocation of the original story's Venetian Carnival setting. What should they now do, Bill asks when they arrive at her place? "How about you just leave it up to me?" Domino, the kindly female dominant in black gloves (a carryover from the sex-scene ending of *A Clockwork Orange*) offers. "I'm in your hands," he replies. But their erotic encounter abruptly ends with just some tentative kissing when Alice rings Bill on his mobile. There you have it: excitation, interruption, postponement now become the narrative pattern.

Later that night, Bill, still haunting the Village, visits the surreal "Rainbow Fashions" costume shop after hours to rent his apparel for the dress-up sex party at Somerton. "Looks like alive, huh?" boasts the shop owner, Mr. Milich (Rade Šerbedžija), of the variously outfitted mannequins that people his showrooms. The mise-en-scène reflects Kubrick's abiding fascination with artificial persons, which goes all the way back to his other New York City film, 1955's *Killer's Kiss* and its climax in a Garment District dress doll factory. That concern with synthetic humans also shows up in another of Kubrick's unrealized projects, *A.I. Artificial Intelligence*. Inspired by science fiction writer Brian Aldiss's story "Supertoys Last All Summer Long," the movie is a fairy tale of an android programmed with the ability to love: a techno Pinocchio. "Please make me a real boy," implores mommy's-boy boy robot David, of the Blue Fairy, "so my mommy will love me and let me stay with her." (Good luck with that, son.) When Kubrick decided to make *Eyes Wide Shut* instead, he bestowed *A.I.* on Steven Spielberg, whose film came out in 2001, posthumously dedicated to Kubrick.

Back at Rainbow Fashions, Bill finds two Japanese men in wigs and makeup—the gesture toward drag is another of the movie's added queer touches, along with the name "Rainbow Fashions" itself—cavorting with Mr. Milich's sylphlike teenage daughter (Leelee Sobieski, updating Sue Lyon's Lolita). That scenario structurally rearranges the three-way that had been proposed to Bill at Ziegler's Christmas party by Nuala (Stewart Thorndike) and Gayle (Louise J. Taylor), the clingy fashion models who alluringly offer to take him "where the rainbow ends." Bill is called away in this instance, however, not by his wife, but as a favor to Ziegler to tend to a naked prostitute, Mandy (Julienne Davis), who has overdosed in Ziegler's parlor-like bathroom. "To be continued?" Bill asks the models before he leaves. Continued it is, under a giant neon rainbow sign at Rainbow Fashions, as a new threesome of two cross-dressing men and a late-stage nymphet: a queerer configuration than that generic *Playboy* fantasy of two girls for one lucky guy. (So is this where the rainbow ends?) The trios in *Eyes Wide Shut* flash back to the scene in *A Clockwork Orange* when Alex brings home the pair of schoolgirls who have been flirting with him in the record shop, where a copy of the *2001: A Space Odyssey* soundtrack is on display. (Everything in Kubrick, at this point, seems to relate to something else in Kubrick.) Threesomes thus present themselves in all three of Kubrick's sex films. A DVD release of *Eyes Wide Shut* bills the whole movie as a kind of ménage-a-trois between its two stars and their director, as the screen flashes in sequence CRUISE, KIDMAN, KUBRICK before the start of the film itself. These three names were also the only copyline on the publicity posters.

As though the protagonist in a pornographic movie, Bill comes across sexual opportunities wherever he goes. We have touched on his brush with the paired fashion models Nuala and Gayle, and also with the prostitute Domino. Then there is Marion (Marie Richardson), the daughter of a just deceased patient of Bill's, who quaveringly confesses her love for him while keeping vigil over her father's body. Eros and thanatos have always been affiliated in Kubrick. In *Eyes Wide Shut*, they are kissing cousins. This never more so than in a later scene at the hospital morgue, when Bill lingers over and appears to be about to kiss the corpse of that beautiful junkie hooker Mandy, presented to him nude on a slide-out metal table.[52] There is also Sally (Fay Masterson), Domino's equally sweet roommate, who lets Bill come on to her, just before she delivers the news that Domino has tested positive for HIV: another link the film makes between sex and death. (Or is this where the rainbow ends?) Kubrick's "blue movie" is not the pornographic grab bag of perversions that Southern's satiric novel is, where it's all played for low humor, including a repellent surround story that involves necrophilia. But the film lends a taboo pedophiliac tinge to its erotic spectrum when Milich's daughter snuggles up to Bill at the costume shop and whispers something we can't hear in his ear (just as Lolita does to Humbert in the bedroom scene at the Enchanted Hunters Hotel in Kubrick's film). The next day Milich himself lets Bill know that the youngster is, like his costumes, also on offer to him for rent. Once again, however, nothing comes of this pornotopia of sexual opportunity, of Bill gone, as Slavoj Žižek terms it, "on a kind of window-shopping trip for fantasies."[53]

The day after the orgy the erotic window-shopper Bill is back on the streets, toting a large "Rainbow" bag that holds his rented costume. Before he returns it, Bill stops at the Hotel Jason, looking for Nick Nightingale (what fairytale names!), his pal from medical school, turned roaming musician for-hire and the one who told him about the secret saturnalia. At the hotel Bill learns from a gay desk clerk—this is how the published screenplay labels him—that Nick (Todd Field), a bruise apparent on his cheek and looking scared, checked out at 5:00 a.m. in the company of "two big guys, . . . *very well dressed.*"[54] Alan Cumming plays this gay hotel clerk and his performance lays it on thick, cruisily coloring every word and exaggerated gesture (Figure 40). This flirty hotel clerk's pre–Production Code, pre-Stonewall forerunner is *Lolita*'s George Swine, night manager of the Enchanted Hunters Hotel, who (très gay) is also a part-time actor and bodybuilder. The drawn-out, three-and-a-half minute encounter at the Hotel Jason in *Eyes Wide Shut* is one of the longest gay scenes in Kubrick. But blank Bill never seems to catch on that another man is here sizing him up, that this is yet another sexual possibility for him. It's one more in a string of Kubrickian homosexual nonevents: something gay, suddenly right there in the story—indeed once again added to the story—but ultimately not all that significant in itself. It's just there, interestingly—for what? Comedy? A touch of queerness? Added men's film texture?

Let us now return at last to the orgy at the mansion, which, if Raphael's account is credited, fairly obsessed Kubrick during development of the screenplay.[55] The film adds several homosexual elements to what Schnitzler mostly leaves—apart from "masked people in clerical costume" (231) and the thrill of all these totally naked women—to the imagination. Nick Nightingale is led blindfolded through a sparsely peopled ballroom where the nocturnal accompanist does not see three masked same-sex couples—two female, one

Figure 40. "Big guys."

male—slow dance to "Strangers in the Night," an atypically obvious and
schmaltzy musical choice. (Deliberately so?) One partner in each pair wears a
tux (shades of that gay specter in his dinner clothes in *The Shining*) and the
other wears nothing at all. While there is no frontal male nudity here, the
orgy is a parade of fetish fashion photography female nudes in high heels and
G-strings. It's hard to tell most of these leggy, Helmut Newton animatrons
apart, save for the fantastic masks that hide their faces.

Michel Chion, sounding rather scandalized, finds that *Eyes Wide Shut* "describes a society in which almost everything is permitted when it comes to the
depiction of sex, in which bisexuality, homosexuality . . . are tolerated."[56] Yet
the only homosexual sex we catch a glimpse of during the orgy is between a few
female participants: two women fondling the breasts of a third and two others
apparently sixty-nining. The latter sight is mostly obscured, like all the explicit
action here, by cloaked figures digitally inserted during postproduction in order
to fend off the dreaded NC-17 rating—toxic at the American box office. (European audiences, of course, got to see "everything.") How far we have fallen from
the days when a film—say, *A Clockwork Orange*—could be rated X, rank in the
year's top ten highest grossing releases in America, and be nominated for multiple Oscars, including best picture, best director, and best adapted screenplay.

While Bill wanders from room to room at the orgy staged in some massive Long Island manor, looking not playing, back home Alice dreams her own bacchanal: a fantasy she will relate to him later that night in detail at his masochistic insistence. It begins with her making love at last to that naval officer. Then it morphs, Alice tells him, into her "fucking other men, so many . . . I don't know how many," the whole time laughing at her husband, who in the dream has to watch it all. "I wanted to make fun of you," she confesses. (It's far worse in *Traumnovelle*, where the wife's sex dream ends with her husband denuded, scourged, and crucified.) Whether the costumed orgy Bill crashes is real or also itself a dream—we will return to that ambiguity later—it is, ironically, the one place he goes where no one is interested in him sexually. Until, that is, he's found out and ordered to strip in front of everyone. And what next for him? That we never learn. For just then, high above the floor where Bill has been encircled by the dark-cloaked attendants, a naked woman steps forward. "Stop," she calls out from behind her mask. "Let him go. Take me. I am ready to redeem him." (This may or may not be Mandy, who in any case winds up afterward in the morgue.)

From this point on, the movie reorients itself generically, overlaying a mystery plot onto its sexual odyssey storyline—as though Kubrick were offering his own, "adult," married-couple version of something like David Lynch's male coming-of-age sexual psychodrama, *Blue Velvet* (1986). As with Lynch's laddish Jeffrey Beaumont—played by Kyle MacLachlan, who sports the same dark brown boyish bangs Cruise wears here—Dr. Bill Harford suddenly becomes an amateur dick. He flashes his New York State Medical Board card like a detective's badge to get to the bottom of mysteries the film is determined to leave unresolved. Such as how did Mandy really die? In a lengthy explanatory scene near the end of the film, Ziegler claims she overdosed alone in her apartment, after she "got her brains fucked out" back at the orgy. Or was she rather "sacrificed" there in place of Bill? And what about Nick Nightingale? Is Ziegler to be believed when he tells Bill that "that little cocksucker" who let him in on the secret of the shadowy sex party is now back home in Seattle, roughed up a bit but none too worse for the wear and "probably banging Mrs. Nick"? And also how does the mask that Bill wears at the orgy end up on the pillow next to his sleeping wife back home? Not that it feels, however, like the film ultimately cares very much about all this, apart from cultivating an air of dangerous mysteriousness.

As for the mystery of what might have befallen Bill at the orgy had not a woman taken his place, the Stanley Kubrick Archive at the University of the Arts London holds some clues. An early draft of the screenplay by Raphael describes "a 'POSSE' of men in black costumes, dressed as if they might be

"Renaissance secret policemen" closing ranks around the trespasser. The men "drive BILL backwards to a long heavy table on which various implements are arranged." "They might be," notes Raphael, "antique medical equipment."[57] Kubrick objected to this turn in the story—not because it was too menacing, but because it wasn't menacing enough. The copy of this draft screenplay I consulted in the Kubrick Archive has attached to the page I have just been quoting from a sticky note on which Kubrick has devastatingly jotted in blue pencil the words "Silly" and "Camp." Next to them, he has also written: "Confrontation lacks danger."

Raphael's proposal of weird medical devices brings to mind David Cronenberg's *Dead Ringers* (1988) and its creepy gynecological "Mantle Retractor." One wonders what might be the male version imagined for use here on the doctor himself in *Eyes Wide Shut*. But Kubrick envisioned a different contemporary cinematic referent: "Should be Pulp Fiction class," reads another of his attached notes. I suspect that he was thinking in particular of the male rape and rape revenge sequence in Tarantino's 1994 movie, which begins with bondage, ball gags, and a pommel horse, and which ends with the victim, who suddenly gains the upper hand, menacingly informing his victimizer: "I'm going to get medieval on your ass." At the top of his note, which is covered with commentary, Kubrick has spelled out that all this "Has to be": "Credible," "Very sexy," "Dangerous," "Contemporary." Another annotation next to this one indicates that Bill, toward this end, should be "Tied naked" and "Buggery, at least should be suggested."

A later draft shows how Raphael accordingly reconceived this climactic scene, now setting it in the mansion's music room, explicitly marked here as "a male domain":

> The MEN come towards and around him with implacable slowness and evident purpose.
>
> They push him onto the billiard table. The balls netted in the pockets somehow suggest what they may have in mind . . .
>
> Some MEN go and choose cues . . .[58]

Kubrick wanted at least the suggestion of what he quaintly terms buggery, and that is what Raphael none too subtly here delivers. "First we bend, then—if need be—we break," a "GREY-HAIRED MAN" in charge determines, in the next draft's version of this scene, now reset in the billiard room. "First we bend, then . . . we break," the rest of the MEN ritually reply in chorus.[59] What if the rainbow had ended here for Bill—bent, broken, sodomized? ("Men have to stick it in every place they can," Alice had observed to her husband in their bedroom scene.) But buggery winds up not being a way station on this film's yellow brick road of outré sexual experiences. I put it that way not only because of all the rainbow talk and imagery in the film. But also because "Oz" was the password to the orgy in an early version of the screenplay: this, before it was changed to "Fidelio," identified in the movie as the name of Beethoven's opera, which is subtitled *The Triumph of Married Love*.

"You saved my ass," says Ziegler to Bill, after Bill, called away at the Christmas party from the two fashion models offering to take him where the rainbow ends, revives Mandy, the nude hooker who overdosed in Ziegler's bathroom. The about to be manhandled Bill could say just the same to Mandy (if indeed she was the one who offered herself in his place) when he is allowed to depart the orgy clothed and unscathed.

Kubrick bought the rights to *Traumnovelle* in 1970, when he was finishing *A Clockwork Orange*, and it was announced as his next project. Yet this film adaptation of Schnitzler would be nearly thirty years in coming, deferred until after Kubrick made *Barry Lyndon*, *The Shining*, and *Full Metal Jacket*. *Eyes Wide Shut* took longer to shoot—a record four hundred days—and made more at the box office—$162 million, most of it overseas—than any other Kubrick movie. Kubrick himself is said to have judged it his best film. But in keeping with the initial reception of nearly all his movies, the reviews were mixed, including some outright pans. The orgy, no surprise, was a flashpoint for critics. Michiko Kakutani complains that it "feels more ludicrous than provocative." A "boring free-for-all," says Andrew Sarris. Amy Taubin dismisses the orgy as "ponderous," a drag on the whole film from which "it never quite recovers." Louis Menand judges that "in *Eyes Wide Shut* nothing works," though he does credit the orgy as "achiev[ing] true bathos." All this sounds measured compared to the verdict of David Denby: "I can state unequivocally that the late Stanley Kubrick, in his final film, 'Eyes Wide Shut,' has staged the most pompous orgy in the history of the movies." Ben Parker, in a droll reflection on Tom Cruise's "star-text," manages to go Denby one better, however. He nominates Kubrick's "synthesizer-scored orgy" as "probably the least sexy scene in cinema history."[60]

Let's allow Parker and Denby their hyperbole. There's something to it. Yet who knows what Kubrick thought he was doing in the first place, whether he actually intended to make these scenes simply sexy. Perhaps he did. The point is that the film's orgiastic tableaux turned out looking and feeling strange, weird in so many ways—and isn't that always how the erotic comes across in Kubrick? Consider what he did to *A Clockwork Orange*, how his dystopic film about sex, violence, and art turned Burgess's parable, with its Big Moral Statement about free will and social conditioning, into a tour de force of gleefully exhibitionist visual style. (The sex in that film, too, is more arty than sexy.) In his adaption, Kubrick was, of course, picking up on something—Burgess's own bravura display of linguistic ingenuity—that was also there in the book. Speaking of source texts, it's likewise questionable whether the costumed orgy in the original Schnitzler story was itself ever meant to be simply sexy and not also (or more so) bizarre, perhaps satiric too. "Where am I? wondered Fridolin. Among lunatics? . . . Have I gotten into the meeting of some religious sect?" (232).

"Two camps have always formed around each of Stanley's movies," Michael Herr rightly observes in his memoir of Kubrick, "and no one in either camp could ever imagine what the other camp thought it was seeing." "In the case of *Eyes Wide Shut*," Herr continues, "the camps were made up of people who knew within minutes that they were watching a dream film and those who didn't."[61] Kubrick explained in an interview that Schnitzler's endeavor to "equate the importance of sexual dreams and *might-have-beens* with reality" is what drew him to this tale about "the sexual ambivalence of a *happy marriage.*"[62] It's the wife's recitation of what is at first a notional fantasy (that she would have given up everything for the naval officer), then a *dream realization* of this fantasy, that impels nearly all her husband's subsequent deeds. *Eyes Wide Shut*, the paradoxical title Kubrick gave to his film translation of Schnitzler's *Dream Story*—a title disliked, incidentally, by Raphael—signals a phenomenological dimension of erotic experience where the distinction between having fantasized or dreamed something and actually having done it wouldn't much matter, where that difference falls away, feels dissolved. I see the film's completely weird orgy as standing for that dissolve. Or rather its *orgies*, for that here imagined to be extreme sexual experience is doubled and paired: his and hers. If the orgy that we get to see is indeed the husband's parallel sexual dream to the wife's that we "only" hear about (but also in which, unlike his, she actually "does it"), his dream winds up like a classic anxiety dream ("Remove your clothes")—which might, of course, also still be someone's wet one. Indeed, it's his: "I'll tell you everything," Bill opens up to his wife afterward in the film's climactic scene, and then, like so many of Kubrick's men before him, he breaks down in tears. "I'll tell you everything," he sobbingly repeats. *Eyes Wide Shut* is another Kubrick melodrama (but aren't they all?) about male vulnerability.

"You have but slumbered here/While these visions did appear. /. . ./No more yielding but a dream," Shakespeare has Puck say at the end of *A Midsummer Night's Dream* (5.1.417–418, 20). But near the movie's end, Dr. Bill (now at last playing Dr. Freud) counters with a line straight out of Schnitzler that "No dream is ever just a dream." Puck's famous epilogue retroactively sets all of Shakespeare's crossed-love marriage comedy—I'd like to say all theater— within dreamspace. The same has been said of *Eyes Wide Shut*. You have been dreaming here all along.[63] That's a way to take the film's many strange, de-naturalizing aspects: everything from its sound-stage simulacrum of New York with imaginary street names (there's no Wren Street in the Village, though it's in keeping with the poetics of a story that also features a Nightingale) to all those passages of what Chion terms "parroted" dialogue (Gayle: "Where the rainbow ends." Bill: "Where the rainbow ends?" Or, Bill: "What did he want?" Alice: "What did he want? Oh . . . what did he want."); from the many scenes that seem to go on several beats too long with little narrative payoff to the some-times stilted, sometimes overdone acting.[64] None of this weird dreamy stuff was much appreciated by the film's naysayers. But then there is its gorgeous irreal rainbow of colors: the expressive gradations of blue, overly vivid reds, and Gustav Klimt gold curtains of light. This is also part of the dream that is *Eyes Wide Shut*, leaving me, for one, spellbound.

Kubrick's version of Schnitzler's *Dream Story* is also a ghost story. The film is haunted, as Lucy Scholes and Richard Martin consider in their illuminat-ing essay "Archived Desires," by many specters.[65] Some hark back to the old Europe of Schnitzler and Freud, others even earlier. Take the Beethoven op-era password to the orgy, Fidelio. Or the Sonata Cafe, where Bill meets Nick Nightingale (*Nachtigall* in the book). Or the heavily accented Eastern Euro-pean costumer Mr. Milich, along with the Hungarian Sandor Szavost (Sky du Mont), who waltzes Alice around the ballroom at Ziegler's Christmas party and eruditely talks of adultery in terms of Ovid. Other hauntings are of the film's here and now. None more so than Kubrick's sudden death on March 7, 1999, as it happened just days after he delivered the film to Warner Brothers. Suspicion that he wasn't really finished with it has shadowed *Eyes Wide Shut* since its premiere on July 13, 1999. Unfinished works and their indices of "*might-have-beens*" (to reuse Kubrick's phrase) have their own allure. But I would like to bring back something else I see haunting Kubrick's final film—another ghostly association—unearthed, like those considered by Scholes and Martin, from the archives.

Let us return one last time to what would or might have happened to Bill had not some beautiful naked woman offered up herself in his place at the orgy. ("You can do it to me . . . All of you . . . Take me instead of him," she declares in an early draft of the screenplay.) I see the specter of Bill's sexual punishment— the "buggery" first called for by Kubrick, then conjured up by his screenwriter at this command, and ultimately exorcised from the actual film—hovering over his final encounter with Ziegler. Letting Bill know that he also was there at the orgy and "saw everything that went on," Ziegler wants to scare off the now ob-sessed doctor/detective from his prying investigations. This thirteen-minute-long scene—which is not in the novella, nor is the sinister Ziegler himself (he's

the screenplay's major characterological invention)—is set in the library of
Ziegler's city mansion. The room's décor marks it as another of those male
spaces in Kubrick: the clubby furniture, the well-stocked tabletop bar, the
model ship, the antique globe, and so forth. But it is dominated by that red pool
table. The older man and the younger man twist and turn about it—sometimes
together, sometimes apart, a paternalistic hand on the shoulder here (add
Ziegler to the roll call of bad father figures in Kubrick), a back turned there—in
ways that recall the maneuverings between Dax and his superior General Broulard in the second to last scene of *Paths of Glory*, a scene to which I keep coming back for its climactic "up yours" provocation. When Bill enters the room
and looks at that lurid red pool table, he asks Ziegler if he is in the midst of a
game. Ziegler replies that no, he had just been "knocking a few balls around."
Once you know about it, how not to think of the draft screenplay's scripted billiard table gangbang that in the end wasn't to be? This long drawn-out, rather
unsatisfying scene with Ziegler, cue in hand, is what is remains of that one.

The return of the repressed? I wouldn't put it quite that way. There is too
much manifest homosexual content in this movie to warrant that kind of reading. Nor do I think Taubin heads down the right path with her invocation of
all "The homosexual panic lurking below putative heterosexuality" in Kubrick's movies, which she sees "played out even more clearly in *Eyes Wide
Shut*."[66] I've been implying throughout these two chapters on male sexuality
in Kubrick that there isn't really all that much homosexual panic therein. At
times, it approaches a homosexual indifference, which, as I have also tried to
suggest, is in itself not nothing. Perhaps there is a charge of sexual panic in
how Antoninus, learned as he is in "the classics," flees his sadistic bisexual master Crassus for another kind of male love embodied by the fatherly Spartacus.
But not in the way that Johnny nonchalantly sets aside the older man Marv's
advances in *The Killing*. Nor in Barry's impassive response to the male couple
bathing together in *Barry Lyndon*. Remember too how in *A Clockwork Orange*
Kubrick drops the scene in the novel when Alex beats to death a fellow inmate who had been fondling him when he was asleep in his bunk. In the film,
Alex is unfazed by all the homosexual attention he attracts; if anything, he
expects it for being young and good-looking. As for *Eyes Wide Shut*, Bill appears more on edge when he is alone with Domino in her apartment and she
wants to get down to business than when he is accosted in the streets by the
college jocks who make him out to be a "faggot."

Currents of male sexual anxiety, churning at times with misogynist aversion and contempt, flow deeply through Kubrick's movies; but this is mainly
attendant on their fraught depictions of heterosexual relations. *The Shining*
(to which this chapter briefly turns next) is his most dreadful example of that

aversion, where it has both supernatural and non-supernatural dimensions. Non-supernatural inasmuch as Jack is possessed with hatred of his wife Wendy, whom he refers to as "the old sperm bank," well before he is actually possessed, and this much sooner and more potently in Kubrick's film than in King's novel. As for the "supernatural," even the desirable naked female phantom Jack encounters in the queasy pea green bathroom of Room 237 deteriorates into a rotting crone in his eyes as soon as he embraces her. (This scene is the other notable exception to the bathroom being the men's room in Kubrick.)

Eyes Wide Shut, which as we have seen has its own ghosts, can be taken in part as a restorative rewriting of that horror show. This film offers a happy ending insofar as for once in Kubrick—after *The Killing, Spartacus, Lolita, A Clockwork Orange, Barry Lyndon*, and *The Shining*—the man and his family survive intact. This conclusion leads us back to the question of where the rainbow *does* end in this movie about wandering from home before returning to it. In Schnitzler's novella, as well as in several of Raphael's draft screenplays, that final scene occurs in the couple's bedroom. But the film replaces it with the literally storybook setting of a supersized, color-saturated children's toy store. Here Bill and Alice, their eyes still red from the teary, sleepless night before, repair with their oblivious young daughter in tow. So what do they do now? The husband asks this of the wife from whom he has strayed, a wife he has come to understand harbors her own sexual fantasies and dreams, some that involve him and some that don't. "I do love you," Alice tells Bill as they drift through the crowded store. "And you know," she continues after a pause, "there is something very important that we need to do as soon as possible?" "What's that?" he asks. Is it something to consider that Bill doesn't seem to know what *that* is, that she has to spell it out for him? It's the "Bad Bad Thing" of the film's purring Chris Isaak song, also the musical soundtrack for the trailer that promised *Eyes Wide Shut* as the sexiest studio movie ever. But even the "Fuck" of conjugal restoration falls in line with this tale's pattern of erotic deferral. That is, out Christmas shopping with their daughter, Bill and Alice can't, of course, do it then and there.[67]

Another "F" word comes up in this scene, but this one Alice demurs uttering. Her distressed husband wants them now to exchange pledges of "Forever." "Forever?" Alice (who never simply plays the part of Penelope in the film's sexual odyssey) repeats, but as a question. "Let's . . . not use that word," she then determines; "it frightens me."

Kubrick's Apparitional Homosexuals

Maybe Alice, whom we find watching movies at home on TV, has seen *The Shining* (1980), where Jack (Jack Nicholson) says that he wishes his own family of three could remain at the Overlook Hotel "forever and ever and ever." This is also what the spectral Grady girls had just intoned to Danny: "Come play with us, Danny. Forever and ever and ever." Note that the traumatized young boy who sees things in *The Shining* has been exchanged in *Eyes Wide Shut*—Kubrick's other family film, the one with something like a happy ending—for a standard-issue adorable little girl, who remains mercifully oblivious throughout to the travails of her parents.[68] But there are no happy endings for father-son (or "father"-"son") stories in Kubrick, and almost always one or the other dies and sometimes both.

Before turning in the final chapter to *Full Metal Jacket*, replete with its own male familial dynamics, I want to linger a moment more with *The Shining*, the most spectacular of father-son stories in Kubrick. Recall that it was a pair of ghosts from that film who initiated this two-chapter consideration of male sexuality and homosexuality in Kubrick. Unlike many of the apparitional homosexuals we have encountered, they are not exactly Kubrick's movie's invention. The image here of a man in an animal costume, kneeling between another man's open legs, is the movie's own visualization of a s/m relationship referred to in Stephen King's novel involving two of the haunted hotel's most perverse denizens: its wealthy, imperious owner Harry Derwent and Roger, a past trick of his. Caretaker of the Overlook Jack Torrance learns all about them while waltzing in its grand ballroom with a female ghost in a cat mask. Harry is "AC/DC, you know. Poor Roger's only DC," she relays. "Harry," Jack's phantom dance partner further recounts, "never goes back for seconds . . . not on his DC side, anyway . . . and Roger is just *wild*. Harry told him if he came to the masked ball as a doggy, a *cute* little doggy, he might reconsider."[69] The movie omits this explanatory scene, while in the book Roger accordingly capers about on all fours, dragging his tail, and playfully barking at the other revelers. But in the movie Harry and Roger do "get a room" (as the saying goes) for when things turn hot and heavy. And that is where Wendy spies them through a door left open, ready to go about their business—ghosts, by nature, being exhibitionists.[70] In the novel, however, the "dogman" appears not to her but to her son Danny: "I'm going to eat you up, little boy," Roger threatens him. "And I think I'll start with your plump little *cock*" (494; emphasis in the original). Kubrick's film further changes things around by putting this queer creature's fairytale lines—"Not by the hair of my chinny-chin-chin" and "I'll huff, and I'll puff, and I'll blow your house in"—in the mouth of Jack, Danny's abusive father, who we learn early in the story had once dislocated his son's shoulder in a fit of drunken anger. Now here in the film, dad, as the Big Bad Wolf, wants to devour him.

Danny's traumatic response to his abuse is also orally oriented: the creation of a protective second self, an imaginary little boy he calls Tony—derived in

Figure 41. Chef Hallorann "shining."

King's novel from this father and son's shared middle name Anthony—who lives in Danny's mouth and hides in his stomach. Forms of splitting and doubling proliferate in *The Shining*, as they do throughout Kubrick's work. Fittingly, the "father function" is also here twinned. To go with his increasingly malevolent real father, Danny is provided with a kindly surrogate father-figure in the Overlook's head chef (what else would he here be?), Dick Hallorann, who addresses Danny as "Doc," just as Danny's parents do in private at home.

Hallorann, played by Scatman Crothers, is the most prominent African American character in Kubrick, his importance marked by the movie's affording his weathered face a sustained frame-filling close-up (Figure 41). Hallorann stands out as more than another good man Black man among the ranks of Kubrick's men, ranging from a minor character like the overly friendly parking lot attendant in *The Killing* to the towering Ethiopian gladiator Draba in *Spartacus*; but his prominence comes at the cost of further stereotyping. Like Danny (though not as powerfully), Hallorann possesses the telepathic power of "shining." "I can remember when I was a little boy . . ." he begins when he sits down alone with Danny over a big bowl of ice cream in the hotel's cavernous kitchen. (So the good father feeds the boy, just as the bad one would consume him.). The folksy way in which Hallorann experiences and explains what it means to shine aligns with the familiar "Magical Negro" trope whereby a Black character in a supporting role assists or saves a white protagonist through the use of some unusual, often animistic power.[71] This relates to Hallorann's other principal narrative function in the film, in addition to his explicating what it means to shine in terms that a child could understand. Paranormally summoned by Danny from all the way down in Florida, Hallorann returns to the Overlook in a fearful blizzard to deliver, coachman-like, the Sno-Cat that will serve as the boy and his mother's means of escape from Jack and the hotel at the film's end.

The character Crothers plays is not only magical, he's sacrificial. Within moments of his summoned return to the Overlook, Hallorann is axed to death by Jack. The scene is shocking and gruesome—and also a major departure from the novel. There, though grievously wounded by Jack, Hallorann survives and himself saves Danny and Wendy, making for a reconstellated family unit at the novel's end. But so not in the film, where the good father is killed by the evil one, who in turn, outsmarted by the son, meets his own snowbound dead end trapped in the maze outside the hotel. In Kubrick's unsparingly antipatriarchal revision of *The Shining*, all fathers must die and the family remains irreparably breached. But that structural imperative doesn't make what happens to the Black man—the only killing in this horror film that we actually see—any less hard to take.

A pair of Black female nudes decorate Hallorann's bachelor pad winter getaway. Softcore porn makes an appearance much earlier in the film when the camera catches Jack distractedly flipping through a copy of *Playgirl* that he happens to find in the lobby of the Overlook. This is while he is waiting to be shown around the hotel by its manager, Mr. Ullman (Barry Nelson), a character multiply marked as gay—homophobically so—in King's novel, though not in Kubrick's film.[72] A skin mag is not the kind of thing one expects to find lying around a hotel lobby, even at the once swinging Overlook. Nor does this *Playgirl* show up in the novel. Who knows just what this male nude monthly, which billed itself as "The Magazine for Women" but always had a sizable undercover gay male viewership, is doing there in the movie. The arcanists among the film's fans tend to spotlight this particular issue's cover story on "Incest: Why Parents Sleep with Their Children" as a deeply embedded, hermetic clue that Jack's abuse of Danny involved sexual abuse.

My inclination is to take this soft-core porn magazine's cameo appearance as synecdochic—as standing for homosexuality, which seems just to happen to be there in some transient, ghostlike way in Kubrick's movies, typically in the background or around the edges, part of their male atmospherics. The homosexual flicker tends to be fainter, more encoded in his Production Code–era

films (the "snails and oysters" of *Spartacus*), more in your face after the Production Code had been done away with (the full male nude prison induction
scene in *A Clockwork Orange*). But its status in Kubrick remains remarkably
the same across that historical division: not treated at length or in depth, but
there. Sometimes male homosexuality is made to serve a particular minor
expositional purpose (the army officers in love in *Barry Lyndon*). And sometimes it's largely for color (the pornographic murals in *A Clockwork Orange*)
or for additional kinky erotic interest (back to that weird dress-up coupling of
male ghosts in *The Shining*). But in Kubrick there is always some added homosexual accompaniment, a revenant bent on returning film after film, from
The Killing on.

5

His Fundamental Core

Full Metal Jacket

There's nothing that soft in *Full Metal Jacket*.

— STANLEY KUBRICK

Arma virumque cano. "I sing of arms and the man," blazons Virgil in the opening words of *The Aeneid*, epic of course being war's genre. (What does it say
that our most exalted poetic form makes war its great subject?) The Kubrick
iteration of this locus classicus of vaunted martial masculinity appears, ironically, in *Full Metal Jacket* (1987), his antiheroic, utterly unsentimental Vietnam War movie. There it is said that even "God has a hard-on for marines."
This remarkable revelation of divine desire is put in the mouth of Gunnery
Sergeant Hartman, the film's most famous character. "God has a hard-on for
marines," intones the oracular drill sergeant, "because we kill everything that
we see. He plays his games; we play ours. To show our appreciation for so much
power, we keep heaven packed with fresh souls!"

   In line with Kubrick's revisionary ways with a genre to which he remained
attracted over the course of his whole career, *Full Metal Jacket* is a very different
kind of war film—also a very different kind of Vietnam War film—beginning
with its form. *2001: A Space Odyssey*, where we left off our consideration of
Kubrick's war films a few chapters ago, unfolds slowly, episodically, as a
moving-picture book about man: what he was and what he might come to be.
Full Metal Jacket, similarly all about men and metamorphosis, is a cinematic
diptych. One narrative panel renders Parris Island, the other Vietnam. This
is a military movie as concerned with the transformational processes of boot
camp as it is with the battlefield. (Parris Island—no mere prelude—steals
the show.)

We have seen a decentering of actual combat in other Kubrick war films. *Paths of Glory* features only one three-minute, albeit harrowing, battle sequence. It occurs fairly early on. The rest of the film, with its court-martial plot, gives scope to what I suggest in Chapter 2 is Kubrick's principal interest in this story: its vexatious rendering of hierarchical male relations in the intensified setting of the military during war. Kubrick's World War I melodrama keeps raising the question of what is expected of soldiers (and officers) as men. *Full Metal Jacket*, a rare war story evacuated of melodrama, clinically works through a more fundamental line of inquiry: How do you convert a teenage boy into a marine, the most hardcore of all American fighting men?

"If you ladies leave my island, if you survive recruit training," Hartman preordains, "you will be a minister of death, praying for war." This is a religious claim, indeed an evangelical one, from a hardened true believer. But it takes this movie forty-five minutes to deliver its ministers of death to the battleground of Vietnam. For the film lingers, as though itself mesmerized, at Parris Island. There, in a succession of viscerally harrowing but visually beautiful set pieces, *Full Metal Jacket* renders the physical drills and psychical operations by which raw recruits are unmade, remade, and incorporated into the Marine Corps, an extended, everlasting male family. "From now on, until you die, wherever you are, every marine is your brother," declares Hartman after their completion of recruit training. "Most of you," he continues, "will go to Vietnam. Some of you will not come back. But always remember this: marines die, that's what we're here for! But the Marine Corps lives forever. And that means *you* live forever!"[1]

While the Corps constitutes an eternal brotherhood, each marine is himself, as Hartman pronounces the night he has his men bed down with their rifles, "married to this piece, this weapon of iron and wood." "And," he orders, "you *will* be faithful!" *Semper fidelis*. The Marine Corps motto stands as an order. So here, then, is the pledge of always, of forever that the husband desires but does not receive from his wife after all their travails at the end of *Eyes Wide Shut*. We have to turn back for it from Kubrick's last film to the one right before it in sequence: another of his essentially all-male military films—the Marine Corps one, positioned in between two different but related traumatic tales about marriage and family, *The Shining* and *Eyes Wide Shut*. This set of films marks a turn, emergent in *Barry Lyndon*, toward the familial in Kubrick's filmography.

Faithfully married to his weapon, the marine becomes one with it: "You will be a weapon," the gunnery sergeant thus foretells of the recruits on their very first day of boot camp. This conversion—mechanical, familial, religious— is the telos, but also (let us confess it from the outset) the pleasure/pain of these transformational operations, ranging from the twisted virtuosity of Hartman's verbal assaults to the precision choreography of male bodies put through their paces, training, marching, and chanting in cadence. Hartman: "I love working for Uncle Sam!" Recruits: "Lets me know just who I am!"

Head Like a Hole

> I remember going in one end and coming out the other. (Anthony Swofford, *Jarhead*)

What, then, here does it mean to be a marine? How are they made? The process of producing marines commences in *Full Metal Jacket* with boot camp's initiatory first rite. To the maudlin steel-pedal guitar strains of Johnny Wright's 1965 country and western hit, "Hello Vietnam," with its wistful refrain of "Kiss me goodbye," the recruits receive their first "jarhead" high-and-tight marine haircuts. Presented without dialogue, *Full Metal Jacket*'s opening barbershop montage makes for some striking male portraiture, still images of which seem like something Kubrick could have taken on assignment back when he worked for *Look* magazine. The clippings that rapidly pile up on the floor around the barber's chair are the detritus of male selves processed for impersonality (Figure 42).

Cut from the barbershop to the squad bay. "You're the lowest form of life on earth," begins Hartman, in a demonic characterization by R. Lee Ermey. His Gunnery Sergeant Hartman is no standard issue Hollywood drill instructor, the kind whose leathery exterior hides a paternal heart of gold. Lou Gossett Jr. played that part to the hilt a few years before in Taylor Hackford's *An Officer and a Gentleman* (1982) and won an Oscar. All that Ermey got for his terrorizing, perfectly one-note performance was a Golden Globe nomination. A former Marine Corps drill instructor and Vietnam veteran, Ermey broke into the movies with small roles in two other Vietnam films: Sidney J. Furie's *The Boys in Company C* (1978) and Francis Ford Coppola's *Apocalypse Now* (1979).[2] Kubrick first hired him as a consultant on *Full Metal Jacket*, but Ermey fought for and won the role of Hartman. Kubrick even let him improvise what turned out to be many of his character's best lines. The only other actor Kubrick allowed that kind of latitude was Peter Sellers.

"You are not even human-fucking-beings!" Hartman carries on. "You are nothing but unorganized grabasstic pieces of amphibian shit!" (Like *2001*, *Full Metal Jacket* begins as an evolutionary tale.) "There is no racial bigotry here! I do not look down on niggers, kikes, wops, or greasers. Here you are all equally worthless!" Hartman's leveling rhetoric continues, as he strides in a masterfully

Figure 42. "Kiss me good-bye."

sustained, deep-focus, wide-angle traveling shot up and down two facing lines of identically dressed and posed petrified young men. He will here bestow upon them, in another turn on the satiric male nomenclature of *Dr. Strangelove*, the mocking nicknames that they retain throughout the movie: Private Joker, Private Cowboy, Private Snowball, Private Toejam, and so on. For their part, the grunts respond to him in a single voice of compliance: "Sir, yes, sir!"

"You want to be different?" Hartman later accuses Leonard Lawrence (Vincent D'Onofrio)—or Gomer Pyle, as he has been here renamed—after Pyle mishandles his rifle during a group drill. Upon Pyle's repeated missteps and his continued failings at physical training, Hartman charges the private's individual shortcomings to the platoon itself: "I have tried to help him, but I have failed because *you* have not helped me! You people have not given Private Pyle the proper motivation! So from now on, whenever Private Pyle fucks up, I will not punish him. I will punish all of you." In the scene that immediately follows, the corporate body takes on its new work of self-regulation. Gagged and strapped to his bed with a sheet, the sleeping Pyle is given a "blanket party." Armed with bars of soap jacketed in towels, the others silently stream by Pyle's bunk on both sides, each serially tendering his blows: an efficient assembly line of discipline and punishment, shot in a disconcertingly beautiful blue

light. Last in line is Private Joker (Matthew Modine) whom Hartman had assigned the task of personally coaching Pyle though his training, a charge Joker
thus far had taken up with a measure of patient compassion.[3] When Joker hesi-
tates in front of Pyle's bed, Private Cowboy (Arliss Howard), Joker's friend,
insists that he "Do it! Do it!" Joker pauses a moment longer, and then lands
repeated, especially savage blows on Pyle's convulsing body. The machine is
fully functional only when every part is doing its part.

   "What do we do for a living, ladies?" Hartman asks. "Kill, kill, kill!" comes
back the reply in a husky chorus. The first casualty of the war machine is the
male self as monad. The platoon's mechanically administered physical battery
of Pyle almost immediately effectuates, if not Pyle's full incorporation, at least
his technologization. Two scenes later, he is shown speaking to and doting over
the precision machinery of his rifle, to which, following Hartman's orders to
the whole platoon, he has given a girl's name: "It's been swabbed . . . and wiped.
Everything is clean. . . . So that your action is beautiful. Smooth, Charlene."
Pyle also now suddenly emerges as an unexpectedly dexterous rifleman, a sharp
shooter, meriting for the first time his drill sergeant's praise: "Outstanding, Private Pyle! I think we've finally found something that you do well!" The shattering array of physical and psychological experiences brought to bear upon
him have succeeded in making Pyle "born again hard!" as Hartman triumphantly, religiously puts it. The former "fatbody" (as the drill sergeant had
termed him), now a hardened killer-to-be, represents this story's most dramatic
and absolute conversion to the machine; indeed, from one vantage, Pyle's re-
birth as a coldly mechanical killer ironically marks this gunny's greatest success.
Ironically, because these two figures—another bad "father"-"son" pairing—
together comprise the necessary sacrificial token in the scene that spectacularly
concludes *Full Metal Jacket*'s first act.

   For this climax, we return to the place where the circuit of boot camp begins, that is, to the head, which in this setting is to say the head that is a hole.
"From now on . . . the first and last words out of your filthy sewers will be 'Sir!'"
Hartman orders in his opening harangue, his conflation of mouth and anus
marking a locus around which so much at once abjectifying and doting attention is here to accrue. In ordering Joker and Cowboy to scrub the barracks
latrine—another head that is a hole—Hartman tells these two "turds" (as he
here addresses them) that he wants "that head so sanitary and squared away
that the Virgin Mary herself would be proud to go in there and take a dump."
Head and hole continue to redouble each other throughout the movie. "I'll
P.T. you until your assholes are sucking buttermilk," Hartman threatens the
whole platoon. "I've got your name! I've got your ass!" he warns Joker; "You
had best unfuck yourself," Hartman continues, "or I will unscrew your head

and shit down your neck." "You'd better get your head and your ass wired together, or I will take a giant shit on you!" Joker is likewise later warned by a colonel.[4] "I will gouge out your eyeballs and skull-fuck you," Hartman puts it to Private Pyle, whose risible nickname evokes Gomer Pyle, the sad-sack marine of the popular 1960s television comedy series played by Jim Nabors, as well as the dung with which he is repeatedly identified. "You are a worthless piece of shit, Pyle," Hartman tells him. "You really look like shit today, Leonard," echoes Joker on another occasion. "Private Pyle, you had best square your ass away and start shitting me Tiffany cufflinks," Hartman comes at him again, in an opulent flight of fecal fancy, "or I will definitely fuck you up!" Nor is Pyle the only recruit so maligned. "Five foot nine? I didn't know they stacked shit so high!" says Hartman as he sizes up Private Cowboy during recruit training. "It looks to me like the best part of you ran down the crack of your mama's ass and ended up as a brown stain on the mattress!"

But these are also the Corps' terms of endearment, as we see when Joker and Cowboy, the only characters the movie retains when it reboots itself in Vietnam, happen to hook up with each other in its second part. "Boy, I hoped I'd never see you again, you piece of shit!" exclaims Cowboy, as they embrace in front of an annular pagoda entrance (Figure 43). This joyful reunion occurs near the front lines of the battle, where Joker, now commissioned as a reporter for *The Sea Tiger*, the Marine Corps newspaper, has been sent to cover the aftermath of the Tet Offensive. As Joker's commanding officer had said, "It's a huge shit sandwich, and we're all gonna have to take a bite." For that matter, any station within the thick of the action, any direct engagement with the enemy, is described as being "in the shit": a state both dreaded and desired as the principal medium in which hardcore "marineness" is tried and proven to oneself and to the Corps. Rafterman (Kevyn Major Howard), the newbie photographer assigned to work with Joker, complains that all he does is take pictures at ceremonies, when what he really wants is "to get out into the shit," "to get some trigger time." "Wasting," the most oft-used term here for what marines are trained best to do—which is to kill—likewise bears an excremental connotation.

All this is to say that the exchanges and affiliations between these men continue to be analized. "You're gonna be all right," Joker tells Cowboy near the film's end, holding his dying buddy in his arms.[5] "Oh, don't shit me, Joker! Don't shit me!" Cowboy gasps. "I wouldn't shit you, man. You're my favorite turd," replies Joker, his scatological elegy echoing the fecal nativity Hartman had accorded Cowboy back in boot camp but here affectionately revalencing it. (In one draft of the screenplay, Hartman accuses Joker and Cowboy of being a couple.) Boot camp's only moment of levity also

Figure 43. Analized male bonds.

comes by way of the ass, when Private Snowball (Peter Edmund) misidenti-
fies the location from which Lee Harvey Oswald—a marine, Hartman
proudly wants his men to know—shot Kennedy as "that book suppository
building, sir!"[6]

Back to front, *Full Metal Jacket* is the anal foil to Kubrick's massively phallic *Dr. Strangelove*.

What is it with Kubrick's marines and male anality? Here I want to turn to
an important early work of antihomophobic male sexual theory: Guy Hocquenghem's *Homosexual Desire*, which asserts not only the various "desire
functions" of the anus, but also the overinvested use to which it—and not just
the phallus—is put socially:

> Every man possesses a phallus which guarantees him a social role;
> every man has an anus which is truly his own, in the most secret
> depths of his own person. The anus does not exist in a social relation,
> since it forms precisely the individual and therefore enables the division
> between society and the individual to be made. . . . One does not shit
> in company. Lavatories are the only place where one is alone behind
> locked doors. . . . The anus is over-invested individually because its
> investment is withdrawn socially.[7]

"The anus," Hocquenghem continues, "is so well hidden that it forms the sub-soil of the individual, *his 'fundamental core'*. . . . Your anus is so totally yours that you must not use it: keep it to yourself" (100; emphasis added). But in *Full Metal Jacket*, Hartman has it otherwise: "You can give your heart to Jesus," he preaches to his men on Christmas morning, "but your ass belongs to the Corps!" As far as the Corps is concerned, the ass *is* a man's soul. Hocquenghem notes that one doesn't shit in company—save within the Corps, where, as *Full Metal Jacket* has it, the very architecture of the head with its facing rows of fully exposed toilets, all religiously maintained, reifies the Corps' claim to every man's ass. This ar-rangement of the head sans privacy is to be appreciated as a thematic and also, I think, an aesthetic determination on the part of Kubrick's film. We might even say that this staging is a theoretical concept, a view of impersonality. The photos that Kubrick's researchers sent back to him in England for set design from the actual Parris Island show side dividers between the toilets, if no front door. But in the movie it's all in the open. "Any social use of the anus, apart from its subli-mated use," posits Hocquenghem, "creates the risk of a loss of identity" (101). Just so, the head that is a hole becomes, in these deprivatizing terms, a transfer point in *Full Metal Jacket* for the disarticulation of the private self into the corpo-rate body, into the Corps: a male body/machine plugged in at the ass.

Where else, then, to stage boot camp's last act but in the head? That set-ting is the film's own idea; it's not taken from Gustav Hasford's harrowing, semiautobiographical novel *The Short-Timers*, *Full Metal Jacket*'s main liter-ary source.[8] There, in the head, Joker, who has drawn patrol duty the night before the platoon's graduation day, discovers Pyle out of his bunk and sitting atop one of these white toilets in his white underwear. Shot in the same blue light as the episode of corporate battery that earlier effected Pyle's technologi-zation, this scene finds him again crooning over his rifle, over "Charlene": "Seven-six-two millimeter, full metal jacket," Pyle spits out. "If Hartman comes in here and catches us," Joker warns, "we'll both be in a world of shit." "I am . . . in a world . . . of shit," Pyle hisses back, as he suddenly snaps to his feet and swings his rifle around his body according to the exacting movements of the Manual of Arms. "What is this Mickey Mouse shit? What in the name of Je-sus H. Christ are you animals doing in my head?" shouts Hartman, likewise in his underwear, as he storms in on the scene. "What is your major malfunc-tion, numbnuts?" he demands of Pyle after Joker has informed him that Pyle's rifle is locked and loaded. Pyle trains on him that famous "Kubrick stare," takes a step back, and blows his commanding officer away, as seen in showy slow motion. Pyle next turns his rifle on Joker, who, the published screenplay indi-cates, is "scared shitless."[9] Whereas Hartman treats Pyle as a machine ("What is your major malfunction?"), Joker attempts to reinvoke the human: "Easy,

Leonard. Go easy, *man*" (my emphasis). Pyle eventually lowers his aim and returns to his seat on the toilet. When he places his rifle in his mouth he fulfills on his own Hartman's "skull-fucking" threat by blowing open a hole through to the back of his head.

"You're so ugly," Hartman had told Pyle on boot camp's first day, "you could be a modern art masterpiece." The colorful insult, which returns us to Chapter 2's concern with the question of (male) taste, predicts this scene's indelible final image: Pyle slumped atop the toilet, mouth open, his blood a red spray against the white, white tiles of the head. A lurid abstract expressionist splatter painting: that might be one "modern art" referent here. Another could be Francis Bacon's *Triptych, May–June 1973*, painted after the suicide of his lover George Dyer, in which a dead male figure likewise collapses on the loo.

Field-Fuck

We have been considering what, in terms of *Full Metal Jacket*, is Marine Corps subjectivity. Let me now ask what here is Marine Corps sexuality? Hartman, whose tour de force tongue-lashing seldom veers from the sexual, accords the recruits both a nascent heterosexuality that is also already past—"Your days of finger-banging old Mary Jane Rottencrotch through her pretty pink panties are over!"—and abiding homosexual inclinations. "Do you suck dicks?" he wants to know from Private Pyle, whose civilian name—Leonard Lawrence—Hartman hears as gay: "Lawrence, what, of Arabia? . . . Only faggots and sailors are called Lawrence!" "Are you a peter-puffer?" he had also just insinuated of another recruit. When Hartman learns that this recruit hails from Texas, he christens him Private Cowboy, determining, "Only steers and queers come from Texas." "I'll bet you're the kind of guy," Hartman further presses Cowboy, "that would fuck a person in the ass and not even have goddam common courtesy to give him a reach-around!" Apparently fraternal manners would require something in return.

Marine fucking marine makes for one of the most memorable scenes in Anthony Swofford's *Jarhead*, his both melancholic and blistering Marine Corps memoir of the first Gulf War. Near the beginning of the book, one of them summons his fellows to a "field-fuck." The field-fuck, explains Swofford, is

> an act wherein marines violate one member of the unit, typically someone who has recently been a jerk or abused rank or acted antisocial, ignoring the unspoken contracts of brotherhood and camaraderie and esprit de corps and the combat family. The victim is held fast in the doggie position and his fellow marines take turns from behind.[10]

This instance devolves from an overheated game of pickup football in the Arabian Desert, with Swofford and his marine jock buddies surreally encased in their MOPP (Mission Oriented Protective Posture) gear and gas masks. Staff Sergeant Siek orders the game to show off to reporters that American fighters in these antichemical-attack outfits "are virtually an unstoppable fighting force." "The Pentagon," writes Swofford, "insists that warriors can fight at 100 percent in full MOPP and gas mask for eight hours. Siek wants us to play ball for an hour" (19).

An overly aggressive tackle on the playing field, however, suddenly turns into a three-way brawl—Kuehn "takes Vann down hard. Vann punches Kuehn in the side of the head, Combs kicks Kuehn in the ass"—which then quickly "degenerates into a laughter-filled dog-pile" involving all the players. "[Staff Sergeant] Siek," Swofford continues, "doesn't like our grab-ass, and he yells at us to resume the game, but we do not listen. He must know what terrible treat will soon be played out for the colonel and the reporters": "Combs pulls Kuehn from the bottom of the pile and yells 'Field-fuck!' Fowler starts the fun, thrusting his hips against Kuehn's ass, slapping the back of his head; when you aren't field-fucking, you're shouting support and encouragement or helping secure Kuehn." "Get that virgin Texas ass! It's free!" someone calls out, taking a page from *Full Metal Jacket* and Hartman's homosexualized hazing of Private Cowboy, another Texan (20–21). Later one marine here teasingly asks of another: "Do you include a reach-around or is it gonna cost me extra?" (110). Life imitates (Kubrick's) art.[11]

As for the field-fuck, everyone takes a turn at Kuehn, the scapegoated member of Swofford's unit who has been selected for "violation" on the desert playing field:

> "I want some of that. I ain't seen boy ass this pretty since Korea."
> "*Semper fi.* Scout-sniper!"
> "Somebody get a picture for his wife. Poor woman."
> Kuehn yells: "I'm the prettiest girl any of you has ever had! I've seen the whores you've bought, you sick bastards!" (21)

Not that Kuehn is really being fucked; one imagines those sealed MOPP suits getting in the way of that. But nothing is left unsaid on this account. *Jarhead's* rendering of the field-fuck comes encased in disavowals of any erotic meaning to what these marines here play at with one of their own. "This is fun, plain mindless fun, the kind grunts are best at," Swofford declares, setting the stage for what is to come, "with guys fighting their way from the bottom to climb back to the top, king of the pile, king of the Desert" (20). Afterward he reflects, "I stand back from a turn with Kuehn. I feel frightened and exhilarated by the scene. The exhilaration isn't sexual, it's communal—a pure surge of passion and violence and shared anger, a pure distillation of our confusion and hope and shared fear" (21).

"The exhilaration isn't sexual." But what does it mean to use the sexual—sexual language, sexual theatrics—to express what isn't sexual? This is a question not just for *Jarhead* but for *Full Metal Jacket* as well. Then again, we might also consider what counts *as sex*, which need not be confined to just "doing it." With respect to the scene in *Jarhead*, another way to reformulate the sexual "versus" nonsexual question is to consider how the nonsexual can come across as so sexy. "We're all in great shape," Swofford interjects here, this after relaying the enticing detail that on the makeshift desert football field there are "those of us, like me [perhaps Kuehn too?] who . . . go naked beneath" their MOPP suits (18).

The chief meaning that Swofford draws out of "the pure surge of passion and violence" of the field-fuck isn't sex, but "shared anger," pent-up youthful male group rage: "We aren't field-fucking Kuehn: we're fucking the press-pool colonel, and the sorry, worthless MOPP suits, and the goddamn gas masks and canteens with defective parts, and President Bush and Dick Cheney and the generals, and Saddam Hussein . . . we're fucking the world's televisions, and CNN." The marines' anger here and throughout Swofford's book is palpable (and irrefutable). But this expression of anger modulates into *Jarhead*'s most ecstatic passage: "We continue to scream, in joy, in revelry, still wearing full MOPP and gas mask . . . and we sound thousands of miles away from ourselves." It is also one in which Swofford keeps writing the sexual, as well as a bittersweet note of male-male seduction, back into the scene he is unfolding, even as he has taken pains to keep it out:

> We're fucking the sand and the loneliness and the boredom and the
> potentially unfaithful wives and girlfriends . . . ; we're fucking our
> confusion and fear and boredom; we're fucking ourselves for signing
> the contract, for listening to the soothing lies of recruiters, for letting
> them call us buddy and pal and dude, luring us into this life of
> loneliness and boredom and fear; we're fucking all of the hometown
> girls we've wanted but never had; we're angry and afraid and acting the
> way we've been trained to kill, violently and with no remorse. (21–22)

Of course, no one is killed in this scene, and no one (presumably) gets off. Swofford's rhythmically insistent, concatenated prose, like the *ad seriatim* all-male gangbang it renders and then explicates for us, is not pointed toward climax. Rather, it culminates in a reaffirmation of Marine Corps fidelity familiar to us from *Full Metal Jacket*, an avowal of the bonds of something that also sounds like marriage: "We take turns, and we go through the line a few times and Kuehn takes it all, like the thick, rough Texan he is, our emissary to the gallows, to the chambers, to death do us part." By then, the field-fuck has stopped; it has made its point. *Semper fi.* And the marines are now stripping out of their MOPP suits and gas masks: "We're bent over at the waist, hands on knees, either naked or in skivvy bottoms" (22). This early chapter of *Jarhead* begins not on or even near the desert playing field, but back in California with Swofford working out at the base gym, "lifting a few hundred pounds over my chest" (9). The "field-fuck" section of it, which ends with naked marines in the Saudi desert, has Swofford staring at his muscular "forearms as though they are a map" (23). *Arma virumque cano.*

Swofford's *Jarhead* was made into a 2005 film directed by Sam Mendes. Whereas in the book the marines' sexual horseplay has a single designated target or "bottom"—"the thick, rough Texan," Kuehn—the movie depicts them all taking turns before and behind each other, as well as giving and receiving "head." This recasting of the field-fuck has the effect, even as it multiplies the sexual acts and roles on display, of diffusing the concentrated eroticism of the scene as it is rendered in the book. The film, too, seems to understand how sexy the spectacle of men playing at male sex can look, and this, I think, is the way it means to say that this scene is not about sex. That is, the film endeavors to defuse the charge that there's anything sexual going on here by circulating the scene's homoeroticism equally among the marines. (They can't all be gay, right?) Also notable is how at the very end of it the buff Jake Gyllenhaal, who plays Swofford, hollers out to the fleeing female reporter, "Come back soon, lady!"—a solicitation not in the book that ends the scene in the movie on a catcalling heterosexual note.

"This Is for Fighting! This Is for Fun!"

We don't ever see the marines of *Full Metal Jacket* alone with a woman. Instead, boot camp buddies Joker and Cowboy talk dirty to each other . . . about Cowboy's sister, who of course is never here to appear, or to be spoken of again. Joker: "I want to slip my tubesteak into your sister. What'll you take in trade?" Cowboy: "What have you got?" Nor is it a surprise that this exchange between marines transpires in the head, where Joker and Cowboy, in their skivvies and with mops in hand, are once again found doing duty (Figure 44). Even when the movie leaves behind the cloistered all-male world of Parris Island, heterosexual expression continues to operate (classically, we might say) as a means toward intensifying male affiliation. This is apparent in the two interrelated vignettes structured around the appearance of Vietnamese prostitutes. The first of them—and the scene that opens the Vietnam installment of the

Figure 44. "The head."

movie—features a streetwalker (Papillon Soo Soo) who makes her entrance in a black leather miniskirt to the tune of Nancy Sinatra's 1966 hit "These Boots are Made for Walking." The song's coltish sadism ("these boots are going to walk all over you") serves as a hinge between boot camp and Vietnam in *Full Metal Jacket*'s semi-detachable, two-paneled narrative. "You've been messin' where you shouldn't have been messin'," Nancy chastises, as if one needed a reminder of the mess left behind in the head in the previous scene, before the film fades to black and then starts over again in Vietnam. Shot from behind, the streetwalker sashays her high-heeled way toward Joker and Rafterman, who are seated at an outdoor café in Da Nang. "You got girlfriend in Vietnam? Me so horny. You party?" she asks, and they start haggling over what it would cost to share her. "Fifteen dollar too boo-coo [beaucoup]," Joker replies.

The second such scene, which takes place in Hue, likewise features a single prostitute, though she is on offer to an entire squad of marines: the Lusthog Squad—"life-takers and heartbreakers"—with Joker and Rafterman now in their number. When she shows up, Joker, copping a line from the first hooker, blurts out, "I'm so horny that I can't even get a piece of hand." Joker's remark also points back to the Lusthog nicknamed "Hand Job" (Marcus D'Amico), who, his fellows report, couldn't keep his hands off himself, even in the waiting room of "the Navy head shrinker." Just before Hand Job is about to be sent home on a Section Eight, he's killed during the film's brief first firefight. The second prostitute—this film's doubling take on "the one woman in a world of men" scenario we find over and over again in Kubrick's movies—shows up a few scenes after Hand Job's death. The Lusthogs repeat the same bartering rite while slumped on a row of theater seats, hauled out of a wrecked Vietnamese cinema that had been showing *The Lone Ranger*, its signage brandishing Hollywood "redskins" on the warpath.

This is a place to raise and address the question of Kubrick and the western, a genre referenced at the end of *Dr. Strangelove* in Major Kong's backward mechanical bull ride on the bomb, whooping and wildly waving his cowboy hat all the way down—a Slim Pickens mini-western as apocalypse now. Like the war film to which it has ties, the western is a classic among men's films and commands a central place in the oeuvre of other men's film auteurs, most notably Clint Eastwood. One answer to where is Kubrick's western is that it's here, inside *Full Metal Jacket*, insofar as these marines cast their own war movie within the war movie as a put-on western. In it, the muscly Animal Mother (Adam Baldwin), the unruliest of the Lusthogs, takes the role of "a rabid buffalo," while Crazy Earl (Kieron Jecchinis) says he'll be General Custer. "Who will play the Indians?" asks Rafterman. "Well, we'll let the gooks play the Indians," Animal Mother determines.

Joker instigates, but also ironizes, this kind of movie talk when at the scene's start he parodically assumes the John Wayne role. "Is that you, John Wayne? Is this me?" Joker dissociatively asks himself, reprising his very first words in the film from back at boot camp, mimicking the deep drawl of that macho Hollywood gunslinger, that jingoistic Green Beret cowboy. *Full Metal Jacket* renders the "westernization" of the Vietnam War, with its transplanted American imperialism and triumphalism, as both misplaced and depleted. That recognition is emblematized within the film itself by the wrecked movie palace that is still promoting but no longer able to show *The Lone Ranger*. It is also encoded in the peculiar terms by which the character known as Cowboy (whom Joker playfully at one point addresses as "Lone Ranger") expresses to an American TV reporter his own sense of not belonging here. "I hate Vietnam. There's not one horse in this whole country. . . . There's something basically wrong with that." In Hasford's novel, Joker has his reunion with Cowboy and is introduced to the Lusthogs at a movie theater showing John Wayne's own Vietnam film, *The Green Berets* (1968): "the funniest movie," reports Joker, "we have seen in a long time" (32).

Let us return now to the second prostitute scene's own movie-house setting: one of many markers, along with the appearance of a TV crew to interview the marines and the cameras that both Rafterman and Joker wear into battle, of the filmic self-reflexivity with which Kubrick loads the Vietnam portion of *Full Metal Jacket*. Consider first how the literal homosocial theater created here provides a stage for a flush of male-to-male affectations and displays, much of this racially inflected. As the scene unfolds its center of attention shifts away from the girl on offer, first to Eightball (Dorian Harewood), one of the two Black Lusthogs, and then to a dispute over the girl between Eightball and his friend Animal Mother, who is white. Eightball takes center stage when the prostitute's ARVN pimp informs him that she "no boom-boom with soul brotha" because they're "too boo-coo, too boo-coo." To a chorus of jocular acclamation from the other marines, Eightball, his back now turned to the camera, opens up his pants to show the girl that "what we have here, little yellow sister, is a magnificent . . . specimen of pure Alabama black snake. But it ain't too goddam boo-coo." As a Vietnam War film, *Full Metal Jacket* features more Black men than any other of Kubrick's films. This scene activates and then defuses a racialized hypermasculine fantasy/anxiety about male "too-much-ness" by saddling the Black marine who has the largest part in the film with that phallic exorbitance and at the same time denying it to him. The way Eightball himself addresses the prostitute also cuts two ways, claiming affiliation with her ("little . . . sister"), while underlining her racial difference ("little *yellow* sister").

After sizing him up, the prostitute agrees to have sex with Eightball, along with his fellows; but before he can haul her away, Animal Mother challenges him, claiming for himself the leadoff position in the sexual "batting order," as another marine puts it. "Back off, white bread," retorts Eightball. With Animal Mother and Eightball each laying hold of her, this "little yellow sister" is literally between men, between marines, one Black, one white, in what amounts to the scene's climax. By introducing us to Vietnam through an encounter with a young streetwalker, and then replaying that scene over again with another, even younger prostitute later in the narrative, when the marines are deeper "in the shit," *Full Metal Jacket* makes Vietnam, as Thomas Doherty recognizes, both battleground and playground for the Americans.[12] But what these marines play at there—contiguous with the homophobic homoeroticism of boot camp—is an intensified homosocial heterosexuality: a heterosexuality whose libidinal circuits appear to be switched on only collectively, with hypersexualized racial difference here part of the jolt.

The night back in boot camp when the recruits go to bed with their rifles, Hartman tells them that "this is the only pussy you people are going to get." Despite the apparent ready availability of sex for hire in Vietnam, this dictum ramifies beyond the deprivation culture of boot camp to remain true for the entire movie. Joker and Rafterman's dealings with the streetwalker are abruptly aborted when, after Rafterman has snapped some shots of Joker and her together, a passing Vietnamese street punk yanks his Nikon from his hands. Before he speeds away on a motorbike, the boy (in the words of the screenplay) "executes a few Bruce Lee moves": another meta-cinematic touch that is also an assertion of an aggressively counter, "foreign" masculinity. While Joker smilingly rolls with punches and offers his own copycat karate moves, Rafterman afterward complains, "We're supposed to be helping them, and they shit all over us every chance they get." Similarly, the restaging of a prostitute encounter in front of the movie house ends when Animal Mother yanks the young girl away from Eightball and pushes her inside the bombed-out building. That is, the sex scene is over, as far as the film is concerned, when the marine exits the makeshift homosocial theater with its audience of other marines.[13]

As the only "pussy" we ever see these marines get, the rifle serves as a switch point in Marine Corps erotics. It is also by means of the rifle that the recruits are able to move through and out of the state of abject effeminization into which they are cast at the beginning of recruit training. Yet if mastery of one's rifle brings with it a new, retooled manhood, how is the tool itself figuratively gendered and eroticized? The marines, we saw, give female names to their rifles and are told to regard themselves as being faithfully married to "this weapon of iron and wood." "Mount!" Hartman directs them as they take to their bunks, rifles in hand over their chests. Then he orders them to "Pray!" They recite in unison the Rifleman's Creed: "This is my rifle. There are many like it, but this one is mine. . . ." This image of marines prayerfully bedding down with their mechanical brides is closely followed by another, equally gripping scene in which Hartman leads his men in marching around the squad bay in T-shirts and boxer shorts. Toting their rifles in one hand and hefting their crotches with the other, they chant in cadence: "This is my rifle! This is my gun! This is for fighting! This is for fun!" (Figure 45). This group rite of passage, which Carol Burke nicely terms "a form of collective autoeroticism,"[14] at once associates and dissociates the rifle and the male member (along with fighting and fun, death and sex). The marine's weapon is a machinic icon of phallic masculinity here named and embraced as a girl. Queerly functioned as both phallus and pussy, the rifle is the engine for an erotics that can't be said to be either homo or hetero—and to which the marine must be utterly faithful.

So despite all the boot camp talk of male cock-sucking, or the film's anal fixation (which outlasts boot camp), I am not suggesting homosexuality or even homoeroticism as the real content of *Full Metal Jacket*'s romance of men and the Corps. (Nor does it seem to me that the exhilarating "fuck you

Figure 45. "This is for fighting, this is for fun."

all" field-fuck of Swofford's *Jarhead* is really about releasing pent-up repressed homosexual desire.) More interesting, I think, is how becoming a marine, structured here as a repudiation of what counts as normal male desire—"I don't want no teenage queen. I just want my M-14," goes another of Hartman's doggerel chants—entails what seems like its own antihumanist sexuality. Think of it this way for a moment. There's homosexuality. Heterosexuality. Bisexuality. And then there's Marine Corps sexuality, which is not exactly straight or figuratively "bi" either, and certainly not normative. I frame it this way heuristically of course, there being more sexualities than these few—potentially no end of them, given how very different people, and also people in groups, may be from each other.[15]

Most of the work on *Full Metal Jacket* by feminist film critics emphasizes the usual male/female opposition: specifically, how abjection and then violent rejection of the female and femaleness is at the heart of the film's shaping of martial male subjectivity. Susan Jeffords puts that point succinctly in *The Remasculinization of America: Gender and the Vietnam War*: "*Full Metal Jacket* [is] a firm delineation of gender boundaries and reinstatement of the masculine in opposition to a feminine enemy."[16] There are aspects of Kubrick's movie that can be read that way; perhaps a feminist approach is rightly bound to read it that way.[17] And the movie's end will have the Lusthog Squad faceoff with a deadly enemy sniper who turns out to be female. We will return to the overwhelming irony of that denouement shortly. But let us here first register that most of the violence in *Full Metal Jacket*, physical as well as psychical, is male-on-male. Related to this point (an obvious one), though not necessarily following from it, is that the most indicative opposition in the film isn't between "maleness" and "femaleness," much less between men and women. It's rather—and we have seen this throughout Kubrick, though here the expression is more extreme and also more violent—*an opposition between kinds of masculinity*. Coextensive with what I have been suggesting about marine sexuality as its own thing, the Corps' version of hypermasculinity is not so much the development and further intensification of whatever sense or expression of being or acting male that the recruits bring with them to boot camp, but rather a radical alternative to it.

This new form of Marine Corps gendering notably maintains, as we have also seen, an intimate figural relation to the female, indeed the matriarchal. Hartman's hazing of the recruits as "ladies" may recede over the course of their boot camp training to be replaced on graduation day by a new discourse of fraternity. But that brotherhood also goes by the name of "Mother Green and her killing machine," as one of the marines proudly invokes his beloved Corps. This loaded marine moniker, coined in Vietnam during the Vietnam War, reinscribes something female into the hypermasculine, which, in a perverse loop, always seems to double back around to what it so hyperbolically appears to want to leave behind. The most fearsome marine in the world of the film, draped in cartridge belts and wielding an enormous machine gun, thus bears the name Animal Mother.[18]

Conformity to the Corps' own version of masculinity entails other kinds of deviations. Consider the mode in which the film's marines come to think about and inhabit their rebuilt, reconceived bodies. The aim all along has been to fashion the self into a state of indomitable hardness. "A hard heart is what allows you to kill," teaches Hartman, the hardest man of all ("Because I am hard, you will not like me!")—until he isn't, until Private Pyle, his greatest transformational success, puts a bullet in him. "I'm Hard" is also inscribed on the helmet of one of the marines we encounter in Vietnam. The movie's title *Full Metal Jacket*—which refers to a special kind of bullet, with a softer core encased in the shell of a harder metal so that it won't disintegrate upon impact—names both what the marine wields and what he would himself become.[19] Yet as hard as they are conditioned to be, these weaponized men remain pliant, open, vulnerable. On this account, recall Hartman's unrelenting threats about penetrating his charges through any of their available orifices, or of tearing open new ones. And it isn't only the hardened drill sergeant. Animal Mother menaces Joker upon first meeting him in the same terms: "I'm gonna tear you a new asshole." Remember, too, how the most affectively charged relations among these marines, affirmative as well as aversive, cluster around sites and figures of anality. One might say, then, that the film's structuring interest becomes the penetrability of the especially hardened male body, that being the basis of desubjectification and with it, interestingly, the very stuff ("Oh, don't shit me, Joker! Don't shit me!") of male communal love. This, I take it, is part of the movie's queer seduction, a matter to which we will return at the end of this chapter.

When Kubrick's Vietnam War film finally arrives at the battlefield, it moves quickly to pare down the war into a protracted, micro-confrontation in Hue. A sole Vietnamese sniper, staked out in the smoldering ruins of a building, proficiently picks apart a squad of marines. Looking to retrieve their wounded, they are lured one by one into the open. There this sharpshooter's bullets— aimed to wound, not yet to kill—pierce their soft flesh in a slow motion explosion of spurting blood and wrenching agony.[20] After several of their number go down in this fashion, including both their squad leader and then Cowboy, his next-in-command, the Lusthogs, now essentially leaderless and utterly disorganized, storm the building looking for "payback." Once inside, Joker comes upon the sniper, who, in another stunning slo-mo shot, is revealed to be a young girl with pigtail braids and an AK-47 rifle. In Hasford's novel as well as the screenplay, she is described as "a slender Eurasian angel": an angel of death, the revenging revenant of colonized Vietnam.[21]

Just before she is about to blow away Joker, the sniper is felled by a burst of gunfire from Rafterman's M-16. "I saved Joker's ass. I got the sniper," the photographer-rifleman exults, kissing his weapon. The Lusthog Squad encircles the mortally wounded girl, who lies heaving at their feet. "What's she saying?" one of them asks. "She's praying," replies Joker, as the film brings back the religious strain gone missing since boot camp. "No more boom-boom for this baby-san," declares another marine; "She's dead meat." "Sh . . . sh-shoot . . . me. Shoot . . . me," the sniper (Ngoc Le) starts pleading in English. Insisting that they can't leave her like this, Joker finally takes out his handgun (compare his earlier jokey remark that he's "so horny that [he] can't even get a piece of hand") and kills her—or "wastes" her, as Animal Mother puts it in the film's excremental rhetoric. While the valences of Joker's deed are ethically uncertain, perhaps undecidable—what began as a desire for battlefield revenge ends with a mercy killing that feels like an execution—the scene's visual layout evokes a gang rape. "Hard core, man. Fucking hard core," one of the men pronounces over the girl's prone body. His epitaph casts this the third of the film's group-sex scenes, and the only one for the marines, trained from boot camp to eroticize death—"Get some! Get some!" here means shoot, kill—to achieve some form of consummation.[22]

"This Is Vietnam, the Movie"

The urban setting of the sniper sequence, *Full Metal Jacket*'s action climax, adds further layers to the film's revisionism. Back in 1979, *Apocalypse Now* established the deep, deep heart-of-darkness jungle as the topos for the Vietnam War movie. Kubrick's version distances itself from the verdant mythopoeticism of Coppola's trippy, mystical epic, as well as the in-the-field naturalism of Oliver Stone's *Platoon* (1986), by relocating the combat zone to a concrete jungle of rubble-strewn, booby-trapped city streets and bomb-scarred buildings on fire.[23] Rainforest green and midnight black give way to industrial grey and a chemically orange-red. For Kubrick's vision also differs from most Vietnam films in delivering a stark daytime view of war. We see everything. The horror, the horror. Kubrick said that he was after "a newsreel effect."[24] This documentary image of combat as street-to-street fighting remains familiar to us from media coverage of America's twenty-first-century wars in Iraq and Afghanistan, along with the movies to come out of those long wars, including Kathryn Bigelow's *The Hurt Locker* (2008).

I single out *The Hurt Locker* here not only because aspects of *Full Metal Jacket* subtend Bigelow's Baghdad film in its look and temperament but also because, as I indicated in the Introduction, Bigelow herself might be thought of as another auteur—a formidable one—of the men's picture. Like Kubrick, she is a genre filmmaker who seems especially drawn to "male" genres, even though Bigelow sometimes makes versions of them that feature a female main character in the male role. Consider her follow-up to *The Hurt Locker, Zero Dark Thirty* (2012), billed as "the greatest manhunt ever." It stars Jessica Chastain as a relentlessly driven CIA agent who is in certain respects one of the guys, which here includes the macho Navy SEALS. Or, from earlier in Bigelow's career, the crime film *Blue Steel* (1990), in which Jamie Lee Curtis in short cropped hair plays a rookie cop who is really into her gun. So is Bigelow's camera. This film's credit sequence is pure gun porn, full metal jacket.

Bigelow's filmography also ticks off other "male" genres. Her 1981 feature debut, *The Loveless*, is an arty male gang film, where the fetish object this time is (Kenneth Anger–like) the motorcycle. Bigelow's *Near Dark* (1987) crosses horror with the western. Her sports/heist film *Point Break* (1991) helped launch Keanu Reeves's career as an action star. It also alludes, I think, to Kubrick's great heist movie, *The Killing*, in the form of the rubber masks worn by its male pack of thieves ("Too much testosterone," says the one woman in this film's world of men), as well as a brief shot of fluttering greenbacks. Bigelow's *Strange Days* (1995) is a sleazy, noir-ish science fiction film about men and their pornographic tech toys, which also features a muscular Angela Bassett as a fierce driver/bodyguard. *K-19: The Widowmaker* (2002) is Bigelow's first movie with a military setting: a Cold War historical action thriller about a Russian submarine armed with nuclear warheads. Things go very wrong and suddenly (*Strangelove* redivivus) there is a risk of a retaliatory U.S. strike and possibly nuclear war.

But it isn't only for her taste in genres and situations that I bring up Bigelow here. There are also all kinds of contact points—imagistic and especially thematic—between Bigelow's predominating interests and what we have been exploring in Kubrick: kinky sex and intense violence, for sure—but also an attention to weapons, uniforms, and machines touching on fetishism; a probing of stressed-out male roles and relations, including their homoerotic undertow; and an interest in male pain and suffering (though Bigelow's men don't cry the way that Kubrick's men do). Of course, there are other important differences between Kubrick and Bigelow as men's film filmmakers. Bigelow is engaged with the action movie in a way that the director of *Barry Lyndon* never was. And with respect to works like *Blue Steel* (where the protagonist's father complains, "I've got a cop for a daughter"), *Zero Dark Thirty*, and to some extent *Strange Days*, one could also, or instead, say that Bigelow is a new kind of women's picture filmmaker—that is, one more informed by men's films than the classic domestic women's films that originally gave us this gendered conception of genre.

Vietnam, it is often said, was the first fully televised war. This historical recognition is built into Kubrick's film by way of two scenes in which the Lusthog Squad is filmed for a television documentary. "Start the cameras. This is 'Vietnam, the Movie!'" Cowboy, playing actor-director, calls out during the first of these metascenes. Ducking low, a centipedal camera and sound crew weaves sideways, panning across Joker, Cowboy, and a long line of marines hunkered down behind a concrete barrier. This is the scene I touched on earlier during which the Lusthogs cast themselves in "Vietnam—the western." Herr remembers this addition to the screenplay as wholly Kubrick's idea.[25] The low-angle, traveling shot of the film crew shooting the marines diegetically inscribes one of Kubrick's visual signatures right into the story. Coppola gave himself a cameo in *Apocalypse Now* as a frenetic TV journalist trying to get a realistic shot: "Don't look at the camera! Just go by like you're fighting. . . . *This is for television!*" The first several times I saw *Full Metal Jacket* I'd think for a moment that Kubrick had here done the same thing, that the unkempt, dark-haired cameraman in the green fatigue jacket with lots of pockets in it, first seen from behind, was the director himself. Not quite. He turns out instead to be his Steadicam operator, John Ward.

Kubrick prepared to make his Vietnam War movie the way that he prepared to make his never-to-be made Napoleon film: reading, studying, and watching. He accumulated a massive amount of documentation on the war—all kinds of books (memoirs, manuals, novels, encyclopedias) and articles, as well as troves of photographs, which Kubrick marked up by hand to highlight interesting details. And he viewed hundreds of hours of documentary film and TV news footage. This extensive research archive, especially the photographs, informed the astonishing fabrication he oversaw of an urban Vietnamese war zone outside of London on the bank of the Thames. There, in Beckton, Kubrick had found a derelict gas works, spread out over a square mile, already slated for demolition. "The architecture," he recounts, "was perfect—thirties industrial functionalism."[26] His designer Anton Furst spent weeks artistically punching holes in buildings with a wrecking ball and then adding some Vietnamese architectural elements to the ruins. When hundreds of real palm trees from Spain and thousands of artificial tropical plants from Hong Kong were imported to this reformatted East London factory site, Kubrick had his stunning cinematic simulation of Hue City after the Tet offensive.[27]

Kubrick's highly mediated Vietnam War film, constructed out of books and photos and full of cameras, not only replaces the jungle with an urban theater of war. The setting for *Full Metal Jacket*'s culminating battle is also (to use Kubrick's term) "industrial." We might think of this sequence as the movie sending its marines, whose minting it had so analytically regarded on Parris Island, back to the factory. And there, despite the eventual taking out of the sniper, much of what boot camp built them to be dramatically falls apart. The purchase on the rigors of recruit training, with its assault on the structures of male selfhood, including the extreme pressure points of gender and sexuality, was to be the production of a more finely tuned and controlled—thus more powerful—fighting force. Their systematic depersonalization allows for the recruits to be subsumed into the Corps, a corporal killing machine whose efficient force outweighs the sum of its parts. "Marines die. That's what we're here for! But the Marine Corps lives forever. And that means *you* live forever!" Hartman promised. You live forever because you're no longer really you; you're a marine, you're a cog in the Corps. And it goes on forever because the cogs the Corps mass-produces are ever replaceable. Throw the marines, famously "the first to fight," into the worst of the conflict and expect heavy casualties. More marines are always there, next in line, to take the place of the fallen. "The Corps came to be called by many," Herr grimly observes in *Dispatches*, "the finest instrument ever devised for the killing of young Americans."[28] (Here, then, is a second sense of the Marine Corps as a killing machine.)

This principle of disposability is reflected in how the film so indifferently treats its characters, swapping nearly every one of the newly made marines from its first act in boot camp for new, though equally generic ones in its second act over in Vietnam. As we have noted, the only exceptions are Joker (here to provide sporadic voiceover musings) and Cowboy (here to be sacrificed in act two). Even they come without any kind of backstory that would further personalize them. Kubrick said that one of the things that drew him to Hasford's *The Short-Timers* in the first place was how "all of the 'mandatory' scenes, explaining who everybody is—that this guy had a drunken father and that that guy's wife is a . . . —are left out."[29] That exclusion also works to cut back *Full Metal Jacket*'s melodramatic quotient to next to nil, something that further sets it apart from *Apocalypse Now*, *Platoon*, and especially that other great Vietnam War movie, yet to be mentioned here, Michael Cimino's operatic *The Deer Hunter* (1978)—but also from Kubrick's own previous war films.

Male sentiment is the clotted air that the war film breathes and heaves. I have been advancing a view that each of Kubrick's war films is an experiment in its own way with the form. Part of the experiment of *Full Metal Jacket* is its formal refusal of sentiment, and with it the tug of melodrama and any attendant emotional release. Ever so briefly the movie brushes up against the sentimental in Cowboy's death scene. But his buddy Joker, unlike so many of Kubrick's men, holds back the tears. And there is nothing at all of this sort back on the assembly line of Parris Island. The "malfunctioning" Pyle blows Hartman away just when the drill sergeant tries to turn this fatal final scene in the head into a personal family drama. "Didn't Mommy and Daddy show you enough attention when you were a child?" he roars, aiming to put the adult-baby Pyle back in his place by pinning on him some kind of legible psychobiography. Pyle's automatized murder-suicide instantly silences such talk.

Nearly all that we know about the marines of *Full Metal Jacket* comes from the dehumanizing drill of boot camp, or what they do once they are let loose in the field as trained killers. Their only story is this story. We might say that they are just marines and only minimally characters, much less versions of supposed real people. Indeed, we know these "jolly green giants, walking the Earth with guns" (more of the movie's grunt-speak) solely by the rebaptized Marine Corps names they are all given. There is an exception, though it's one that reinforces this view. Again that would be Pyle, who utters his civilian name, Leonard. But this recruit—the one Hartman accuses of "want[ing] to be different"—doesn't make it out of boot camp. He is also, incidentally, the only one to cry here, this after the brutalizing "blanket party" the platoon throws for him. Otherwise, *Full Metal Jacket* keeps the male tears to a minimum, rare for a Kubrick film.

The sequence of interviews with the Lusthogs—the second part of "Vietnam, the movie" within the movie—does render some gestural character-delineating strokes. Here the marines talk directly to the camera, offering in turn their own sound-bite opinions on questions like America's involvement in the war. ("Do I think America belongs in Vietnam? Um . . . I don't know. *I* belong in Vietnam. I'll tell you that," reports one.) But by this point we already know that this war film hardly depends on—and doesn't even seem much interested in—who its fighting men are, if by that one means their individual psychologies or personal histories.[30] The quick succession of these one-man talking pictures, with the film crew's camera and boom mike protruding into the frame, recalls the male portraiture of *Full Metal Jacket*'s opening sequence in the barracks barbershop, likewise shot in medium close-up, which begins with a jar-head haircut the Corps' process of deindividuation.

Kubrick's determination to cast *Full Metal Jacket* with relative unknowns (apart from Modine) also bears on this point. This stands in contrast to all his films from *The Killing* back in 1956 onward. Here there is no towering, taciturn Sterling Hayden. No earnest, firebrand, chest-baring Kirk Douglas. No dueling Shakespeareans the likes of Olivier, Laughton, and Ustinov. No sly, metamorphic Peter Sellers or blustery George C. Scott. No handsome, blue-eyed, blank-faced Ryan O'Neal. No always already possessed Jack Nicholson. No earnest man-boy Tom Cruise. Lacking in star power and star turns, Kubrick's Vietnam War/Marine Corps movie is a Fordist male ensemble film.[31]

It's a different story, however, once the film's marines come under fire. The Lusthogs stumble into the sniper's shooting gallery in the first place because they have misread the map and bypassed their checkpoint. They also wildly misidentify this lone sniper for a larger enemy force. Their desperate calls for reinforcement, then rescue, in the form of a tank go unheeded. More deleterious still is the insubordination, the utter breakdown in command that almost immediately follows these mistakes, resulting in suicidally ineffective individual heroics and further casualties. "Stand down, Mother! That's a direct order!" yells Cowboy, as he tries to hold together the squad over which he has now, if only momentarily, assumed command. "Fuck you, Cowboy! Fuck all you assholes," says Animal Mother, as he leads the rest of the Lusthogs in breaking rank and Cowboy to his death. That *Full Metal Jacket* depicts Mother Green and her killing machine as so disordered and vulnerable in the encounter with a single enemy gunman makes the film a demystification and a critique of the mechanistic system with which it is so clearly fascinated. That this sure-shot enemy gunman is female—a stunning redeployment against these marines of Hartman's order to give their weapons a girl's name—puts gender at the core of such a critique. And this is so in ways that a simplistic sense of the movie's masculinism isn't, I'd say, very well positioned to engage. For what does it mean that a teenage female sniper turns out to be a better marksman and a more efficient killer than any of these marines? "I don't want no teenage queen. I just want my M-14," Hartman has his men chanting in cadence in boot camp. But in the field Joker's rifle jams, and he is nearly killed by a girl. Think of her as the return with a vengeance, here in the last of Kubrick's war films, of that one woman in a world of men trope we have been tracking throughout them.

In *Full Metal Jacket*'s closing scene, Joker has rejoined his platoon, marching in formation through Hue as it burns. "We hump down to the Perfume River to set in for the night," he relays in his final voiceover, as his own thoughts "drift back to erect nipple wet dreams about Mary Jane Rottencrotch and the Great Homecoming Fuck Fantasy." Joker's homecoming fantasy anticipates the "F-word" ending of the Kubrick film that follows this one, Kubrick's last. But Joker's is the raunchy, male adolescent version of what the beautiful, knowing wife in *Eyes Wide Shut* deems she and her chastened wayward husband must do as soon as they make it home. When Alice utters "Fuck" she and Bill are in, of all places, a kids' toy store. Joker's pornographic reverie is likewise juxtaposed against his platoon's juvenilizing rendition of the Mickey Mouse Club song: a regressive, haunted reprise of the "Mickey Mouse shit" that went on in the head as boot camp comes to its end. "I'm in a world of shit . . . yes. But I am alive," Joker concludes, while the marines intone: "Come along and sing this song and join our family." The film fades out again, just as it did after that messy scene in the head, and the Mouseketeer theme song gives way, as its final note, to another anthem, a bad boy one: the Rolling Stones' anti-redemptive "Paint It Black."[32]

This final scene, with its wet dreams, returns us to the question of arousal, which subtends all of Kubrick's war and military films. "Sing this song and join our family": is this the film's embedded acknowledgment that it is also a form of enticement, a come-on? That reportedly was the director (and World War II infantryman) Samuel Fuller's view. He felt that teenage boys would leave Kubrick's movie thinking that all this was cool.[33] Versions of that response are registered here and there in the self-professed marine-chaser Steven Zeeland's contemplation of *The Masculine Marine*, a connoisseurial assemblage of cultural analysis, "true confessions" sex stories, some military beefcake snapshots, and unexpectedly poignant interviews with current and former marines.

"Did you join the Marines to be a man?" Zeeland here questions "First Lieutenant Frank." "Yeah. Very much so," the lieutenant responds. "I was seventeen when I signed up. And away I went to Parris Island." "Was it like the movie?" Zeeland asks. "There is no truth in advertising. It was not like that goddamned film!"[34] (Note that in this exchange "*the* movie" need not even be named.) My own sense, anecdotally derived over the years and confirmed by the acute disappointment of this particular marine recruit, is that *Full Metal Jacket* has itself taken on the status of a fetish object, a talisman of extreme male experience and bonds. This may be nowhere more so (at least as Zeeland's book has it) than among marines, notwithstanding ever-ongoing official reforms intended to make the experience of recruit training more humane, and, as such, evidently less gratifying to some recruits. "Were you ever physically struck?" Zeeland asks another marine, "Corporal Jack." "No. Like I was talking to you earlier about *Full Metal Jacket*—I kind of wish it was more like that" (173).

This is Kubrick's "Vietnam—the movie" as military recruiting film, yet another kind of men's film. Swofford, who introduces himself in *Jarhead* as "a young man raised on the films of the Vietnam War" (7), works out this reception of *Full Metal Jacket* to its end: a ghastly, though lyrically rendered, epiphany. Vietnam War films, determines Swofford, "are all pro-war, no matter what the supposed message, no matter what Kubrick or Coppola or Stone intended." Some "Mr. and Mrs. Johnson in Omaha or San Francisco or Manhattan," he continues, "will watch the films and weep and decide once and for all that war is inhumane and terrible." But not "Corporal Johnson at Camp Pendleton and Sergeant Johnson at Travis Air Force Base and Seaman Johnson at Coronado Naval Station and Spec 4 Johnson at Fort Bragg and Lance Corporal Swofford at Twentynine Palms Marine Corps Base." They "watch the same films and are excited by them, because the magic brutality of the films celebrates the terrible and despicable beauty of their fighting skills." "Filmic images of death and carnage," Swofford concludes, are "pornography for the military man; with film you are stroking his cock, tickling his balls with the pink feather of history, getting him ready for his real First Fuck" (6–7). (So much for just "finger-banging old Mary Jane Rottencrotch through her pretty pink panties.") Swofford's platoon, on standby for their deployment in Operation Desert Storm, stages its own motivational "Vietnam War Film Fest," which of course features Kubrick (9). Swofford recounts how these aroused young men would rewind and replay the subgenre's signal scenes again and again: from the Wagner-propelled helicopter gunships blowing away a Vietnamese village in *Apocalypse Now* to the "me so horny" streetwalker scene in *Full Metal Jacket* (6).

This investiture of allure and inspiration into "*the* movie," into *Full Metal Jacket*, can't simply be dismissed as some jarhead's vacant misrecognition of what is meant to be analysis and critique for (false) advertisement (Zeeland's "First Lieutenant Frank" and "Corporal Jack") or a turn-on ("Lance Corporal Swofford"). What these various marines implicitly grasp is that Kubrick's anatomy of the Corps, for all the pain and bloodshed, is itself an indulgence in the potent pleasures of both the war machine and the war movie. So much so that *Full Metal Jacket* dials it all the way back, before the rocket's red glare and the other excitements of battle, to the very beginning in boot camp, to the metamorphic processes by which the nervous boy next door is made into that hardened (yet still vulnerable) killer, the marine.

Swofford finds that Vietnam War films, including this one, function as porn for the lusty young warriors of *Jarhead*. It's not only them. Kubrick's movie can also be quite stimulating for an aficionado of what I have been treating here as the men's film. "There is more to say about war," Kubrick remarked in an interview when *Full Metal Jacket* came out in 1987, "than it is just bad."[35] That observation serves as the epigraph for Chapter 2, on Kubrick's other war movies. Affording the last movie that he made in this genre—the genre to which he most often returned throughout his moviemaking career—its own chapter seems appropriate not only because nearly all of this book's concerns with Kubrick's men come back in some form here. It's also because this movie's treatment of masculinity is so excruciatingly pressurized, its rendering so fascinatingly distortive. *Full Metal Jacket* takes us through a technology of extreme self-refashioning, whose antihumanism—a major strain throughout Kubrick—entails a rupture of gender, sexuality, subjectivity, and sociality. Here, in the crucible of the Corps during war, what it means to be male is at once violently undercut and intensified beyond the breaking point. Penned on Animal Mother's helmet are the words "I am become death." That dictum, which is scriptural, may serve for this film's negativist mantra.[36]

Coda

Visual Pleasure in Kubrick

There is a further reason why I have allotted *Full Metal Jacket* its own chapter, which has to do with the heightened aestheticism of Kubrick's strange and
alluring antihumanist final war film. And how else to conclude this book but
with the question of art and style, with how Kubrick's movies about men and
masculinity in extremis *look*—with the question, that is, of visual pleasure in
Kubrick?

According to the long prevailing theoretical account of it, cinematic visual
pleasure turns voyeuristically on bodily display. This is true to an extent with
regard to Kubrick's art, where it involves, as I have sought to show, the male
form as well as the female. Among the revelations for me in studying Kubrick's
works—his films but also his early photography—immersively and to the best
of my ability all together at once is the bounty of bared, exposed male bodies.
(The other thing that I had not expected were all those scenes here of men
crying, though not in the hardcore anti-melodrama of *Full Metal Jacket*). There
is much flesh, male and female, on display in Kubrick. But visual pleasure in
Kubrick's movies is predominantly about the composition of the image—and
here I mean any image, every shot. It's the perfect camera work and the as-
tounding lighting. It's the masterful art direction and set design, in which so
many fascinating art objects, as we have been noting all along the way, have
their featured roles, like those giant landscape paintings in *Paths of Glory*, the
Herman Makkink pieces in *A Clockwork Orange*, or the mysterious black
monolith in *2001: A Space Odyssey*, itself a reference to minimalist sculpture.

Especially interesting are those works by Kubrick where visual style verges
on overbearing plot and meaning too. *A Clockwork Orange*, Kubrick's most
notorious film, again comes to mind. There it's the style that takes hold of us,

not any message about free choice and society or the state. But the affective disjunction between expression and subject may be just as pronounced in *Full Metal Jacket*, the film with which this study concludes. Most of the story is horrifying (though sometimes at the same time funny too) and the meaning deeply nihilistic; yet the look of it all is always rivetingly beautiful. There are other "too" beautiful war films, like Terrence Malick's *The Thin Red Line* (1998), with its stunning tropical settings. But Kubrick's movie makes art of boot camp, even the head. Take the study in seriality afforded by the repeating identical white toilets, each ringed by a contrasting black toilet seat, with matching rectangular white water tanks above. Remember that this isn't "found art." Kubrick was not copying the way it is at the real Parris Island. This is his vision of the head. As we have found time and time again, Kubrick's movies like to present things multiplied and lined up in rows. People too, and mostly men. Sometimes these arrangements are static, like the two facing lines of freshly scalped, depersonalized recruits Hartman confronts in the opening squad bay scene here in *Full Metal Jacket*; sometimes they are in motion, like the handsomely uniformed infantry lines in *Barry Lyndon* mechanically marching to their deaths.

All this is horrible and beautiful. So is (to stay with *Full Metal Jacket*) the cerulean blue light that bathes Private Pyle's cruel "blanket party," which, along with the other expressionist fluorescent color lighting effects in the barracks, put me in mind at times of a Dan Flavin installation. Or the Turner-esque turn at film's end in the nighttime torching of Hue, the scene's "Paint It Black" screen canvas spotted here and there, like the work of that great English painter of destruction, with fearful shades of burning orange. The sheer aestheticism of these renderings does not short-circuit *Full Metal Jacket*'s operations foremost as analysis and secondarily (perhaps) as critique, but it is in excess of them.

Kubrick repeatedly said that for him as a filmmaker it was all about finding a good story.[1] And what stories his movies tell! They take us, epically, all the way back to "The Dawn of Man" in *2001: A Space Odyssey* and fast-forward all the way to the "wargasmic" obliteration of life on earth in *Dr. Strangelove*. In between man's beginning and end in Kubrick are all kinds of other male journeys, encounters, and battles. But Kubrick's moviemaking could also be said to be just as much or even more about the interest of the image. No matter the story, and perhaps especially when there hardly is one by mainstream standards, Kubrick's movies always arrest the eye. It is clear that he could put a narrative through its paces. His early feature *The Killing* is a prime example of exacting, propulsive storytelling. *Dr. Strangelove* and the final third of *The Shining* provide two more. But other films such as *2001* and *Barry Lyndon* spectacularly illustrate something else, namely that this is a filmmaker willing to sacrifice dramatic urgency for the lingering visual pleasure of a shot or mise-en-scène.[2]

So what is visual pleasure in Kubrick? It is, in short, the sheer style and technique of it all. James Naremore's *On Kubrick* proffers its subject as one of cinema's last modernists. My inflection of that claim is to put forth Kubrick—with his portraits of men multiplied, hyperbolized, strained, distorted, metamorphosed—as one of cinema's great formalists, indeed among the great image-makers of his time.

Acknowledgments

This book's subject has been a preoccupation of mine for some years now. I am abidingly grateful for the indulgence of friends as I have gone on about its concerns. The resulting work has benefitted significantly from their enlightening responses to ideas I first tried out, this way and that way, with them. No less valuable and enabling has been the familiar support and good cheer that they have been so expert in providing me with over this time. You all know who you are, but it gives me much pleasure to put forth your names here. My heartfelt thanks to: Amanda Anderson, Mark Beard, Matt Bell, Hal Brody, Richard Burt, Patricia Cahill, Janice Carlisle, Cathy Caruth, Brian Clamp, Stuart Curran, Brent Dawson, Bob DeFiore, Lee Edelman, Jon Fields, Mary Jo Foley, Stephen Foley, Leela Gandhi, Jonathan Goldberg, Stephen Greenblatt, Jay Grossman, David Halperin, Scott Handwerker, Janet Halley, Coppélia Kahn, Ken Levin, Robert Levy, Eng-Beng Lim, Kevin McLaughlin, Douglas Mao, Jeffrey Masten, Ourida Mostefai, Marc Redfield, Ravit Reichman, Joseph Roach, Bill Roberts, Mark Robbins, Melissa Sanchez, Harry Shuman, Jesse Solomon, Steven Swarbrick, Ramie Targoff, Whitney Taylor, Amy Toy, and Joseph Wittreich.

I have also benefitted from the opportunity to present portions of this book as work-in-progress at Bridgewater State, Brandeis (on two occasions), Brown (also on two occasions), Columbia, Dartmouth (again on two occasions), Emory Law School, Harvard Law School, Johns Hopkins, Louisiana State University, Pitzer, Princeton, Rice, the University of Buffalo Law School, and the University of Rhode Island. Thank you to everyone in those audiences, and especially to those who invited me to campus and there supplied such warm hospitality: namely, Matt Bell, Ramie Targoff, Alexander Lash, Eng-Beng Lim,

Martha Fineman, Janet Halley, Drew Daniel, Benjamin Kahan, Alexandra Juhasz, Bradin Cormack, Matthew Ritger, Gary Wihl, Helena Michie, Martha McCluskey, and Travis Williams. Special thanks to Kathryn Schwarz for opening the space for me to talk about Kubrick and Shakespeare at an Annual Meeting of the Shakespeare Association of America.

This book began to take shape as a book during a most welcome year spent as a senior fellow at Emory's Bill and Carol Fox Center for Humanistic Inquiry. I am very grateful for its support, along with the interest accorded my work by the other fellows also then in residence, especially Shane Vogel and Deborah Elise White.

Most of this book was written since I joined the faculty at Brown, where I have relished being part of such a stimulating—and extraordinarily sociable—academic community. Within it, Timothy Bewes, Stuart Burrows, Michelle Clayton, Joan Copjec, Philip Gould, Bonnie Honig, Christine Montross, Deak Nabers, Ben Parker, and Ellen Rooney have been especially supportive of and engaged with this particular project. Among my English Department colleagues, I want appreciatively to single out and thank Jacques Khalip, James Kuzner, and Adam Golaski for reading sizeable portions of the manuscript. So did Joseph Litvak, James Meyer, and Anthony Swofford. The thoughtful commentary and inspiring encouragement they each provided vastly improved the finished product. Grace Zabriskie not only scrutinized sections of this book but also took me to the opening of the 2013 Stanley Kubrick exhibition at LACMA. It is always a thrill to be in her company, whether we're talking movies, art, or poetry.

Teaching at Brown has been a deeply gratifying vocational pleasure. Thanks are due for all that I have learned from the students who have taken my Kubrick seminar. I would name everyone here if I could. A special nod to those who have over time continued with me the conversations we first began around the seminar table at Brown, including Tristan Baer, Allegra Chapman, Benjamin Cunningham, India Ennenga, Baylor Knobloch, Alexandra Kordas, Charlotte Lindemann, Madison Lygo, Minoshka Narayan, Ryan Paine, Yasmina Price, and Francesca Sabel. Thanks to Tammuz Frankel, my research assistant, and to Natalie Mesa and Zachary Barnes for help with images.

A semester-long fellowship at Brown's Cogut Institute for the Humanities afforded me the time and chic space to complete work on this book in inspiringly interdisciplinary company. Brown also generously supported several invaluable research trips to the Stanley Kubrick Archive housed at the University of the Arts London. Thanks to the staff there, headed by Richard Daniels, for their kind and informed assistance.

Fordham University Press blessed me with two readers—Robert Corber and Sharon Willis—whose work in film studies I have long admired. I am not sure that I was able to make good on all their astute and probing suggestions, but I hope that it is as apparent to them as it is to me that this book in its final form is better for what they asked of it.

As for my remarkable editor, Richard Morrison, we are now several books and several decades into a working relationship that has also long been a valued friendship. I am grateful to him for his sustained and sustaining interest in my work throughout its various turns. Thanks too to the production team at Fordham.

I have always loved and benefited from talking about movies—Kubrick's included—with my remarkable mother, Rosalie Rambuss. Deep thanks to her.

Though I'm not sure that I have yet turned him into the enthusiast of its subject that I am, this book, perforce, is dedicated to my husband, Charles Vincent O'Boyle, Jr. We began dating back in Atlanta as I wrote and published my first piece on Kubrick and the question of masculinity. He quickly—inevitably—became my most valued critic, my most searching interlocutor, and of course my closest companion. For me, there could be no other. So this book, at last, is for you, Chuck, with gratitude, with admiration, and with all my love.

Earlier versions of some of the material here first appeared in the essays "Machinehead," *Camera Obscura* 42 (1999): 96–123, and "After Male Sex," in *After Sex? On Writing Since Queer Theory*, ed. Janet Halley and Andrew Parker (Durham, NC: Duke University Press, 2011), 192–206. I am grateful to Duke University Press for permission to reproduce elements of those publications here.

Notes

Introduction: Kubrick and the Men's Film

1. See, for instance, Pam Cook, "Melodrama and the Women's Picture," in *Gainsborough Melodrama*, ed. Sue Aspinall and Robert Murphy (London: British Film Institute, 1983): "There is no such thing as 'the men's picture,' specifically addressed to men; there is only 'cinema,' and 'the woman's picture,' a sub-group or category specifically for women, excluding men; a separate, private space designed for more than half the population, relegating them to the margins of cinema proper. The existence of the women's picture both recognises the importance of women, and marginalises them" (17). Or Molly Haskell in *From Reverence to Rape: The Treatment of Women in the Movies*, 3rd ed. (Chicago: University of Chicago Press, 2016), 154: "A film that focuses on male relationships is not pejoratively dubbed a 'man's film' (indeed, this term, when it is used, confers—like 'a man's man'—an image of brute strength), but a 'psychological drama.'" More recently, A. O. Scott and Manohla Dargis have reflected upon how "Hollywood remains committed to granting the presumption of gravitas almost exclusively to stories about men," with the "unfortunate consequence of this bias . . . [being] that genuinely interesting movies about men sometimes fall under a cloud of ideological suspicion." See "The Pros and Cons of Nostalgia," *New York Times*, January 6, 2020.

2. Mary Ann Doane, *The Desire to Desire: The Woman's Film of the 1940s* (Bloomington: Indiana University Press, 1987), 3. As some such problems, Doane specifies those "revolving around domestic life, the family, children, self-sacrifice, and the relationship between women and production vs. that between women and reproduction." What problems (to adapt Doane's formulation) might be defined as "male"? That is one of the questions this book about male melodrama and male metamorphosis looks to address.

3. Here it might be noted that Max Ophüls, the master melodramatist and director of such female-centered classics as *Letter from an Unknown Woman* (1948), *The Earrings of Madame de . . .* (1953), and *Lola Montès* (1955), was one of Kubrick's own favorite directors, possibly his very favorite.

4. It is striking that as the first woman to win a Best Director Oscar (something Kubrick himself never garnered), Bigelow won it for a war film, *The Hurt Locker* (2008), focused entirely on male relations. I will return to Bigelow and the men's film in the final chapter.

5. I am grateful to Anthony Swofford for helping me understand this dimension of them.

6. Eve Kosofsky Sedgwick, "'Gosh, Boy George, You Must Be Awfully Secure in Your Masculinity!'" in *Constructing Masculinity*, ed. Maurice Berger, Brian Wallis, and Simon Watson (New York: Routledge, 1995), 16.

7. Thanks to Joseph Litvak for bringing this point into focus for me.

8. Terry Castle, *The Apparitional Lesbian: Female Homosexuality and Modern Culture* (New York: Columbia University Press, 1993).

9. "I swore that if I ever got out of this place," Spartacus declares about the gladiatorial "school" in which he is a captive, "I'd die before I watched two men fight to the death again. Draba made that promise, too. He kept it. So will I." See Ina Rae Hark, "Animals or Romans: Looking at Masculinity in *Spartacus*," in *Screening the Male: Exploring Masculinities in Hollywood Cinema*, ed. Steven Cohan and Ina Rae Hark (London: Routledge, 1993), 159.

10. In Jack Kroll, "1968: Kubrick's Vietnam Odyssey," *Newsweek*, June 29, 1987.

11. I explore this concern in more theoretical terms in Richard Rambuss, "After Male Sex," in *After Sex? On Writing Since Queer Theory*, ed. Janet Halley and Andrew Parker (Durham, NC: Duke University Press, 2011), 192–204.

12. D. A. Miller, *Hidden Hitchcock* (Chicago: University of Chicago Press, 2016). On "too-close reading," see especially 50–51.

13. See, for instance, Nathan Abrams, *Stanley Kubrick: New York Jewish Intellectual* (New Brunswick, NJ: Rutgers University Press, 2018), which frames that concern in terms of Jewish masculinities.

1. Men's Pictures

1. Joyce Carol Oates, *On Boxing* (Garden City, NY: Dolphin/Doubleday, 1987), 93.

2. In *Camera Lucida: Reflections on Photography*, trans. Richard Howard (New York: Hill and Wang, 1981), Barthes differentiates what he calls the *punctum*—an apparently extraneous, perhaps accidental detail—from a photograph's overall meaning or intended purpose, which he terms *studium*:

> The second element will break (or punctuate) the *studium*. . . . It is this element which rises from the scene, shoots out of it like an arrow, and pierces me. A Latin word exists to designate this wound, this prick, this mark made by a pointed

instrument: the word suits me all the better in that it also refers to the notion of punctuation, and because the photographs I am speaking of are in effect punctuated, sometimes even specked with these sensitive points; precisely, these marks, these wounds are so many *points*. This second element which will disturb the *studium* I shall therefore call *punctum*; for *punctum* is also: sting, speck, cut, little hole—and also a cast of the dice. (26–27)

I am moved to cite Barthes at such length because his terms resonate so powerfully with the paradoxical effects—the *puncta*, if you will—of Kubrick's at once soft and hard-edged, wounding and wounded boxer who opens this study, not to say the penetrable hypermasculine marines of his *Full Metal Jacket*, who will close it. Note too how Barthes brings his *punctum* around to gaming and chance ("a cast of the dice") which matter so much to Kubrick's men, ranging from the con men of *The Killing* to the disreputable likes of Barry Lyndon.

3. Richard Meyer, *Outlaw Representation: Censorship and Homosexuality in Twentieth-Century American Art* (Oxford: Oxford University Press, 2002), 191. *The Perfect Moment* is the title of a 1988–1989 traveling retrospective of Mapplethorpe's work that was cancelled by the Corcoran Gallery of Art in Washington, DC, three weeks before the exhibition was to open there.

4. See Thomas Waugh, *Hard to Imagine: Gay Male Eroticism in Photography and Film from Their Beginnings to Stonewall* (New York: Columbia University Press, 1996), 28. See also Chapter 3 for a history of the genre of sports photography and its homoerotic currency.

5. In Michel Ciment, *Kubrick: The Definitive Edition*, trans. Gilbert Adair (New York: Faber and Faber, 2001), 196. Philippe Mather cites an effusive fan letter published in *Look*, which offers, "Many thanks for giving us that wonderful story and picture spread on Monty Clift. Three cheers should go to Stanley Kubrick, the photographer, for taking the best natural pictures of the most natural actor on the stage." See "Stanley Kubrick and *Look* Magazine," in *Stanley Kubrick: Essays on His Films and Legacy*, ed. Gary D. Rhodes (Jefferson, NC: McFarland and Company, 2008), 19–20.

6. Rainer Crone compiles an impressive anthology of these images in *Stanley Kubrick Drama and Shadows: Photographs 1945–1950* (London: Phaidon Press, 2005). See also the encyclopedic *Through a Different Lens: Stanley Kubrick Photographs*, ed. Donald Albrecht and Sean Corcoran (Cologne: Taschen, 2018). The photographs gorgeously reproduced in this volume are in the collection of the Museum of the City of New York. Philippe Mather's *Stanley Kubrick at Look Magazine* (Chicago: Intellect, 2013) provides the most deeply informed study of the topic.

7. In *Kubrick's Total Cinema: Philosophical Themes and Formal Qualities* (New York: Bloomsbury, 2012), Philip Kuberski is persuasive regarding "the importance of female nudity in Kubrick's subsequent films," which "can hardly be exaggerated— both as an example of the breakdown of censorship in the 1960s and in the

development of his own imaginary film language." He further asserts that "Kubrick's use of the female nude is never coy or sentimental, the usual ways in which the illicit and the sexual are domesticated in popular representations. Instead, it is unembarrassed and, risking the charge of depersonalization, detached and objective" (88). Kuberski shows no interest, however, in the undressed male body in Kubrick. Flesh for him is figurally female flesh even when male. Regarding the recruits in *Full Metal Jacket*, for instance, Kuberski writes: "It is as this form of female flesh that they are subject to the fierce gaze of their drill instructor and the sexualized humiliation that is directed their way. This fiction that civilian men are in effect female flesh guides the strategy and tactics of the training section of the film" (96–97). In my reading of that film in Chapter 5, I suggest that the gendering and sexualization of these pliant male bodies signifies more complexly.

8. Thomas Waugh, "Strength and Stealth: Watching (and Wanting) Turn of the Century Strongmen," *Canadian Journal of Film Studies* 2 (1991): 1.

9. See Christine Lee Gengaro, *Listening to Stanley Kubrick: The Music in his Films* (Lanham, MD: Scarecrow Press, 2013), 2–3. Fried also provided music for Kubrick's first four feature films.

10. Richard Combs, "*Day of the Fight*," *Monthly Film Bulletin* 47, no. 563 (December 1980): 249.

11. Cited in John Baxter, *Stanley Kubrick: A Biography* (New York: Carroll & Graf, 1997), 37.

12. As recounted by Vincent Cartier to Vincent LoBrutto in *Stanley Kubrick: A Biography* (New York: Da Capo Press, 1999), 59.

13. Michael Herr, *Kubrick* (New York: Grove Press, 2000), 27.

14. Regarding the martial analogy, Herr comes right out and says it: "Movie directors are like generals." In *Full Metal Jacket: The Screenplay by Stanley Kubrick, Michael Herr and Gustav Hasford, Based on the Novel The Short-Timers by Gustav Hasford* (New York: Knopf, 1987), v. Consider also James Naremore's conception of Kubrick "guiding his actors through grisly battle scenes like a field general" in his highly rewarding, comprehensive study *On Kubrick* (London: British Film Institute, 2007), 48. Regarding Kubrick, the director, as a computer, again see Herr in *Full Metal Jacket: The Screenplay*, where he describes Kubrick as "a regular mental warrior" whose "means are telephonic. He has tremendous information, and he loves to process it" (v). Ken Adam, set designer for *Dr. Strangelove* and *Barry Lyndon*, compares Kubrick to "a chess player with a computer-like brain." See "For Him, Everything Was Possible: Interview with Ken Adam," in *Stanley Kubrick, Kinematograph*, 2nd rev. ed., (Frankfurt: Deutsches Filmmuseum, 2007), 89. Gene Siskel observes that "Kubrick is well-known for being plugged into all manner of information through his voracious reading and extensive computer system," in "Candidly Kubrick," in *Stanley Kubrick: Interviews*, ed. Gene D. Phillips (Jackson: University of Mississippi Press, 2001), 185. Consider also Gilles Deleuze's related observations about how Kubrick's films portray the world as brain in *Cinema 2: The Time-Image*, trans. Hugh Tomlinson and Robert Galeta (Minneapolis: University of

NOTES TO PAGES 26–36   207

Minnesota Press, 1989): "For, in Kubrick, the world itself is a brain, there is identity of brain and world, as in the great circular and luminous table in *Doctor Strangelove*, the giant computer in *2001: A Space Odyssey*, the Overlook hotel in *The Shining*. The black stone of *2001* presides over both cosmic states and cerebral stages." See 205–206. In an interview with Joseph Gelmis, Kubrick himself referred to a director as "a kind of idea and taste machine" (and actors as "essentially emotion-producing instruments"). See Gelmis, *The Film Director as Superstar* (Garden City, NY: Doubleday & Company, 1970), 314 and 311.

15. Cited in LoBrutto, *Stanley Kubrick: A Biography*, 58.

16. "The boxer meets an opponent who is a dream-distortion of himself. . . . He is my shadow-self, not my (mere) shadow" (*On Boxing*, 12). Oates evokes the structural twinship of boxers in her book's scene-setting first sentence: "They are young welterweight boxers so evenly matched they might be twins" (1). Later Oates reinflects this coupling in the ring homoerotically: "No sport is more physical, more direct, than boxing. No sport appears more powerfully homoerotic: the confrontation in the ring—the disrobing—the sweaty heated combat that is part dance, courtship, coupling—the frequent urgent pursuit by one boxer of the other in the fight's natural and violent movement toward the 'knockout.'" (30).

17. Does the dolorous recent sports film *Foxcatcher* (dir. Bennett Miller; 2014) have this early film of Kubrick's on its mind when it places its combat athlete—in this case a wrestler—in front of that movie's version of the fighting man's mirror? Like Kubrick's short-form sports documentary, Miller's feature film is about two real-life brothers (though not twins): Mark and Dave Schultz, both Olympic gold medalists. Early on, after a practice bout with his brother that gets out of hand, we see Mark (Channing Tatum) doubled as he contemplates his handsome puffy face in a split mirror (this film's own surreal touch), poking, pulling, and eventually flailing at it in ways that repeat and exceed Kubrick's boxer's own curious self-manipulations.

18. See Alexandra von Stosch, "Beyond the Looking Glass: Kubrick and Self-Reflexivity," in Crone, *Stanley Kubrick: Drama and Shadows*, 246.

19. It's as though the pictorial was shot to illustrate Jacques Lacan's "The Mirror Stage," which theorizes the child's encounter with himself in the mirror as a stage in his developing sense of individuation. See again van Stosch: "In Kubrick's photo-essay, the mirror becomes the threshold in which the self is represented as the other. The irritation in the last picture reflects the jarring experience of stepping beyond oneself through the mirror, of transcending one's consciousness. . . . In many ways, Kubrick's photographs of the baby serve as a mirror itself of the mirror stage." Von Stosch, "Beyond the Looking Glass," 246, 248.

20. Bill Krohn, *Stanley Kubrick*, rev. English ed. (Paris: Cahiers du Cinéma Sarl, 2010), 16.

21. Oates, *On Boxing*, 30.

22. Naremore remarks "a subtle racial implication" to Vince and Gloria's coupling, "as if Kubrick were trying to create a frisson of forbidden sexuality." "Here,

as in *Fear and Desire*," he continues, "Frank Silvera is cast in the role of a primitive, his somewhat African features played in sharp contrast with Irene Kane's aristocratic blondness and extremely white skin, which is displayed by her backless dress." *On Kubrick*, 60.

23. Boxing would also be the subject of Sackler's 1967 Pulitzer Prize– and Tony Award–winning play *The Great White Hope*, modeled on the story of Jack Johnson, the first African American world heavyweight champion. Sackler's play was turned into a movie in 1970, starring James Earl Jones, whose first film role was a small part in *Dr. Strangelove* six years before that. Sackler, another high school friend of Kubrick's, also wrote the screenplay for *Fear and Desire*, Kubrick's debut feature film.

24. Laura Mulvey, "Visual Pleasure and Narrative Cinema," *Screen* 16 (1975): 15–16.

25. See Dan Streible, *Fight Pictures: A History of Boxing and Early Cinema* (Berkeley: University of California Press, 2008), 7.

26. Cited in Alexander Walker, *Stanley Kubrick, Director*, rev. ed. (New York: Norton, 1999), 16.

27. See, in particular, Catherine Malabou, *What Should We Do with Our Brain?*, trans. Sebastian Rand (New York: Fordham University Press, 2008). Drawing on Deleuze, Malabou here mentions Kubrick, along with Alain Resnais, as a "filmmaker of the brain" (39).

28. This paragraph is indebted to discussions with Jacques Khalip.

29. See her autobiography, published under her married name, Chris Chase, *How to Be a Movie Star, or A Terrible Beauty is Born* (New York: Harper & Row, 1968). 22, 16. Speaking of boyish female leads and looking ahead, at one point Kubrick conceived of his screen Lolita more along the lines of a preteen tomboy, and thus more in keeping with aspects of her character in Nabokov's novel. "Lolita—moods of naiveté and deception, charm and vulgarity," Kubrick jotted down descriptively on his pre-production index cards, "goofing off–diffused dreaming in a boyish hoodlum way." Cited in Karyn Stuckey, "Re-Writing Nabokov's *Lolita*," in *Stanley Kubrick: New Perspectives*, ed. Tatjana Ljujić, Peter Krämer, and Richard Daniels (London: Black Dog, 2015), 127.

2. War Films: *Fear and Desire, Paths of Glory, Dr. Strangelove, 2001: A Space Odyssey*

1. Carl von Clausewitz, *On War*, ed. and trans. Michael Howard and Peter Paret (Princeton, NJ: Princeton University Press, 1984), 75.

2. Reproduced in Eva-Maria Magel, "The Best Movie (N)ever Made: Stanley Kubrick's Failed *Napoleon* Project," in *Stanley Kubrick*, rev. ed., *Kinematograph* 20 (2007): 158.

3. Joseph Gelmis, *The Film Director as Superstar* (Garden City, NY: Doubleday & Company, 1970), 298.

4. Alison Castle's epic compilation *Stanley Kubrick's Napoleon: The Greatest Movie Never Made* (Cologne: Taschen, 2011) reproduces a trove of these images.

5. Gelmis, *The Film Director as Superstar*, 298.

6. Eva-Maria Magel, "'Everything a Good Story Should Have': Stanley Kubrick and Napoleon," in Castle, *Stanley Kubrick's Napoleon*, 35.

7. Gelmis, *The Film Director as Superstar*, 297.

8. Magel, "'Everything a Good Story Should Have,'" 38.

9. Gelmis, *The Film Director as Superstar*, 297.

10. *Napoleon: A Screenplay by Stanley Kubrick*, scene 43; reproduced in Castle, *Stanley Kubrick's Napoleon*, 696.

11. Ibid., 688–689.

12. Ibid., 675–676.

13. Reproduced in Magel, "The Best Movie (N)ever Made," 158.

14. *Napoleon: A Screenplay by Stanley Kubrick*, scene 137, 787, in Castle, *Stanley Kubrick's Napoleon*.

15. "Stanley Kubrick/Felix Markham Napoleon Dialogues," annotated by Geoffrey Ellis, in Castle, *Stanley Kubrick's Napoleon*, 113.

16. A facsimile of Kubrick's memo is reproduced in Magel, "The Best Movie (N)ever Made," 157.

17. See Gelmis, *The Director as Superstar*, 295.

18. See Vincent LoBrutto, *Stanley Kubrick: A Biography* (New York: Da Capo Press, 1999), 324.

19. Magel, "The Best Movie (N)ever Made," 164.

20. Gelmis, *The Director as Superstar*, 296.

21. Ibid., 296–297.

22. When asked by Gelmis, "Why are you making a movie about Napoleon?" Kubrick replied: "I find that all the issues with which it concerns itself are oddly contemporary—the responsibilities and abuses of power, the dynamics of social revolution, the relationship of the individual to the state, war, militarism, etc., so this will not be just a dusty historical pageant but a film about the basic questions of our own times, as well as Napoleon's." *The Director as Superstar*, 297.

23. Stanley Kubrick, Letter to Joseph Burstyn dated November 16, 1952. Consulted in the Stanley Kubrick Archive at the University of the Arts London.

24. Geoffrey Cocks, *The Wolf at the Door: Stanley Kubrick, History, and the Holocaust* (New York: Peter Lang, 2004), 79. James Naremore adds, "The battle-weary faces of Kubrick's four soldiers were much closer in appearance to newsreel images of GIs in Korea than to the characters in almost any war movies Hollywood had produced during the 1950s." *On Kubrick* (London: British Film Institute, 2007), 52.

25. William Shakespeare, *The Tempest* 3.2.134–135, in *The Complete Pelican Shakespeare*, ed. Stephen Orgel and A. R. Braunmuller (New York: Penguin Books, 2002). Further references supplied in the text.

26. Montaigne, "Of Cannibals," in *The Complete Essays of Montaigne*, trans. Donald M. Frame (Stanford: Stanford University Press, 1965), 150–159.

27. Paolo Cherchi Usai's informative piece on *Fear and Desire* likewise has its relation to *Full Metal Jacket* in mind. See "Checkmating the General: Stanley Kubrick's *Fear and Desire*," *Image (Journal of Photography and Motion Pictures of George Eastman House)* 38 (1995): 19, 23, 25.

28. Naremore, *On Kubrick*, 11.

29. The original letter is in the Stanley Kubrick Archive, where I consulted it.

30. See Justin Stewart, "Kubrick's First Feature: Paul Mazursky Q&A on *Fear and Desire*," *Film Comment*, March 26, 2012, accessed online at https://www .filmcomment.com/blog/kubricks-first-feature-paul-mazursky-qa-on-fear-and-desire (accessed October 1, 2020). Kubrick pays Mazursky a compliment in *Eyes Wide Shut* by having Alice watch Mazursky's marriage comedy *Blume in Love* (1973) at home on TV.

31. There is a similar incident—though there it is indeed a recognition scene—in Derek Jarman's 1989 screen adaptation of Benjamin Britten's *War Requiem*. Britten's piece intermingles the mournful, trenchantly unsentimental World War I poetry of Wilfred Owen with the Latin Mass for the Dead. In Jarman's film, the character known as "the Unknown Soldier" at death recognizes himself in his German counterpart whom he has killed and who has killed him. As Owen writes in "Strange Meeting": "I am the enemy you killed, my friend." Jarman, incidentally, also made a film of *The Tempest* in 1979.

32. See John Baxter, *Stanley Kubrick: A Biography* (New York: Carroll & Graf, 1997), 54.

33. See Alexander Walker, *Stanley Kubrick, Director*, rev. ed. (New York: Norton, 1999), 15–16.

34. Cited in Janet Maslin, "Critic's Choice/Film; A Young and Promising Kubrick," *New York Times*, January 14, 1994.

35. Jeremy Bernstein, "Profile: Stanley Kubrick," in *Stanley Kubrick: Interviews*, ed. Gene D. Phillips (Jackson: University of Mississippi Press, 2001), 27.

36. In a note at the end of the novel, Cobb declares: "All the characters, units, and places mentioned in his book are fictitious." "However," he continues, "if the reader asks, 'Did such things really happen?' the author answers, 'Yes.'" Cobb then refers the reader to "a special dispatch" to the *New York Times*, July 2, 1934, with the headline: "FRENCH ACQUIT 5 SHOT FOR MUTINY IN 1915; WIDOWS OF 2 WIN AWARDS OF 7 CENTS EACH." *Paths of Glory* (New York: Viking Press, 1935), 265. Further references to the novel are in the text.

37. See Wilhelm Roth, "Generals and Censors: *Paths of Glory* and the Games of Power," in *Stanley Kubrick*, rev. ed., *Kinematograph* 20 (2007): 44–55, especially 50–54. *Paths of Glory* was finally released in Paris in 1976.

38. In a perceptive unpublished paper titled "Aesthetic Choices in *Paths of Glory*," Jonathan Goldberg, who also approaches Kubrick's film as melodrama, pushes the association between Dax and both Mireau and Broulard even harder, relating them as fellow sadists in various military settings. Moreover, Goldberg sees

as complicit with the sadism of these characters the aesthetic choices of the film itself, especially "the imperturbability of Kubrick's camera work."

39. See the excellent chapter on "War" in Philip Kuberski, *Kubrick's Total Cinema: Philosophical Themes and Formal Qualities* (New York: Bloomsbury, 2012). "Where classical war is organized according to a geometric logic," he notes, "modern war draws on the nascent sciences of statistics and systems theory" (62).

40. Walker, *Stanley Kubrick, Director*, 74.

41. Paul Fussell, *The Great War and Modern Memory* (1975) (New York: Oxford University Press, 2000), especially ch. 1: "Every war is ironic because every war is worse than expected. Every war constitutes an irony of situation because its means are so melodramatically disproportionate to its presumed ends. . . . But the Great War was more ironic than any before or since" (7–8). Anthony Frewin, Kubrick's personal assistant, reports that the director admired Fussell's work as "a book without peer." See Frewin, "Stanley Kubrick: Writers, Writing, Reading," in *The Stanley Kubrick Archives*, ed. Alison Castle (Cologne: Taschen, 2004), 518. Fussell, it is worth noting in this context, was trained as a specialist in eighteenth-century English literature and was an US Army officer in World War II.

42. Walker, *Stanley Kubrick, Director*, 20.

43. Naremore, *On Kubrick*, 95.

44. Vivian C. Sobchack, "Décor as Theme: A *Clockwork Orange*," *Literature/Film Quarterly* 9 (1981): 93–94.

45. Thomas Allen Nelson's account of *Paths of Glory* is rich in observations and details with which I too am here concerned. See his *Kubrick: Inside a Film Artist's Maze, New and Expanded Edition* (Bloomington, IN: Indiana University Press, 2000), especially 44–45, 48. See also Mario Falsetto, *Stanley Kubrick: A Narrative and Stylistic Analysis* (Westport, CT: Praeger, 1994), 39–40. Noting that "it is the presentation of space, decor and camera . . . that gives the film its stylistic distinction," Falsetto argues that "the film's formal design makes war itself an abstraction" (42–43).

46. Others too have written on how the film is both steeped in ritual and deeply concerned with hierarchy. See, in particular, Walker, *Stanley Kubrick, Director*, 84–93, 103; Nelson, *Kubrick*, 54; and Robert Kolker, *A Cinema of Loneliness: Penn, Stone, Kubrick, Scorsese, Spielberg, Altman*, 3rd ed. (New York: Oxford University Press, 2000), 110–114. My own interest in ritual more specifically turns on gender— on what is indicatively male about these thematics as they are given scope in Kubrick's military film.

47. Bill Krohn, *Stanley Kubrick*, rev. English ed. (Paris: Cahiers du Cinéma Sarl, 2010), 22; Walker, *Stanley Kubrick, Director*, 74.

48. Naremore, *On Kubrick*, 85.

49. Barry Keith Grant, "Of Men and Monoliths: Science Fiction, Gender, and *2001: A Space Odyssey*," in *Stanley Kubrick's 2001: A Space Odyssey—New Essays*, ed. Robert Kolker (New York: Oxford University Press, 2006), 78.

50. This reconnaissance mission that Dax dispatches to take the lay of the land before the next day's assault on the Ant Hill provides *Paths of Glory*'s subplot and is emblematic of the movie's refusal to traffic in any battlefield saving graces. This three-man patrol, headed by the drunken and cowardly Lieutenant Roget is a study in bad soldiering, bad faith, and dysfunctional, albeit still rigidly enforced, hierarchical male relations. "Say, what's [Roget] got against you anyway?" Lejeune (Kem Dibbs), one of the two corporals assigned to this dangerous detail, asks the other, after they have been briefed about the mission. Replies Corporal Paris: "He thinks that I don't have enough respect for him. He's right." Paris's disregard for his superior is validated by the operation itself. Roget splits up the patrol by sending Lejeune off alone, ahead of the other two, toward the German wire: a violation, Paris protests to no avail, of procedure. Then, in his cowardly retreat at the first sign of enemy fire, Roget blindly sends a grenade into the darkness, killing Lejeune. The corporal's death at the hand of his commanding officer signals early on the military machine's propensity for killing its own and portends more such deaths to come. In the scene that follows back in the bunker, Paris angrily confronts Roget, who is already officiously at work writing a falsified report about the patrol. Paris: "You ran like a rabbit after you killed Lejeune." Roget: "Killed Lejeune? What are you talking about? I don't like your tone. You're speaking to an officer. Remember that." Paris: "Oh, well. I must be mistaken, then, sir. An officer wouldn't do that. *A man wouldn't do it.*" Roget later seizes the opportunity to dispatch the one witness of his battlefield malfeasance by picking Paris as the scapegoat from his company to face court-martial and then the firing squad.

51. Here I am thinking especially of the villainous Phillip Vandamm's (James Mason) interest in art and antiques in Hitchcock's own Cold War thriller, *North By Northwest* (1959). And then there are Bruno Antony (Robert Walker) in *Strangers on a Train* (1951) and Brandon Shaw (John Dall) and Philip Morgan (Farley Granger) in *Rope* (1948), homicidal aesthetes all.

52. Yvonne Tasker, "Soldiers' Stories: Women and Military Masculinities in *Courage Under Fire*," in *The War Film*, ed. Robert Eberwein (New Brunswick, NJ: Rutgers University Press, 2005), 180.

53. Nelson, *Kubrick*, 44.

54. Kirk Douglas, *The Ragman's Son: Autobiography* (New York: Simon & Schuster, 1988), 317.

55. This is as good a place as any to register the anal/excremental thematic that runs through Cobb's novel from the beginning. Indeed, it is in terms of the bowel that the effect of war is here first registered on men's bodies and minds. "See that sort of greyish tint to their skin?" an older soldier asks a younger one. "They're nearly all of them constipated." "Now I know you're fooling me," the other replies. "Everybody always says the front line acts on you just the other way." The older soldier further explains: "The Germans have got all our trench latrines registered. And we've got theirs, too. Now a soldier doesn't like to go to a place that's registered. What's more, he doesn't like to take his breeches down because when his breeches

are down he can't jump or run. So what does he do? He bakes it. . . . When men get scared they get tense and things inside them solidify. Functions stop. Secretions dry up. When you hear a shell coming straight at you, you hold everything." Cobb, *Paths of Glory*, 3–5. Later in the book, another soldier complains of a pain "in the tail" (54). Compare Kirk Douglas's scatological estimation of Kubrick after working with him on *Paths of Glory* and then on *Spartacus*. "Stanley Kubrick," writes Douglas in *The Ragman's Son*, "is a talented shit" (333).

56. By the way, Allan Bérubé reports that the all-female play by Clare Boothe Luce upon which Cukor's likewise all-female film is based was a popular performance piece in the all-male GI wartime theater repertory. He also notes that the talent these military men in drag displayed in putting on such soldier shows of *The Women* mightily impressed Luce and prompted her "to interpret the GI production as an important wartime critique of traditional gender roles." See Bérubé, *Coming Out Under Fire: The History of Gay Men and Women in World War Two* (New York: Free Press, 1990), 88–89.

I would be remiss if I did not also mention here Fred Zinnemann's *The Men* (1950). The particular institutional setting of this affecting male melodrama—a VA hospital—is a variation on the usual military one. *The Men* stars Marlon Brando (his screen debut) in a wheelchair as a paraplegic World War II soldier, making it an interesting forerunner of the Vietnam War disabled veteran films *Coming Home* (dir. Hal Ashby, 1978) and *Born on the Fourth of July* (dir. Oliver Stone, 1989).

57. Tim Cahill, "The *Rolling Stone* Interview: Stanley Kubrick," in Phillips, *Stanley Kubrick: Interviews*, 190.

58. Gelmis, *The Director as Superstar*, 309. Mick Broderick's deeply researched *Reconstructing Strangelove: Inside Kubrick's "Nightmare Comedy"* (London: Wallflower Press, 2017) provides a valuable sourcebook on how Kubrick's "nightmare comedy" came to be made.

59. As I set forth earlier, the question of arousal is fundamental to my consideration of Kubrick's way with the war film. And sometimes it is disgust in addition to desire that is aroused. This would seem, as Joseph Litvak pointed out to me, to have its objective correlative in how the dick might also become a turd, as when here Kong drops from the plane straddling the bomb. This film's satiric anal-excremental preoccupation congeals into a kind of poetics in *Full Metal Jacket*, the subject of the book's last chapter.

60. So reports Terry Southern, one of Kubrick's collaborators on the screenplay, in "*Strangelove* Outtake: Notes from the War Room," *Grand Street* 49 (1994): 69.

61. See LoBrutto, *Stanley Kubrick*, 247. But at least President Reagan had seen Kubrick's cautionary movie. This might be more than one could assume of Donald Trump, who as a candidate for that office wondered why the United States couldn't, wouldn't use its nuclear weapons when it had so many of them. Trump has made *Dr. Strangelove* an alarmingly urgent *must-see* all over again. When he took office, the Bulletin of the Atomic Scientists advanced its "Doomsday Clock" to two and a half minutes to midnight. The Strangelovian conceit of a Doomsday Clock conveys

pictorially how close we are to destroying our world with dangerous technologies of our own making, especially nuclear weapons. The Doomsday Clock ticked forward again in each year of Trump's presidency.

As for other world leaders who need a schooling in *Strangelove*, during his 2017 Showtime documentary *The Putin Interviews*, Oliver Stone asks the Russian president if he knows Kubrick's film. When Putin says he doesn't, Stone arranges to watch it with him on DVD. The scene cuts to Putin for a reaction shot at the movie's end. His usual impassivity is no match for what he has just seen.

62. See Richard Kostelanetz, "One-Man Think Tank," *New York Times Magazine* December 1, 1968, 94. See also Sharon Ghamari-Tabrizi, *The Worlds of Herman Kahn: The Intuitive Science of Thermonuclear War* (Cambridge, MA: Harvard University Press, 2005), 363n90. Kahn himself may have gotten the idea for the Doomsday Machine from Peter George's (as Peter Bryant) novel *Red Alert* (New York: Ace Books, 1958), upon which Kubrick's film is based. In the film, Strangelove reports that he commissioned a study of a Doomsday device from the BLAND Corporation. Kahn had worked for the RAND Corporation.

63. For the "pornography for officers" claim, see Paul Johnson, review of *On Thermonuclear War, New Statesman*, May 1, 1961, 754, as cited in Alex Abella, *Soldiers of Reason: The RAND Corporation and the Rise of the American Empire* (Orlando: Harcourt, 2008), 103. The term "Wargasmic," which I used earlier, derives from Kahn, who once told the generals at the Strategic Air Command that they dreamed of a "wargasm." See Louis Menand, "Fat Man: Herman Kahn and the Nuclear Age," *The New Yorker*, June 27, 2005, 95. For that table enumerating "Tragic But Distinguishable Postwar States," see Herman Kahn, *On Thermonuclear War* (Princeton, NJ: Princeton University Press, 1960), 20.

64. As is the case with just about all these characters, the portrayal of the president is quite different in George's novel, where he is a decisive, rather heroic figure—a man among men. Even the Russian ambassador "had been immensely impressed with the firm grasp the President had on the reins of government. He achieved absolute command without his leadership becoming obtrusive or unpleasant. Yet he was instantly obeyed." (*Red Alert*, 178).

65. *Dr. Strangelove* is obviously spoofing extreme right-wing conspiracy theorists who saw water fluoridation as a plot to weaken American bodies and minds for a coming communist takeover. Some anti-fluoride crusaders also contended that it caused infertility and that the Nazis had experimented with it on female concentration camp prisoners. In keeping with the film's overt masculinism, the (paranoid) concern here, however, is essentially with fluoride's physical and psychological effects *on men*. Ripper's toxic fluoride revelation comes to him "during the physical act of love," when he was overtaken by "a profound sense of fatigue, a feeling of emptiness," "a loss of essence." Beyond its immediate Cold War context, the film taps into a classic male complaint, as old as the ancients, that every ejaculation costs a man a day of his life and leaves for him, as John Donne

memorably puts it in his seventeenth-century postcoital depression poem "Farewell to Love," "A kind of sorrowing dullness to the mind."

66. Bosley Crowther, "*Dr. Strangelove*: Kubrick Film Presents Sellers in 3 Roles," *New York Times*, January 30, 1964, and "Is Nothing Sacred?" *New York Times*, February 2, 1964.

67. Chalmers M. Roberts, "Film with A-War Theme Creates New World Problems for U.S.," *Washington Post*, February 21, 1964. Were Kubrick's film to be "shown around the world," warns Roberts, it could "cause the United States as much harm as many a coup or revolution."

68. Nora Sayre, *Running Time: Films of the Cold War* (New York: Dial Press, 1982), 219. Compare also Ghamari-Tabrizi, *The Worlds of Herman Kahn*, 275: "Nearly every critic framed his or her review of the film as an entry in the public etiquette of the cold war. Was *Dr. Strangelove* funny? Was it immoral and improper? Just what was the right response to the nuclear grotesque?" For more on the film's initial reception, see Margot A. Henriksen, *Dr. Strangelove's America: Society and Culture in the Atomic Age* (Berkeley: University of California Press, 1997), 327–331.

69. Gelmis, *The Director as Superstar*, 309.

70. Peter Baxter, "The One Woman," *Wide Angle* 6 (1984): 35, 36.

71. In his autobiography, Jones recounts how "in 1963, film director Stanley Kubrick had come to see George C. Scott play Shylock in Central Park when he was casting *Dr. Strangelove*. Kubrick also saw me playing the Prince of Morocco: 'I'll take that black one, too.' I got the role of Lieutenant Lothar Zogg." James Earl Jones (and Penelope Niven), *Voices and Silences, with a New Epilogue* (New York: Limelight, 2002), 135–136. Jones later adds about his role in *Strangelove*, "I was the bombardier, and the only one who questioned the patriotic mission we were on. I liked the fact that the black man was the one who asked the hard questions. To my great disappointment, those lines wound up cut out of the script before we even shot them" (311).

72. Crowther, "*Dr. Strangelove*," 24.

73. Pauline Kael, review of *Bonnie and Clyde*, *The New Yorker*, October 21, 1967, 170. Kael blames *Dr. Strangelove* for opening "a new movie era" of "black comedy," in which "everything is gross, ridiculous, insane; to make sense would be to risk being square" (171). Crowther thought so too: "[Kubrick] is firing his blasts of derision and mockery at everyone." "Hysterical Laughter: Further Thoughts on *Dr. Strangelove* and Its Jokes about the Bomb," *New York Times*, February 16, 1964.

74. Eric Nordern, "*Playboy* Interview: Stanley Kubrick," in Phillips, *Stanley Kubrick: Interviews*, 68–69. Kubrick was still talking about this threat some twenty years later, when he did the publicity for *Full Metal Jacket*. In a 1987 interview with Gene Siskel he reflects, "Of course the worst danger in the world today is still nuclear war. . . . But I think the only way this could happen now is by some inadvertent use of nuclear weapons by accident, miscalculation, or madness." See Phillips, *Stanley Kubrick: Interviews*, 185.

75. Kuberski, *Kubrick's Total Cinema*, 56. See also Susan White, "Kubrick's Obscene Shadows," in Kolker, *Stanley Kubrick's 2001: A Space Odyssey*: "Kubrick's hominids move toward civilization by learning to kill efficiently" (128).

76. Minimalist-conceptualist artist Robert Morris's double-paneled *Dust Gets in Your Eyes* (2018) understands the relay that I am pushing here between *Dr. Strangelove* and *2001* as films about the threat of nuclear war. Morris's epically scaled, UV-printed Kubrick montages superimpose the former film's doomsday scientist and the latter's weapon-wielding protohumans on the same sickening yellow and burnt orange irradiated landscape. In one panel, it's Moon-Watcher who hurtles the deadly bone/weapon skyward against a backdrop of mounting fiery dust clouds. In the other panel, it seems to come from Strangelove's Nazi-saluting black gloved hand. I am grateful to James Meyer for directing me to Morris's "Banners and Curses" 2018 show at the Castelli Gallery and to Barbara Bertozzi Castelli for further conversation about Morris.

77. Arthur C. Clarke, *2001: A Space Odyssey* (1968) (New York: Penguin, 2016), 226.

78. Grant, "Of Men and Monoliths," in Kolker, *Stanley Kubrick's 2001*, 76–77.

79. Arthur C. Clarke, "Christmas, Shepperton," in *The Making of 2001: A Space Odyssey*, selected by Stephanie Schwam (New York: Modern Library, 2000), 37. Regarding HAL's "sexuality," see Ellis Hanson's pathbreaking essay: "Technology, Paranoia, and the Queer Voice," *Screen* 34 (1993): 137–161. See also Dominic Janes's wide-ranging and suggestive piece, "Clarke and Kubrick's 2001: A Queer Odyssey," *Science Fiction Film and Television* 4 (2011): 57–78. More recently, Nathan Abrams has put forth the claim that "HAL's 'androgynous,' 'equivocally gendered,' and 'oddly asexual' qualities . . . all play into the stereotype of the 'queer' or 'sissy Jew.'" See "What was HAL? IBM, Jewishness and Stanley Kubrick's *2001: A Space Odyssey* (1968), *Historical Journal of Film, Radio and Television* 37 (2017): 430.

3. Male Sexuality and Homosexuality I: *Lolita, The Killing, Spartacus*

1. Frank Rich, "Stanley, I Presume," *New York Times Magazine*, August 15, 1993, Endpaper/Public Stages. The movie also depicts the encounter with Rich, though it replaces the drama critic's newspaper friends with his wife, the writer Alex Witchel, who is played by Marisa Berenson, Lady Lyndon in Kubrick's *Barry Lyndon*. *Color Me Kubrick* is replete with many such "in-the-know" references.

2. Patrick Webster likewise proposes in passing, albeit more tentatively, that "it would appear reasonable to argue that all of Kubrick's work was, to some degree, imbued with what Leslie Fiedler called a 'delicate homosexuality.'" See *Love and Death in Kubrick: A Critical Study of the Films from Lolita to Eyes Wide Shut* (Jefferson, NC: McFarland, 2011), 24.

3. This is the subject of Rodney Ascher's fascinating 2013 documentary *Room 237*.

4. See *The Stanley Kubrick Archives*, ed. Alison Castle (Cologne: Taschen, 2004), 333 for a rare on-set still of Sellers done up as Miss Pratt.

5. Vladimir Nabokov, *Lolita: A Screenplay* (New York: McGraw-Hill, 1974), 96.

6. Reprinted in Pauline Kael, *I Lost It at the Movies* (1965) (New York: Marion Boyars, 1994), 206–207.

7. James Mason, *Before I Forget* (London: Hamish Hamilton, 1981), 320.

8. Vladimir Nabokov, *Lolita* (1955) (New York: Vintage Books, 1997), 181, 17. Further references to the novel will be supplied parenthetically in the text.

9. See Webster, *Love and Death in Kubrick*, 25.

10. The novel elaborates. Quilty, reports Lolita, "was a complete freak in sex matters, and his friends were his slaves." He wanted her, as Lolita lays it out for an aghast Humbert, to do "weird, filthy, fancy things," including an intergenerational bisexual orgy: "I mean, he had two girls and two boys, and three or four men, and the idea was for all of us to tangle in the nude while an old woman took movie pictures." Humbert is appalled, but he also seems fascinated, parenthetically noting here that "(Sade's Justine was twelve at the start)" (276). As for those "painters, nudists, writers, weightlifters," they evoke various human-interest subjects Kubrick shot while he worked at *Look*.

11. In the novel, when Humbert learns that Quilty is dead, he reflects, "the only satisfaction it gave me, was the relief of knowing I need not mentally accompany for months a painful and disgusting convalescence interrupted by all kinds of unmentionable operations and relapses, and perhaps an actual visit from him, with trouble on my part to rationalize him as not being a ghost" (306). The film's ghost-making flashback, tape loop–like structure, as I later discuss, deprives Humbert of even that last satisfaction.

12. "Homosexual Subtexts," in *The Encyclopedia of Stanley Kubrick: From Day of the Fight to Eyes Wide Shut*, ed. Gene D. Phillips and Rodney Hill (New York: Checkmark Books, 2002), 164–165.

Mason himself was even more perturbed by this scene than the character he here plays. Complaining that Kubrick was "so besotted with the genius of Peter Sellers that he seemed never to have enough of him," Mason recalls: "There was one scene in which Sellers, immersed in the character of Quilty which he was playing, pretended to be an undercover detective for a full nine minutes while poor Humbert Humbert had nothing to do but look uncomfortable. I was Humbert Humbert" (*Before I Forget*, 318). Mason's extreme annoyance induces some exaggeration on his part. The scene out on the veranda runs just short of five minutes, which is, nonetheless, considerable.

13. See Nabokov, *Lolita*, 39: "In the course of the sun-shot moment . . . [Humbert's] glance slithered over the kneeling child (her eyes blinking over those stern dark spectacles)." A few scenes later, Lolita lands on his lap. While this child-Eve chomps on an apple, the slithering Humbert gets off from frottage: "'Give it back,' she pleaded, showing the marbled flush of her palms. I produced Delicious. She grasped it and bit into it, and my heart was like snow under thin crimson skin. . . . I cautiously increased the magic friction. . . . Her legs twitched a little as they lay across my live lap; I stroked them; there she lolled in the right-hand corner, almost asprawl, Lola the bobby-soxer, devouring her immemorial fruit, singing through its juice" (58–59).

14. Richard Corliss, *Lolita* (London: British Film Institute, 1994), 31–32. In Nabokov's novel, Humbert pictures himself as quite the looker, as "a great big handsome hunk of movieland manhood" (39): "clean-cut jaw, muscular hand, deep sonorous voice, broad shoulder" (43); he is "lanky, big-boned, wooly chested Humbert Humbert with thick black eyebrows and a queer accent" (44).

15. James Naremore, *On Kubrick* (London: British Film Institute, 2007), 111; Thomas Allen Nelson, *Kubrick: Inside a Film Artist's Maze*, new and expanded ed. (Bloomington, IN: Indiana University Press, 2000), 69.

16. Naremore, *On Kubrick*, 109.

17. Nelson too notes this in *Kubrick*, 71, though to a different end. On the film's ending, see also Corliss, *Lolita*, 85–86.

18. "The faint dislike [Johnny] had felt for the other man [Unger] from the very first was rapidly developing into a near hatred." Lionel White, *The Killing*, originally published in 1955 as *Clean Break* (Floyd, VA: Black Curtain Press, 2013), 34.

19. Mario Falsetto also comments on this timekeeping "error," though his concern with it is basically narratological. Not that he fails to mention in passing "the delicacy of the homosexual subtext in [Marv's] unrequited relationship with Johnny," which Johnny in "a typical 1950s display of machismo . . . treats . . . as something of a good-natured joke." *Stanley Kubrick: A Narrative and Stylistic Analysis* (Westport, CT: Praeger, 1994), 9, 11. Apparently the movie's voiceover narrator, whose "masculine, authoritative tone" Falsetto also remarks (10), is less amused by such things, whether played for delicacy or machismo, and attempts to efface the whole thing chronologically.

20. Bill Krohn, *Stanley Kubrick*, rev. English ed. (Paris: Cahiers du Cinéma Sarl, 2010), 22.

21. Joseph Gelmis, *The Film Director as Superstar* (Garden City, NY: Doubleday & Company, 1970), 307. In a *Playboy* interview with Eric Norden in 1968, however, Kubrick seems more open about other sexual possibilities. There he speculates that by the year 2001 "we may eventually emerge into polymorphous sexual beings; with the male and female components blurring, merging and interchanging." "The potentialities for exploring new areas of sexual experience are," he continues, "virtually boundless." See Gene D. Phillips, ed., *Stanley Kubrick: Interviews* (Jackson: University of Mississippi Press, 2001), 66.

22. Howard Fast, "Author's Note" accompanying an excerpt of *Spartacus* in *Masses and Mainstream*, July 1951, 21.

23. Ibid.

24. Howard Fast, *Spartacus* (1951) (London: The Bodley Head, 1952), 97 (italics in the original). All further references are to this edition and will be supplied parenthetically in the text.

25. See Martin M. Winkler, ed., *Spartacus: Film and History* (Malden, MA: Blackwell, 2007), particularly Allen M. Ward's "*Spartacus*: History and Histrionics," 97–98, and W. Jeffrey Tatum's "The Character of Marcus Licinius Crassus," 138. See

also Natalie Zemon Davis, *Slaves on Screen: Film and Historical Vision* (Cambridge, MA: Harvard University Press, 2000), 32.

26. Kirk Douglas, *The Ragman's Son* (New York: Simon & Schuster, 1988), 304, 314.

27. In Gelmis, *The Film Director as Superstar*, 314.

28. Naremore, *On Kubrick*, 16–17.

29. Sam B. Girgus critiques the liberal politics of this scene in a chapter titled "The Black Gladiator and the Spartacus Syndrome" in *America on Film: Modernism, Documentary, and a Changing America* (Cambridge: Cambridge University Press, 2002), 94–95.

30. Michel Foucault, *The Use of Pleasure, The History of Sexuality*, vol. 2, trans. Robert Hurley (New York: Vintage Books, 1990), 50–51.

31. Douglas, *The Ragman's Son*, 319–322.

32. Tony Curtis and Barry Paris, *The Autobiography* (New York: William Morrow, 1993), 186.

33. Philip Kuberski, *Kubrick's Total Cinema: Philosophical Themes and Formal Qualities* (New York: Bloomsbury, 2012), 30. Notwithstanding this perspective, Kuberski denigrates *Spartacus* for its "palpable stupidities" (30), which he finds amounting to little more than "sentimental and irritating kitsch" (93). For gay male viewers, another referent for this virile encounter at the baths is the work of 1950s gay physique painter and illustrator George Quaintance, whose work appeared in Bob Mizer's *Physique Pictorial*.

34. Trumbo wrote a mass-marriage scene for Spartacus and Varinia and the other escaped slaves. It was to take place before the final battle and would show "that even slaves, sub-humans, despised and rejected and illiterate though they may be, can aspire toward the noblest concepts of their betters. These men and women are yearning toward the ideal of the family, of the dignity of a formal union between man and woman, of legitimacy for their children and the continuity of their seed." Kubrick, however, balked at the idea, which was historically highly improbable. See Natalie Zemon Davis, "Trumbo and Kubrick Argue History," *Raritan* 22 (2002): 178–179. Duncan L. Cooper provides an exhaustive account of the many intense battles over writing, filming, and editing *Spartacus*—battles not only between Trumbo and Kubrick, but involving just about everyone who had a hand in its production. See his "Who Killed the Legend of Spartacus? Production, Censorship, and Reconstruction of Stanley Kubrick's Epic Film," in Winkler, *Spartacus: Film and History*, 14–55.

35. See Michael Parenti, "Roman Slavery and the Class Divide: Why Spartacus Lost," in Winkler, *Spartacus: Film and History*, 150–151.

36. Letter dated November 20, 1959; cited in Davis, "Trumbo and Kubrick Argue History," 188 (my italics).

37. On this subject, see also Ina Rae Hark's discerning essay, "Animals or Romans: Looking at Masculinity in *Spartacus*," in *Screening the Male: Exploring Masculinities in Hollywood Cinema*, ed. Steven Cohan and Ina Rae Hark (London: Routledge, 1993), 151–172.

38. Douglas recollects: "We needed sound—male voices saying 'Hail, Crassus!' and 'I am Spartacus' in English. We needed thousands of voices. We came up with the idea of getting the lines at a college football game during half-time. We settled on Michigan State in East Lansing, because, as I said, 'It's only natural for Spartacus to go to the Spartans for help.' So, on Saturday, October 17, 1959, 76,000 screaming fans at the Michigan State–Notre Dame football game made history when they yelled and made noises that were recorded on three-channel sound equipment and laid into the *Spartacus* soundtrack back in Hollywood" (*The Ragman's Son*, 325–326).

39. Letter from Marx to Engels, London, February 27, 1861, in *Karl Marx—Frederick Engels: Collected Works* (London, 1985), 41:264–265. See also Brent D. Shaw, *Spartacus and the Slave Wars: A Brief History with Documents* (Boston: Bedford/St. Martins, 2001), 14–15.

40. For more on this "Spartacus" (Dimitri Svigelj), also the director of early gay hardcore films, see Finley Freibert, "Spartacus," in *Physique Pictorial* 52 (Spring 2020), 34–39. See also 64–71 for additional examples of "Spartacus's" work.

41. See Theresa Urbainczyk, *Spartacus* (London: Bristol Classical Press, 2004), 14.

42. See David Hughes, *The Complete Kubrick* (London: Virgin Publishing, 2000), 81–82.

43. This gay coming-out story may have come to its *Spartacus* moment of solidarity by way of *To Wong Foo, Thanks for Everything! Julie Newmar* (dir. Beeban Kidron, 1995), a comedy about three drag queens on the run from the law who take refuge in a small Midwestern town. Rather than give them up, the townsfolk come forward in turn, declaring, "I am a drag queen," or some variation on the theme.

4. Male Sexuality and Homosexuality II: *Barry Lyndon, A Clockwork Orange, Eyes Wide Shut, The Shining*

1. Before selecting Ryan O'Neal, Kubrick is said to have considered both Robert Redford and Clint Eastwood for the leading role. One can only imagine.

2. "Homosexual Subtexts," in *The Encyclopedia of Stanley Kubrick: From Day of the Fight to Eyes Wide Shut*, ed. Gene D. Phillips and Rodney Hill (New York: Checkmark Books, 2002), 166.

3. Vito Russo, *The Celluloid Closet: Homosexuality in the Movies*, rev. ed. (New York: Harper & Row, 1987). Russo briefly discusses the censored bath scene between Crassus and Antoninus in *Spartacus*, but not the skinny-dipping in *Barry Lyndon*.

4. An exception is Maria Pramaggiore's rewarding study, *Making Time in Stanley Kubrick's Barry Lyndon: Art, History, and Empire* (New York: Bloomsbury, 2015). See 103, 107.

5. Michel Ciment, *Kubrick: The Definitive Edition*, trans. Gilbert Adair (New York: Faber and Faber, 2001), 171–172, emphasis added. *The Encyclopedia of Stanley*

Kubrick interestingly misquotes Kubrick's interview by replacing his invocation of "the comic situation" with "the dramatic situation" (see 166). I address the question of gays and "the comic" later in this chapter.

6. Kubrick's addition of a gay element to the scene he invents to liberate Barry more expeditiously from the army may have been prompted by a brief queer moment in the corresponding scene in the novel, which, as Kubrick explains, is much more involved. There Barry brings the wounded Lieutenant Fakenham to a house in a small German town, and having himself sustained a head injury, pretends to go mad: "One night I whispered to him that I was Julius Caesar, and considered him to be my affianced wife Queen Cleopatra, which convinced him of my insanity." William Makepeace Thackeray, *The Memoirs of Barry Lyndon, Esq., of the Kingdom of Ireland*, ed. Andrew Sanders (New York: Oxford University Press, 1999), 75. Further references to the novel are in the text.

7. D. A. Miller, 8½ (New York: Palgrave Macmillan, 2008), 57.

8. Vincent LoBrutto's biography of Kubrick includes fascinating material from the author's interview with the English comic actor Jonathan Cecil, who plays Jonathan in the film, about the evolution of his role. Cecil was first cast as "a sort of upstage, snotty, upper-class young officer," which is more in keeping with Thackeray's Jonathan Fakenham. That part was eventually cut, but he was called back to play "a gay soldier in a love affair with another officer." Cecil recalls that he and his partner in the scene, Anthony Dawes (Frederick), did sixty takes and that the two-minute scene "took a full twelve-hour day to shoot." *Stanley Kubrick: A Biography* (New York: Da Capo Press, 1999), 391–395.

9. Andrew Sarris, "What Makes Barry Run?" *The Village Voice*, December 29, 1975, 111.

10. Alan Spiegel, "Kubrick's *Barry Lyndon*," *Salmagundi* 38–39 (1977): 204. See also Pramaggiore, *Making Time*: "There is a tragic sense of incompleteness to *Barry Lyndon*, which relates to its narrative of masculine loss, through gentlemanly violence, war, accident, and cupidity" (47). It is the demands of war that cause the separation between these two male lovers.

11. Ciment, *Kubrick*, 167.

12. Joseph Litvak, *Strange Gourmets: Sophistication, Theory, and the Novel* (Durham, NC: Duke University Press, 1997), 56.

13. Fifteen wigs were made for Ryan O'Neal alone (LoBrutto, *Stanley Kubrick*, 382), who also reportedly had some fifty-one costume fittings (James Howard, *Stanley Kubrick Companion* [London: B.T. Batsford, 1999]), 139.

14. Naremore, *On Kubrick* (London: British Film Institute, 2007), 183–184.

15. See ibid., 183 for Sir Charles; 176 for the Reverend Runt; and 179 for the narrator. Though these characterizations are all fetched from Naremore, other commentators employ similar descriptive terms.

16. Ibid., 183, 184.

17. The film's epilogue is adapted, with some changes, from a pronouncement in the novel's first chapter. See *The Memoirs of Barry Lyndon*, 10.

18. Malcolm McDowell had already showed his all in his first film: another male youth picture, Lindsay Anderson's *If . . . .* (1968), which is what drew Kubrick's attention to the peculiarly charismatic young actor.

19. Philip Strick and Penelope Houston, "Modern Times: An Interview with Stanley Kubrick," in *Stanley Kubrick: Interviews,* ed. Gene D. Phillips (Jackson: University of Mississippi Press, 2001), 128.

20. Anthony Burgess, *A Clockwork Orange* (1962) (New York: Norton, 1986), 97. Further references to the novel are in the text.

21. See Ciment, *Kubrick,* 149.

22. Ibid., 149, 151.

23. The name for this behavioral modification treatment becomes another bit of Kubrick autoreferentiality when in *Barry Lyndon* Barry picks out for purchase a painting from a fictitious artist named Ludovico. "I love the use of blue," Kubrick's dimwitted Blue Boy here declares.

24. Alexander Walker, *Stanley Kubrick, Director,* rev. ed. (New York: Norton, 1999), 218.

25. See Peter Krämer, *A Clockwork Orange* (New York: Palgrave Macmillan, 2011), 104–105.

26. The other "muscle" in the film comes in the form of the statuesque, bulging bouncers, dressed in basket-showing white jumpsuits, in the opening scene in the Korova Milk Bar. These immoveable male forms appear as doubles of the Korova's female furniture. One of the bouncers is played by the 6′5″ Pat Roach, later cast as a bellicose soldier in *Barry Lyndon,* whom Barry surprisingly thrashes in a boxing match.

27. Most commentators simply refer to this notorious artwork/weapon as a molded penis, a murderous mega-phallus. But Makkink's bi-sexed sculpture, like the scene in which it appears, is queerer than that.

28. Ciment, *Kubrick,* 151.

29. Thomas Allen Nelson, *Kubrick: Inside a Film Artist's Maze,* new and expanded ed. (Bloomington: Indiana University Press, 2000),151.

30. Ibid., 152.

31. Ibid., 151.

32. Christopher Ricks, "Horror Show," *The New York Review of Books,* April 6, 1972; Naremore, *On Kubrick,* 160.

33. Nelson, *Kubrick,* 152.

34. See Ciment, *Kubrick,* 163.

35. Anthony Burgess, *You've Had Your Time: The Second Part of the Confessions* (New York: Grove Weidenfeld, 1990), 142.

36. Ibid., 246.

37. Anthony Burgess, *A Clockwork Orange* (London: Bloomsbury, 2012), 50–51. Several all-male (and all the more homoerotic) stage productions of Burgess's story have been mounted recently and this to some acclaim, especially Alexandra Spencer-Jones's toned, gym-bodies iteration, which came to Broadway in 2017.

38. Penelope Houston, "Kubrick Country," in Phillips, *Stanley Kubrick: Interviews*, 111.

39. See here Robert Hughes's astute review of the film, "The Décor of Tomorrow's Hell," *Time*, December 27, 1971; reprinted in *Stanley Kubrick's A Clockwork Orange*, ed. Stuart Y. McDougal (Cambridge: Cambridge University Press, 2003), 131–133.

40. William Blake, *The Marriage of Heaven and Hell* (c. 1790–93). Kubrick had his own literary analogy for his charismatic villain, fetched not from Milton but from Shakespeare. "Alex," he explains in an interview, "is certainly one of the most surprising and enjoyable inventions of fiction. I can think of only one other literary or dramatic comparison, and that is with Richard III. Alex, like Richard, is a character whom you should dislike and fear, and yet you find yourself drawn very quickly into his world and find yourself seeing things through his eyes. It's not easy to say how this is achieved, but it certainly has something to do with his candor and wit and intelligence, and the fact that all the other characters are lesser people, and in some way worse people." Houston, "Kubrick Country," 110.

41. Lucy McKenzie has recreated the film's council flat mural as a vast acrylic on canvas painting titled *If It Moves, Kiss It* (2002).

42. Behind the mask and cloak is Kubrick's longtime personal assistant Leon Vitali, who also played the adult Lord Bullingdon in *Barry Lyndon*.

43. Cited in John Lewis, "Real Sex: Aesthetics and Economics of Art-house Porn," *Jump Cut* 51 (2009), accessed online: https://www.ejumpcut.org/archive/jc51 .2009/LewisRealsex/text.html.

44. Terry Southern, *Blue Movie* (New York: World Publishing, 1970), 35, 14.

45. See Thessaly La Force's interview with Southern in the *Paris Review*, June 7, 2010. That heralded blow job takes up more than four pages in the novel (*Blue Movie*, 103–107).

46. See Peter Loewenberg's rich essay, "Freud, Schnitzler, and *Eyes Wide Shut*," in *Depth of Field: Stanley Kubrick, Film, and the Uses of History*, ed. Geoffrey Cocks, James Diedrick, Glenn Perusek (Madison: University of Wisconsin Press, 2006), 257.

47. Arthur Schnitzler, *Dream Story*, in *Night Games and Other Stories and Novellas*, trans. Margret Schaefer (Chicago: Ivan R. Dee, 2002), 202. Further references to the novella are to this edition and supplied in the text.

48. Geoffrey Cocks also picks up this detail in *The Wolf at the Door: Stanley Kubrick, History, and the Holocaust* (New York: Peter Lang, 2004), 145.

49. Russo, *The Celluloid Closet*, 68. In his insightful treatment of Brooks's novel and its film adaptation by Dmytryk, Robert J. Corber finds the latter "a concrete example of the way in which gay men were expelled from the realm of representation in the Cold War era." See his *Homosexuality in Cold War America: Resistance and the Crisis of Masculinity* (Durham, NC: Duke University Press, 1997), 85.

50. Quoted in Douglass K. Daniel, *Tough as Nails: The Life and Films of Richard Brooks* (Madison: University of Wisconsin Press, 2011), 46.

51. Frederic Raphael, *Eyes Wide Open: A Memoir of Stanley Kubrick* (New York: Ballantine Books, 1999), 59. "In the end," Raphael continues, "Fridolin was to be given the surname Harford, which—with Freudian neatness—does not sound very different from Hertford(shire), the county in which Stanley lived (or indeed from Harrison Ford)."

52. The eroticism of the corresponding scene in Schnitzler is even more pronounced. "Instinctively, as though compelled by and directed by an invisible power, Fridolin touched the forehead, the cheeks, the shoulders, and the arms of the dead woman with both hands, and then entwined his fingers with those of the corpse as though in love play" (269).

53. Slavoj Žižek, *The Fright of Real Tears: Krzysztof Kieślowski Between Theory and Post-Theory* (London: British Film Institute, 2001), 174.

54. Stanley Kubrick, *Eyes Wide Shut: A Screenplay by Stanley Kubrick and Frederic Raphael and the Classic Novel That Inspired the Film, Dream Story by Arthur Schnitzler* (New York: Warner Books, 1999), 117.

55. See Raphael, *Eyes Wide Open*, 93, 99, 137–138, and 143–146, for instance.

56. Michel Chion, *Eyes Wide Shut* (London: British Film Institute, 2002), 87–88.

57. SK/17/1/3, SKA. See page 97 of this draft script.

58. SK/17/1/5, SKA. See page 74 of this draft script.

59. SK/17/1/6. See page 82 of this draft script.

60. Michiko Kakutani, "A Connoisseur of Cool Tries to Raise the Temperature," *New York Times*, July 18, 1999; Andrew Sarris, "Eyes Don't Have It: Kubrick's Turgid Finale," *Observer*, July 26, 1999; Amy Taubin, "Imperfect Love," *Film Comment* 35, no. 5 (September/October 1999): 33; Louis Menand, "Kubrick's Strange Love," *New York Review of Books*, August 12, 1999; David Denby, "Last Waltz," *New Yorker*, July 26, 1999; and Ben Parker, "Cruise Control," *Paris Review*, February 6, 2013.

61. Michael Herr, *Kubrick* (New York: Grove Press, 2000), 83.

62. Ciment, *Kubrick*, 156 (italics in the original).

63. See in particular: Lucy Scholes and Richard Martin, "Archived Desires: *Eyes Wide Shut*," in *Stanley Kubrick: New Perspectives*, ed. Tatjana Ljujić, Peter Krämer, and Richard Daniels (London: Black Dog, 2015), 350–355; Naremore, *On Kubrick*, 230–232; Philip Kuberski, *Kubrick's Total Cinema: Philosophical Themes and Formal Qualities* (New York: Bloomsbury, 2012), 97–100; and Robert P. Kolker and Nathan Abrams, *Eyes Wide Shut: Stanley Kubrick and the Making of His Final Film* (New York: Oxford University Press, 2019), especially the epilogue. Kolker and Abrams also importantly here stress that *Eyes Wide Shut* is an art film.

64. On the "parroting," see Chion, *Eyes Wide Shut*, 71–76.

65. Scholes and Martin, "Archived Desires," 343–356.

66. Taubin, "'Imperfect Love," 30.

67. Loewenberg makes a similar point in "Freud, Schnitzler, and *Eyes Wide Shut*," in *Depth of Field*, ed. Cocks, et al., 275–276.

68. The figure of the supersensitive boy would have hauntingly come back in Kubrick had he not passed off *A.I.* to Spielberg and instead made *Eyes Wide Shut.* As for the latter, I have just suggested that the oedipal release of replacing the son who sees things with a daughter who doesn't has something to do with its other than tragic ending. But, then again, what of that little girl's desire to stay up late to watch *The Nutcracker* while her parents attend Ziegler's Christmas party, where things between them start to fray? That is, what of that *"Nutcracker* wish" in view of the casually castrative remark to come later in the film from the bad "father" Ziegler to the daughter's own father about "knocking a few balls around"? Maybe she's on her way to seeing things too.

69. Stephen King, *The Shining* (1977) (New York: Anchor Books, 2013), 514. Further references in the text. The title of this section, as I noted in the Introduction, is an appreciative nod to Terry Castle's *The Apparitional Lesbian: Female Sexuality and Modern Culture* (New York: Columbia University Press, 1993), which makes the case that the ghost of homosexual love between women has long haunted Western literature and culture. Patricia White's *unInvited: Classical Hollywood Cinema and Lesbian Representability* (Bloomington: Indiana University Press, 1999) persuasively extends that claim to Hollywood film. See especially chapter 3, "Female Spectator, Lesbian Specter," where White works out compelling readings of Hollywood ghost stories as refracted through the question of lesbian invisibility. My concern with apparitional (male) homosexuality in Kubrick is, in some respects, the obverse; that is, why is it so visible here, even if, ghostlike, only fleetingly so?

70. The novelist Diane Johnson, who coauthored the screenplay with Kubrick, attributes this bizarre scene, wholly extraneous to the plot, entirely to him: "There were certain images in the script which I think were always in his mind," Johnson tells John Baxter. "There was that very strange dark bit where at the very end Wendy sees kind of strange images of what looks like oral sex between two men . . . ; that had nothing to do with me." John Baxter, *Stanley Kubrick: A Biography* (New York: Carroll & Graf, 1997), 311.

71. Kubrick appears to endorse these very terms in an interview with Ciment: "Halloran is a simple, rustic type who talks about telepathy in a disarmingly unscientific way. His folksy character and naïve attempts to explain telepathy to Danny make what he has to say dramatically more acceptable than a standard pseudo-scientific explanation. He and Danny—[the Black man and the white child]—make a good pair" (*Kubrick*, 192). Kubrick's account of Hallorann's narrative functionality reverberates with his explanation (also in an interview with Ciment) of why he added the gay scene to *Barry Lyndon* as no more than simply an efficient solution to a storytelling problem. See note 5.

On Hallorann as a "Magical Negro" in both Kubrick's film and King's novel, see Naremore, *On Kubrick,* 201–202, as well as Roger Luckhurst's rewarding BFI book *The Shining* (London: Palgrave Macmillan, 2013), 80–81. There is much more work to be done on racial signification in Kubrick's films, though some time ago Dennis Bingham gave the subject an important jumpstart in an extended endnote for his essay "The Displaced Auteur: A Reception History of *The Shining*," in *Perspectives on Stanley Kubrick*, ed. Mario Falsetto (New York: G. K. Hall, 1996), 304–305.

72. See, for example, King, *The Shining*, 130–131, 136, 142, 144, and so on—to the point of overkill.

5. His Fundamental Core: *Full Metal Jacket*

1. My reading of *Full Metal Jacket* makes the Marine Corps look like a single-sex institution, which is not the case. Women became part of the regular Corps in 1948, and in 2016 the Department of Defense ordered the Corps to open all combat jobs to them. I treat the Marine Corps as an all-male institution because Kubrick's film does.

And because I don't know of any female Marine Corps movies. The military retooling of the female recruit is, however, the subject of Ridley Scott's *G.I. Jane* (1997), which owes more than a little to Kubrick's movie. It engages the question of the full integration of women into the American combat forces through the high-profile test case of a female career Navy officer (Demi Moore), who, to the surprise, even the dismay, of nearly everyone else in the film, successfully completes the harrowing training regimens of the elite Navy SEALs division—"the most intensive military training," we're here told, "known to man." But the film's interest in gender is mostly confined to showing that a woman (or at least this exceptionally tough and determined one) is capable of enduring the rigors of SEAL training: that there can be, in other words, a G.I. Jane who is more or less the equal of a G.I. Joe. Indeed, this particular G.I. Jane proffers what the G.I. Joe some of us know from our childhood—a doll for boys to play with—was disappointedly found to lack. "Suck my dick," G.I. Jane thus retorts, in a climactic moment of defiance, to an abusive and sexist male drill instructor (Viggo Mortensen) who had made it his own mission to brutalize her out of the program. When the other members of her training squad take up G.I. Jane's ballsy rejoinder as a chant—"Suck my dick! Suck my dick!"—we know that she has arrived as one of the boys. (For me, that initiation had already happened earlier in the film, when she expertly gives herself a buzz cut in the barracks barbershop.) What more it might mean that a G.I. Jane lays claim to the (martial) phallus goes unexplored, however, beyond how immediately after this not only rhetorical victory she becomes the object of a lesbian witch hunt—one that the narrative patently fabricates *as just that* so as to guarantee what is here referred to as Jane's "solvent heterosexuality." (Bear in the mind that Scott's movie dates from the era of "Don't ask, don't tell.") For immediately after these false charges surface, we suddenly find Jane out of the blue domestically reunited with the high-ranking naval officer boyfriend she had discarded at the beginning of the film in order to join up with the "cock-swinging-commandos" of the Navy SEALS, as her (as it turns out only temporarily) abandoned male love interest termed them. Eventually reinstated, Jane goes on to spearhead the heroic rescue of her drill instructor, who has been wounded during a covert Libyan mission. This act could be seen as a

redemptive rewriting of the much bleaker conclusion of *Full Metal Jacket*, where, as
we will later consider, a somewhat similar rescue situation triggers a failure in the
chain of command and results in a number of deaths, including those of the squad's
leaders.

2. Sidney J. Furie's *The Boys in Company C* (1978), well worth a look, prefigures
the two-part boot camp then battlefield narrative structure of *Full Metal Jacket*.

3. Modine had already played sensitive military "boy" roles in Robert Altman's
1983 *Streamers* and Alan Parker's 1984 *Birdy*, both Vietnam War films. Modine's
achingly strange and affecting performance in the latter was what brought him to
Kubrick's attention for the role of Joker.

4. Just what it means, discipline-wise, to have one's head and ass wired together is
evocatively left unspecified. But it calls to mind a scene in a preliminary draft of the
screenplay (with typos that I have silently corrected) titled "SIXTY SECOND
DUMP." "There is a right way, a wrong way and the Marine Corps' way to do
everything," Hartman here instructs the privates:

> Defecation discipline in a combat situation could be the deciding factor
> between victory and defeat. Therefore it is every Marine's obligation to
> God, Country and Corps to master and maintain control of his bodily
> functions. The Recruit Training Schedule allows you people to sit and stink
> in the morning from 5.30 to 5.31 and in the evening from 20.30 to 20.31. Two
> minutes a day. . . .
> On the preparatory command, "Ready," you will move your hands up and
> hook your thumbs into the waistband of your skivvies. On the command of
> execution, "Seats," you will push your drawers down to your knees, and at the
> same time seat yourself on the commode. You may commence your dump on
> the command "At ease." . . . Any questions? . . . Move your asses, you got
> one minute."

5. That image reiterates a minor visual motif in Kubrick. Picture Barry cradling
the mortally injured Captain Grogan on the sidelines of the first battle scene in
Barry Lyndon, along with the way that the fatherly Spartacus embraces Antoninus as
he thrusts his sword into his "son" to save him from the worse death of crucifixion: a
pater dolorosa. Picture also the solemn, silent mechanical pietà rendered in *2001*,
when Dave uses the long-armed space pod to retrieve and clutch Frank's lifeless
floating body.

6. Tarantino's *Pulp Fiction*, which came up in Chapter 4 in relation to *Eyes Wide
Shut*, adds a father-son, generational dimension to the concept of anally routed male
bonds while retaining the military framework we have been considering here. At the
beginning of "The Gold Watch" segment of the film's multistrand narrative, a boxer
indicatively named Butch (Bruce Willis) has a flashback dream to a primal scene from
his boyhood: a visitation from a mysterious Air Force officer named Captain Koons
(Christopher Walken). He shows up while Butch happens to be watching the cartoon
TV show *Clutch Cargo* to present the boy with his great-grandfather's gold "war

watch." Butch learns that his great-grandfather wore the watch as a good luck charm throughout World War I, where he served as a marine, and then passed it on to his son for him to do the same and so on. Holding forth this talismanic male heirloom, Captain Koons tells Butch that it was on Butch's daddy's wrist when he and Koons were captured and put in a Vietnamese prison camp. Butch's dad knew, Koons further explains, that the watch—"his boy's birthright"—would be taken from him there:

> So he hid it in the one place he knew he could hide something. His ass. Five long years, he wore this watch up his ass. Then when he died of dysentery, he gave me the watch. I hid this uncomfortable hunk of metal up *my ass* two years. Then, after seven years, I was sent home to my family. And now, little man, I give the watch to you.

Clutch cargo, indeed.

In *Full Metal Jacket*, anality is a rhetorical device for expressing intensified male relations of various kinds. This deeply sentimental tale from *Pulp Fiction* literalizes the device—it puts the male ass to real use on this account—and that is so with a few more turns of the screw to come. Before skipping town to avoid Marsellus (Ving Rhames), a powerful crime boss he has double-crossed by not throwing a fight as agreed, Butch ill-advisedly returns to his apartment to fetch the precious gold watch. Doing so sets in motion a wild chain of events, culminating in Marsellus's being sodomized: a scene, I noted earlier, that Kubrick apparently found cinematically effective when he was contemplating what Bill should be threatened with in the orgy scene of *Eyes Wide Shut*. In *Pulp Fiction*, that (actual) scene of anal sex also leads to Marsellus and Butch's reconciliation. For after Butch shows up in medias res to save Marsellus from further violation in the pawn shop dungeon, Marsellus determines to let their bygones be bygones, and instead turns his avenging fury against his rapist. It might also be noted that Butch's commando-style heroics in going back to rescue Marsellus also have something of a return-and-rescue-mission air about them. The relations between Kubrick's movies and Tarantino's remain underexplored. Here we find, among other matters, their overlapping interest in boxers, war, intense homosociality, and, yes, male anality.

Sharon Willis observes in her astute treatment of the bathroom, anality, and aggression in Tarantino that Christopher Walken, who plays the amulet-bearing vet, "himself operates as a certain icon of 70s re-readings of the Viet Nam war, through his performance in [*The*] *Deer Hunter*," reproducing in *Pulp Fiction* "the deranged voice and look of his character in the earlier film." She suggests that Walken himself is thus "part of the detritus that is being recycled here"—a notion that also makes useful again the cultural remains of the Vietnam War, or at least films the canonical films about it. Willis, "The Father's Watch the Boys' Room," *Camera Obscura* 11 (1993): 45–46.

7. Guy Hocquenghem, *Homosexual Desire* (1972) trans. Daniella Dangoor, with a new introduction by Michael Moon (Durham, NC: Duke University Press, 1993), 97. Hocquenghem's notion of the anus as the first organ to be privatized—indeed as

expressing "privatisation itself"—is drawn from Gilles Deleuze and Félix Guattari's *Anti-Oedipus*, which Hocquenghem notes just before the passage I have quoted here (96). Further references are in the text.

8. In the novel, this scene is set in front of Pyle's bunk in the squad bay. See Gustav Hasford, *The Short-Timers* (New York: Harper & Row, 1979), 22–27. Further references are in the text.

Kubrick received his final Oscar nomination for the adapted screenplay, written in collaboration with Michael Herr—author of *Dispatches*, an acclaimed 1977 collection of sometimes fictionalized first-person essays from Herr's time in Vietnam as a civilian war correspondent for *Esquire*, bits of which are worked into *Full Metal Jacket*—and Hasford, whose novel opens with an epigraph taken from Herr's book. Like Joker, the narrator of his novel, Hasford himself served in Vietnam as a Marine Corps combat correspondent.

9. Stanley Kubrick, *Full Metal Jacket: The Screenplay by Stanley Kubrick, Michael Herr and Gustav Hasford, Based on the Novel The Short-Timers by Gustav Hasford* (New York: Knopf, 1987), 49.

10. Anthony Swofford, *Jarhead: A Marine's Chronicle of the Gulf War and Other Battles* (New York: Scribner, 2003), 20–21. Further references are in the text.

11. This remains true for subsequent Marine Corps literature such as Matt Young's compelling *Eat the Apple: A Memoir* (New York: Bloomsbury, 2018), in which the influence of Swofford's already classic book is also legible. Here where we find lines like "You had better unfuck yourself" (75) and references to "a Private Pyle lookalike": "Refer to this person as Lawrence in reference to the massive fuckup from *Full Metal Jacket*, Private Leonard Lawrence" (38, 147). Kubrick's Marine Corps film is named after a kind of bullet; Young frames himself as one: "I have acted like a bullet. I entered lives and bounced and ricocheted and broke and tore." (219). And whereas *Full Metal Jacket* begins with the marine haircut, Young's book, no less a reflection on men and masculinity, essentially ends with it. In an allusive chapter titled "A Real Boy," he writes: "If there's anything I've learned, it's to keep my hair long. It's the differentiating factor between the gung-ho brainwashed eighteen-year-old I was when I joined and the civilian I desperately want to be. The high and tight is what people notice first. . . . They look at me and think, Jarhead" (242).

12. Thomas Doherty, "Full Metal Genre: Stanley Kubrick's Vietnam Combat Movie," *Film Quarterly* 42 (1988–89): 28.

13. In the fascinating ruminative journal he kept while making the film, Matthew Modine records how he told Kubrick that *Full Metal Jacket* had "Everything but sex." "Where would you put it?" Kubrick then wanted to know. Kubrick eventually determined that Joker should go to bed with the Da Nang streetwalker—though even then, as he imagined it, "the scene [would be] post-coital":

KUBRICK: She's on her back. She's naked and she's rubbing your shoulders. Then she tells you she's still horny and she wants more boom boom. What do you think?

MODINE: I think it's great. It's hysterical. Do I say anything?

KUBRICK: Yeah. You say one of those classic lines from an old Hollywood movie. Something you've memorized. What was the movie with Bette Davis where she's on a boat? The guy with her lights two cigarettes and asks her to marry him?

MODINE: I'm not sure.

KUBRICK: Davis says something like, "My darling, we have the moon . . ."

Neither the director nor the actor gets the star's famous line from the classic women's film *Now, Voyager* (1942) quite right. What Davis says is: "Oh Jerry, don't let's ask for the moon. We have the stars." Nor did that missing "sex scene"—which, reports Modine, was indeed shot—make it into the finished film. See Matthew Modine, *Full Metal Jacket Diary* (New York: Rugged Land, 2005), 231, 238–243.

14. Carol Burke, "Marching to Vietnam," *Journal of American Folklore* 102 (1989): 427.

15. Here I have in mind "Axiom 1" with which Eve Kosofsky Sedgwick launches her field-shaping study of sexuality, *Epistemology of the Closet* (Berkeley: University of California Press, 1990): *"People are different from each other"* (22). That elemental claim, as I see it, remains the most powerful proposition to come from queer studies.

16. Susan Jeffords, *The Remasculinization of America: Gender and the Vietnam War* (Bloomington: Indiana University Press, 1989): 175.

17. On allowing for divergence between feminist readings and other approaches no less concerned with gender and sexuality, see Richard Rambuss, "After Male Sex," in *After Sex? On Writing Since Queer Theory*, ed. Janet Halley and Andrew Parker (Durham, NC: Duke University Press, 2011), 192–193.

18. That moniker "Mother Green and her killing machine" also integrates the machinic and organic, death and life. "What makes the grass grow?" Hartman had asked the recruits. "Blood! Blood! Blood!" came back the horrible answer.

19. Kubrick himself was responsible for the title, found in a gun catalogue. According to Herr's foreword in *Full Metal Jacket: The Screenplay*, Kubrick found the phrase to be "beautiful and tough, and kind of poetic" (vii).

20. Sarah Hagelin also explores the construction of male vulnerability in *Reel Vulnerability: Power, Pain, and Gender in Contemporary American Film and Television* (New Brunswick, NJ: Rutgers University Press, 2013), with *Full Metal Jacket* one of works she insightfully considers. A difference between our approaches to Kubrick's film is that I remain uninclined to take male vulnerability here as necessarily feminizing. See, for instance, the terms in which Hagelin contrasts "Joker's masculine violence and Pyle's feminized vulnerability." There is Joker, "who talks back when Hartman assaults him, and Pyle, who suffers and cries." "Vulnerability, figured as female," Hagelin concludes, "provides the leverage Kubrick uses to enlist his audience's disgust at military cruelty" (60–61). But, as we have seen, Pyle is just one of many male weepers in Kubrick. And doesn't Kubrick

make almost of all his men suffer? What's more, while he is infantilized and homosexualized, Pyle isn't personally effeminized by Hartman in a way that sets him apart from the other recruits—"ladies" all, as far as the drill sergeant is concerned. In a way, what bothers Hartman about the recruit he renames "Gomer Pyle" and associates with Lawrence of Arabia is that he *is* male, corruptingly so: "I'm gonna rip your balls off," Hartman threatens, "so you cannot contaminate the rest of the world!"

21. Hasford, *The Short-Timers*, 98; Kubrick, *Full Metal Jacket: The Screenplay*, 113.

22. In Hasford's novel, Joker finishes off the sniper by putting a bullet through her eye. (We don't see this in the film, as the camera remains focused on Joker's face when he shoots her.) Killing the sniper in this fashion here earns Joker the admiration of his fellows: "Joker, that's a well done. You're hard." But it also provokes a competitive response from Animal Mother, who "zips out his machete . . . and chops off her head . . . and holds it high." "Hard? *Now* who's hard?" he boasts. *The Short-Timers*, 101–102. Kubrick filmed a version of this scene, but in the end did not use it, sparing us that concluding note of ghastly misogynist male one-upmanship while keeping the question of war ethics unresolved. It might also be noted that in the novel there is a premonition of what Joker does here when Hasford has him kill the wounded Cowboy to end his dying friend's suffering.

23. Philip Kuberski emphasizes to strong effect the guerilla war dimension of the conflict as it here is rendered in *Kubrick's Total Cinema: Philosophical Themes and Formal Qualities* (New York: Bloomsbury, 2012), 64–66.

24. Gene Siskel, "Candidly Kubrick," in *Stanley Kubrick: Interviews*, ed. Gene D. Phillips (Jackson: University of Mississippi Press, 2001), 182.

25. "Interview with Michael Herr, screenwriter," in Michel Ciment, *Kubrick: The Definitive Edition*, trans. Gilbert Adair (New York: Faber and Faber, 2001), 251.

26. Ibid,, 243.

27. Richard Daniels offers the fullest archival account of this remarkable feat of large-scale set design in "Stanley Kubrick's *Full Metal Jacket*: Constructing War-Torn Vietnam in England," in *Mythologizing the Vietnam War: Visual Culture and Mediated Memory*, ed. Jennifer Good, Paul Lowe, Brigitte Lardinois, and Val Williams (Newcastle upon Tyne: Cambridge Scholars Publishing, 2014), 79–105.

28. Michael Herr, *Dispatches* (1977) (New York: Vintage, 1991), 102.

29. Siskel, "Candidly Kubrick," 180.

30. Those terms are borrowed from Carla Freccero's "Daddy's Girl—on Leo Bersani," *GLQ* 17 (2011): 350, which offers a brief but compelling reading of Claire Denis's *Beau travail* (1999). Denis's film is a loose resetting of Melville's homoerotic *Billy Budd* in the French Foreign Legion that I see as also streaked with touches of *Full Metal Jacket*, especially in its mesmeric martial ballet of drilled male bodies rhythmically set in motion.

As its title indicates, Freccero's piece is a reading of *Beau travail* through Leo Bersani's own reading of the film in his "Father Knows Best," *Raritan* 29 (2010): 92–104. Bersani sees Denis's highly aestheticized "pseudodocumentary account" of the Legionnaires as "testing definitions and conditions of intimacy, and, in so doing . . . proposed new or at least unfamiliar relational configurations" (96). Aspects of what Bersani terms "the family-world" (100) of the Legionnaires as a collectivity of impersonality resonate with my reading of the Marine Corps of Kubrick's film.

31. I am thinking here of the industrialist Henry Ford's assembly-line conception of humanity as comprising few heads and many hands. See Henry Ford, *My Life and Work* (Garden City: Doubleday, Page & Co., 1922), especially chs. 6–7.

32. To be noted here is that the film's shooting script has Joker himself as its final casualty, his battlefield death in a burst of automatic gunfire intercut with parallel images of the eight-year-old Joker playing with a plastic toy rifle. In this version, the movie ends in a semi-heroicizing military funeral for Joker, with his father tearfully reading A. E. Housman's poem "Epitaph." As Modine tells it in his *Full Metal Jacket Diary*, Kubrick came to feel that this ending—yet more male tears!—was too sentimental. Asked repeatedly by Kubrick how *he* thought the film should conclude, Modine (who had admitted that he liked the original ending) finally retorts: "You want to know what should happen? He should live. He should have to spend the rest of his life thinking about Pyle blowing his brains out. He should have to spend the rest of his life reliving his drill instructor getting shot in a latrine. He should have to spend the rest of his life thinking about how the one guy that was his friend died in his arms. . . . Joker should live." "That's the ending," Kubrick replied (206). So there is nothing sentimental or redemptive, then, about the film's survivalist final note ("But I'm alive"), nothing but—paint it black—that "world of shit."

33. See Bill Krohn, "*Full Metal Jacket*," in *Incorporations*, Zone 6, ed. Jonathan Crary and Sanford Kwinter (New York: Zone Books, 1992), 430.

34. Steven Zeeland, *The Masculine Marine: Homoeroticism in the U.S. Marine Corps* (New York: Harrington Park Press, 1996), 84–85. Further references are in the text.

35. Siskel, "Candidly Kubrick," 185.

36. "I am become death, the destroyer of worlds" is Krishna's utterance from the Bhagavad Gita, but also a citation of Robert Oppenheimer at Los Alamos—and thus a phantom trace that leads from *Full Metal Jacket* back to Kubrick's first Cold War film, *Dr. Strangelove*. My notion of ascesis here is informed by a rewarding exchange with David Halperin over an earlier version of this material.

Coda: Visual Pleasure in Kubrick

1. See, for instance, Michael Herr, *Kubrick* (New York: Grove Press, 2000), 6–7; and Gene Siskel, "Candidly Kubrick," in *Stanley Kubrick: Interviews*, ed. Gene D. Phillips (Jackson: University of Mississippi Press, 2001), 180.

2. Long ongoing discussions about Kubrick's aesthetics with James Meyer have been for me both inspirational and influential, especially in terms of these concluding reflections.

Index

RICHARD RAMBUSS is Nicholas Brown Professor of Oratory and Belles Lettres and chair of the Department of English at Brown University. He is the author of *Closet Devotions* and *Spencer's Secret Career* and the editor of *The English Poems of Richard Crashaw*.

CPSIA information can be obtained
at www.ICGtesting.com
Printed in the USA
JSHW031107090221
11748JS00002B/116